For Steve,

— a real pleasure to
see you in Jerusalem
                                    guy
                    October 96

HIDDEN WISDOM

STUDIES

IN THE HISTORY OF RELIGIONS

(*NUMEN* BOOK SERIES)

EDITED BY

H.G. KIPPENBERG · E.T. LAWSON

VOLUME LXX

HIDDEN WISDOM

ESOTERIC TRADITIONS AND THE ROOTS OF CHRISTIAN MYSTICISM

BY

GUY G. STROUMSA

E.J. BRILL
LEIDEN · NEW YORK · KÖLN
1996

The paper in this book meets the guidelines for permanence and durability of the Committee on Production Guidelines for Book Longevity of the Council on Library Resources.

Library of Congress Cataloging-in-Publication Data

Stroumsa, Gedaliahu A. G.
    Hidden wisdom : esoteric traditions and the roots of Christian mysticism / by Guy G. Stroumsa.
      p. cm. — (Studies in the history of religions, ISSN 0169-8834 ; v. 70)
    Includes bibliographical references and index.
    ISBN 9004105042 (alk. paper)
    1. Occultism—Religious aspects—Christianity—History of doctrines—Early church, ca. 30-600. 2. Discipline of the secret. 3. Mysticism—History—Early church, ca. 30-600. I. Title. II. Series: Studies in the history of religions ; 70.
BR195.O33S77   1996
261.5'1—dc20   96-3330
                                        CIP

Die Deutsche Bibliothek – CIP-Einheitsaufnahme

Stroumsa, Guy G.:
Hidden wisdom : esoteric traditions and the roots of Christian mysticism / by Guy G. Stroumsa.– Leiden ; New York ; Köln : Brill, 1996
    (Studies in the history of religions ; Vol. 70)
    ISBN 90–04–10504–2
NE: GT

ISSN   0169-8834
ISBN 90 04 10504 2

© *Copyright 1996 by E.J. Brill, Leiden, The Netherlands*

PRINTED IN THE NETHERLANDS

For Rachel and Daphna

CONTENTS

PREFACE

Although the existence of secret traditions in the earliest strata of Christianity is now recognized by most scholars, the importance of these traditions is not always appreciated. These traditions disappeared in late antiquity, and their traces are to a great extent blurred. But the existence, at the same period, of esoteric trends in other religious traditions such as the Greek mysteries, Zoroastrianism or Judaism, strengthens the hypothesis of significant esoteric trends in early Christianity.

In the last decade or so, some of my efforts have been dedicated to the study of esoteric trends in early Christianity as well as among Gnostics and Manichaeans. As I proceeded in my research I realized, however, that the question was not yet ripe for a synthetic study to be written. I have opted, therefore, for a series of investigations on various aspects of esotericism in the first Christian centuries. These investigations are intended as forays—or *Vorarbeiten*—to check the terrain. It is hoped that presented together, their results will provide accumulated circumstantial evidence, and carry a weight that will encourage further discussion of the material.

My interest in these questions owes a great deal to many colleagues and friends. At the Hebrew University, I have learned much, in particular, from Galit Hasan-Rokem, Moshe Idel, David Satran, Shaul Shaked, David Shulman and R.J. Zwi Werblowsky. Some of the ideas developed here were first tried in a graduate seminar on esoteric traditions in ancient Mediterrranean religions, taught together with Yehudah Liebes a few years ago.

Versions of the chapters of this book were presented before various audiences. I am grateful for the oral and written comments I received on these occasions. In particular, I should like to thank Hans Dieter Betz, Alain Le Boulluec, Carsten Colpe, Peter Kingsley, Kurt Rudolph, and Werner Sundermann. Robert Lamberton and Charles Kahn kindly read two chapters and made various useful comments. I also wish to recall the memory of Jonas Greenfield, Shlomo Pines, Morton Smith and Ioan Culiano, with whom I discussed some of the issues dealt with here.

A sustained and systematic effort to understand the nature, role and transformation of Christian esotericism in late antiquity demands a comparative approach, which is best done in collaborative ventures. I was privileged to be associated with two such collective enterprizes, which sought to develop cross-cultural approaches to the study of secrecy and esotericism. In 1993, Hans Kippenberg and I organized a workshop on "Secrecy and concealment in Mediterranean and Near Eastern religions," the proceedings of which have recently been published in the *Numen* Book Series. The contributions cover much of the Greek background of the topics dealt with here, the New Testament, and the repercussions of ancient esotericism up to Shi'ite traditions. I have therefore felt it unnecessary to cover again, much less authoritatively, the same material.

Jan and Aleida Assmann (Heidelberg and Konstanz) organized a series of three interdisciplinary conferences on various aspects of secrecy. I have learned much from participating in the second and the third of these conferences, held in 1992 and 1993.

I am indebted to Tamar Osnat Avraham, who compiled the index with diligence. Finally, I wish to thank the editors of *Numen* Book Series for accepting this book, and Elisabeth Erdman-Visser and Hans van der Meij at Brill for their patience and competence.

More than ten years ago, in the Preface of my *Another Seed: Studies in Gnostic Mythology*, I thanked Sarah Stroumsa for her interest in "arcane topics." Meanwhile, this interest has extended to the *arcana* themselves. For that, and for her loving support, I am deeply grateful. This book is dedicated to our daughters, in appreciation of their wisdom.

Jerusalem, August 1995

ABBREVIATIONS

AGAJU	Arbeiten zur Geschichte des antiken Judentums und des Urchristentum
ANRW	*Aufstieg und Niedergang der römischen Welt*
BEHE	Bibliothèque de l'Ecole Pratique des Hautes Etudes
BGBT	Beiträge sur Geschichte der biblischen Theologie
BHTh	Beiträge zur historischen Theologie
CG	Cairensis Gnosticus
CMC	*Cologne Mani Codex*
COP	Cambridge Oriental Monographs
DHGH	*Dictionnaire d' Histoire et de Géographie Ecclésiastique*
DS	*Dictionnaire de Théologie Catholique*
EPROER	Etudes Préliminaires aux Religions Orientales dans l'Empire Romain
FRLANT	Forschungen zur Religion des alten und neuen Testaments
GCS	Die griechischen christlichen Schriftsteller der ersten dreiJahrhunderte
HR	*History of Religions*
HSCP	*Harvard Studies in Classical Philology*
HTR	*Harvard Theological Review*
JAC	*Jahrbuch für Antike und Christentum*
JBL	*Journal of Biblical Literature*
JTS	*Journal of Theological Studies*
LCL	Loeb Classical Library
NHS	Nag Hammadi Studies
NTS	*New Testament Studies*
OTM	Oxford Theological Monographs
PG	Patrologia Graeca
PL	Patrologia Latina
PW	*Paulys Realencyklopädie der klassischen Altertumswissenschaft,* G. Wissowa *et al.*, eds.
RAC	*Reallexikon für Antike und Christentum*
RB	*Revue Biblique*
RHR	*Revue de l' Histoire des Religions*
RSR	*Revue des Sciences Religieuses*
RTP	*Revue de Théologie et de Philosophie*

RVV   Religionsgeschichtliche Versuche und Vorarbeiten
SBL   Society of Biblical Literature
SC   Sources Chrétiennes
TDNT   *Theological Dictionnary of the New Testament*, ed. G. Kittel
TRE   *Theologische Realencyklopädie*
TSAJ   Texte und Studien zum antiken Judentum
ZPE   *Zeitschrift für Papyrologie und Epigraphik*

Savoir et Salut G.G. Stroumsa, *Savoir et Salut* (Paris: Cerf, 1992)

Secrecy and Concealment H.G. Kippenberg and G.G. Stroumsa, eds., *Secrecy and Concealment: Studies in the History of Mediterranean and Near Eastern Religions* (*Numen* Book Series 65; Leiden, New York, Köln: Brill, 1995)

INTRODUCTION

> Yet among the mature we do impart wisdom, although it si not a wisdom of this age or of the rulers of this age, who are doomed to pass away. But we impart a secret and hidden wisdom of God [*theou sophian en mustèriôi, tèn apokekrumenèn*], which God decreed before the ages for our glorification. (I Cor 2:6-7)

As a concept, esotericism is relatively new. 'Ésotérisme' seems to have been used for the first time by Jacques Matter in his *Histoire du gnosticisme*, published in 1828. The practice of keeping religious or philosophical doctrines within a small group of initiates and out of reach from others, however, has been in existence since antiquity.

Esotericism is now fashionable, as even a quick browsing through the specialized shelves in many bookstores will show. Modern esotericism, however, has little to do with secret doctines and practices in ancient religions. It refers, rather, to a pot-pourri of various elements in European trends since the early modern period, such as Renaissance Hermetism, Rosicrucians, "Illuminés", Freemasons, Tarot, the Theosophical Society, and the Anthroposophists.

This book deals with "hidden wisdom" and cognate doctrines in early Christian thought. To be sure, some links exist between the phenomena dealt with in this volume and modern avatars of the *philosophia perennis*. These links are reflected in various medieval mediations, especially in Islamic and in Jewish thought.[1] Whereas dualist and gnostic trends seem to have had a much stronger impact on Christianity than on Judaism or Islam, esoteric traditions seem to have fared in these two religious traditions better than in Christianity. The reasons for this fact, which reflect the different structures of these religions, still remain to be fully elucidated.

Since the Reformation, the study of early Christian esoteric traditions has been highly problematic for both Catholic and Protestant scholars. For Catholics, for whom secrecy is associated with heresy and perceived to be in opposition to the openness and the public nature of the tradition of the Great Church, the existence of such traditions

---

[1] On the important case of Shi'ite esotericism, see E. Kohlberg, "Taqiyya in Shī'ī Theology and Religion", *Secrecy and Concealment*, 345-380.

is difficult to accept. For Protestants, the traditions of the Catholic Church, which is suspected of being tainted with esoteric doctrines, reflect a degeneration of the pristine *kerygma* of Jesus and of his apostles. To both denominations, secret doctrines seem alien to the spirit of a religion which offers salvation to all humankind through a simple act of faith. According to this perception, common to scholars and believers alike, Christians have no need for a specialized knowledge. Consequently, any suggestion that Jesus, Paul and their disciples partook of esoteric doctrines encounters deep suspicion.

Early Christian esotericism, or rather "the Christian mysterium", has often been compared to the Greek mysteries. The existence of esoteric trends in Greek religion and culture is well-known. It is suggested already by the myth of Tantalus, who, having been invited to dine with the gods, disclosed their secrets to mankind. For this sin, he was punished in the Underworld. Indeed, we know of such trends from various sources, such as the references to Orphic doctrines and to the Mystery cults. Also well known is the existence of philosophical esotericism, from the Pythagoreans to the Platonists.[2] In this context one should underline the interplay between oral traditions and literary texts in various sects and schools. Greek literature preserves the often blurred traces of such esoteric trends and teachings.[3]

The peculiarity of Greek esotericism lies in the fact that revelation was unknown in the Greek religious world; in such a context, what is kept hidden is the *arcana naturae*, not the *arcana dei*. In a revealed religion, on the other hand, the status of secret teachings is fundamentally different, since in principle God has already revealed, in the past, what He wanted mankind to know. This status is particularly problematic in a religion such as Christianity, which claims to offer salvation to all.

The comparative study of Christian esotericism with the Greek

---

[2] See for instance J. Pépin, "L'arcane religieux et sa transposition philosophique dans la tradition platonicienne", in *La storia della filosofia come sapere critico* (Milan: Angeli, 1984), 18-35, as well as A.H. Armstrong, "The Hidden and the Open in Hellenic Thought", *Eranos Jahrbuch* 54 (1987), 83ff.

[3] Various aspects of such esoteric dimensions throughout Hellenic culture are reflected in five studies in *Secrecy and Concealment*. One of the most audacious arguments in this respect is that of Reinhold Merkelbach, about the religious dimensions of Hellenistic romances, which according to him reflect mystery cults; see his *Roman und Mysterium in der Antike* (Munich, Berlin: Beck, 1962), and *Die Hirten des Dionysos: Die Dionysos-Mysterien römischen Kaiserzeit und der bukolische Roman des Longus* (Stuttgart: Teubner, 1988).

mysteries reflects the heritage of the arguments between Catholic and Protestant scholars. It insists on secrecy in *cult* (the Christian *mysterium*, or the *disciplina arcani*) rather than on secret *doctrines*. This approach is deeply mistaken on at least two counts. It ignores the Jewish background of Christianity, and it does not explain satisfactorily the disappearance of the esoteric trends in late antiquity.

Indeed, although Paul's "hidden wisdom" is a Greek expression, we should probably seek its meaning in Paul's Jewish education. We know of various esoteric traditions in late Second Temple Judaism, especially in apocalyptic circles. We know further of the existence of esoteric traditions, associated with visionary mystical practices, within Rabbinic Judaism of the first two centuries C.E. These esoteric trends seem to have soon aroused suspicion in main stream Rabbinic Judaism, probably because they were adopted by both Christians and Gnostics.

The main argument of the present book can be summarized as follows:

1. We can detect the existence of esoteric doctrines since the earliest stages of Christianity, and throughout the first centuries.

As mentioned above, the existence of esoteric doctrines in early Christianity has often been played down. A typical Catholic attitude is reflected by Gustave Bardy's lapidary formula: "l'arcane appartient aux hérétiques." This traditional approach relies on allusions of the heresiologists, in particular Irenaeus, to the esoteric doctrines and secret rites of Gnostic and dualist heresies. It tends to ignore, however, various Patristic sources, which insist on the paradox of the hidden character of the new revelation. In the second century, already, Ignatius of Antioch could write: "What is hidden is what is revealed..." (*ad Eph.*, 19.1). For John Chrysostom, similarly, in the late fourth century, "the most characteristic trait of mystery is the fact that it is announced everywhere." Christian mystery is 'unspeakable' (*aporrhèton*), "since even to us, the believers, it is not given in full clarity and knowledge." (*Hom. in I Cor*, 7). Chrysostom alludes here, of course, to the cultic *arcana*, i.e., to the fact that before the celebration of the Eucharist the doors of the Church were closed to non-baptized, catechumens included. But it is not only to cultic *arcana* that we find allusions in the writings of the Church Fathers. Thus Cyril of Jerusalem, in the middle of the same fourth century, can write: "For to hear the Gospel is not permitted to all: but the glory of the Gospel is reserved for Christ's true children only." In other words, the *musteria* are not to be divulged to catechumens. But then he adds: "Therefore, the Lord spoke in parables to those who could not hear: but to the disciples He explained the parables in private." (*Cathechesis*, 6.29). Cyril suggests here the existence of a direct link between cultic and doctrinal esotericism, the former being directly dependent upon the latter. The Church Fathers knew quite well that according to the Gospels, Jesus had taught his disciples esoteric doctrines which he would not disclose to the crowds. Here lies, of course, the rationale of Jesus's parables according to the synoptic Gospels (Mat 13:10-17; Mc 4-10-13; Lk 8:9-10).[4]

2. The origin of these early Christian esoteric traditions is to be found in the immediate background of Christianity, i.e., in first-century Judaism.

In the second half of the nineteenth century, many scholars thought that the mystery cults and oriental religions had represented the most serious challenge to early Christianity. Mithra and Christ were perceived as competing for the conquest of souls in the Roman empire. This perception of things, now rejected, has left as its legacy the identification of the Christian *mustèrion* with cult, or *dromena*, rather than with doctrines, *legomena*, to use the vocabulary of the Greek mystery cults. Christian *mustèrion*, indeed, has been studied mainly in pagan context. Now that the Jewish matrix of nascent Christianity is commonly recognized, this approach seems outdated more than ever.

We know much about esoteric traditions in Palestinian Judaism, both among the Pharisees and the Essenes. These traditions, and not the Greek mystery cults, form the background of the "secret words" of Jesus and of the "advanced doctrines" of Paul. In other words, we are now able to recognize the Jewish roots of Christian esoteric doctrines. This Jewish esotericism has its own roots in apocalyptic literature, in texts which often claim to reveal the divine secrets.[5] It is further reflected in the Dead Sea Scrolls, in particular in their insis-

---

[4] On the motif of Jesus's secret teachings, see G. Theissen: "Die pragmatische Bedeutung der Geheimnismotive im Markusevangelium: ein wissensoziologischer Versuch", in *Secrecy and Concealment*, 225-246).

[5] From a large body of recent literature, see for instance S.R.A. Morray-Jones, "Paradise Revisited: The Jewish Background of Paul's Apostolate", *HTR* 86 (1993), 177-217; 265-292; and M. Idel, "Secrecy, Binah and Derishah", *Secrecy and Concealment*, 311-343, with bibliography.

tence on "secrets" (*sod, raz*). It is natural to see such texts and their conceptions as the obvious and immediate background of Paul's *mustèrion*. Paul, moreover, was privy to revelations in mystical experiences, to which he alludes in II Cor 12:1-6. At the present, a lively debate is being held concerning the closeness of the relationship of these experiences to the experiences described or alluded to in early Jewish esoteric mystical texts (the *Heikhalot* literature), which also contain strong magical elements.[6] Such texts refer to the secrets of the Torah, and in particular to the secrecy of the divine name (*ha-sod ha-gadol*). In their present redaction, the Hebrew texts are all posterior to Paul's letters, but probably contain earlier material. Their late redaction date should not therefore prevent us from recognizing the close affinities between them and Paul's allusions to esoteric doctrines.

3. The early Christian esoteric traditions were adopted and developed by various groups which we usually call Gnostics, and were at the basis of their mythology.

There are two sides to esoteric doctrines. The first side is of course the secret itself, the hidden knowledge about the divinity, which is revealed only to a few. In a sense, we can speak of "objective" esotericism when this aspect is emphasized. The other side relates to the partakers of the secrets. The accent is put here not on the secrets themselves, but rather on those who are privileged to know them, on the community of the elect. In Qumran or among the Gnostics and the Manichaeans, for instance, what counts most is the identity of the group of "knowers." In the present book, I have not dealt in a systematic manner with the sociological dimensions of esotericism.[7] From the evidence dealt with here, however, it would appear that together with the growing importance of the sociological aspect of esotericism, we witness a weakened emphasis on the 'objective' secret. When what counts most is the identity of those who know the divine secrets and the protection of their special status, the secrets themselves seem to loose some of their importance. This neutralisation of esoteric beliefs through the insistence on the status of the *electi* is evident in the case

---

[6] On the links between secrecy and magic, see H.-D. Betz, "Secrecy in the Greek Magical Papyri", *Secrecy and Concealment*, 153-175.

[7] Such an approach, in the line of Georg Simmel, the first sociologist to have analyzed the social dimensions of secrecy, informs many of the studies in *Secrecy and Concealment*. See in particular the introduction, "Secrecy and its Benefits", pp. XIII-XXIV.

of Manichaeism. The whole community knows the *ipsissima verba* of
Mani, and yet we have no evidence of any esoteric traditions among
the elect. In this context, it should be pointed out that esotericism is
inherently prone to instability: if the secret is disclosed, it is no longer
a secret; if it is not divulged, it looses its power and impact, and eventually disappears.

4. Already before the end of the second century, the esoteric traditions were played down, blurred and denied by the Church Fathers,
until they eventually disappeared.

It seems that there are two main reasons for the disappearance of
esoteric traditions from early Christianity. The first reason lies in the
predilection of various "heretics", in particular the Gnostics, for these
traditions. Since Christian intellectuals, such as Irenaeus, were
fighting Gnosticism with all available weapons, this predilection entailed the imperious necessity for them to deny the existence of esoteric traditions within "orthodox" Christianity. The second reason is
the growing understanding, among these intellectuals, that in order
for Christianity to be perceived as a religion offering salvation to all,
it must not keep certain beliefs out of reach from most believers.

5. After the disappearance of the early esoteric traditions, their vocabulary served as building blocks for the emerging mystical doctrines within Eastern, and then Western Christianity.

In the first centuries of Christianity, we witness a gradual process
of de-mythologization, the clearest result of which is the rejection of
Gnosticism. Hans Jonas has argued that this process is accompanied
by the birth and growth of a new phenomenon: Christian mysticism.
Jonas has shown how such a transformation is reflected particularly
well in Origen. Origen and his Alexandrian predecessor, Clement,
were particularly close to the world of Gnosis; esoteric patterns of
thought were of great importance for both of them. The birth of
Christian mysticism is directly related to the contemporary development of a new conception of the person, a new approach to subjectivity and the inner man, in other words to the birth of a Christian
anthropology.[8] It should come as no surprise that the birth of Chris-

---

[8] See for instance G. G. Stroumsa, " *Caro Salutis Cardo*: Shaping the Person in Early
Christian Thought", *HR* 30 (1990), 25-50.

tian mysticism is contemporaneous with the disappearance of Christian esotericsm and with the defeat of dualist and mythologizing trends in early Christianity.

Esotericism has a language of its own, which cultivates paradox, allusions, images, metaphors. This language is meant to reveal without revealing, to hide while at the same time hinting at or insinuating. Esotericism itself is paradoxical: the best way to keep a secret is to avoid making any allusions to it, or at least not to multiply them.[9] With the disappearance of esoteric doctrines, we witness the transformation of Christian religious language and of its reference. The new *imaginaire* born in late antiquity was to dominate ways of expression and patterns of thought at least until the end of the Middle Ages. From the hidden nature of God alluded to in esoteric traditions, early Christian mysticism moved to emphasize mystical darkness. Darkness and shadow do not only protect the hidden nature of God, as for instance in Gregory of Nyssa's *Life of Moses*; they also emphasize and broaden the radical dichotomy between God and the world.

Augustine epitomizes this passage to a new mode of thought. For him, the real secrets are no longer those of God, but those of the individual, hidden in the depth of his or her heart, or soul. With him, we witness more clearly than elsewhere, perhaps, the link between the end of esotericism and the development of a new interiorization. This process of interiorization is *ipso facto* a process of demotization: there remains no place for esoteric doctrine in such an approach.

The order in which the chapters of this book are presented is meant to highlight the general argument as delineated above.

Chapter 1 introduces the hermeneutics of myths in the early Roman empire, and briefly presents some ways in which intellectuals coped with the cognitive dissonance stemming from their cultural tradition. In order to retain the value of myths in which they could no longer believe, they had to develop a code whereby to decipher them. The myths hid a secret truth that the hermeneutics endeavoured to reveal by translating it into plain language.

Chapter 2 presents in general terms the main thesis of the book,

---

[9] A close parallel to the language of esotericism is provided by the secret language of the shamans, sorcerers, or priests in secret societies. See for instance B.L. Bellman, *The Language of Secrecy: Symbols and Metaphors in Poro Ritual* (New Brunswick: Rutgers University Press, 1984).

concerning the existence of esoteric traditions in early Christianity. It insists on the complex relationship between oral traditions and written literature in this respect.

Chapter 3 deals with the problem of esoteric myths and the implications of esoteric traditions among the Gnostics. It points out the transformation of myths into metaphors, and the disappearance of esoteric traditions in later Gnostic trends.

In Chapter 4, I seek to trace the few references to esoteric traditions in Manichaean literature, and in particular among the Jewish-Christian groups, such as the Elchasaites, the milieu within which Mani was born and raised. I further seek to explain the disappearance of esoteric traditions in Manichaeism.

Chapter 5 studies aspects of the creation of orthodoxies within Judaism and Christianity during the second century, and attempts to show that this process was accompanied by the expurgation of esoteric texts and traditions.

In a sense, Chapter 6 completes Chapter 1, by showing that Christianity also meant a new kind of discourse and a new hermeneutical attitude, as well as a particular conception of esotericism. I seek to show that the borrowing of Greek hermeneutical vocabulary by Christian intellectuals also entailed the development of new ambiguities, and that the Gnostic challenge partly explains why Christianity opted out of esotericism.

Clement and Origen reflect the passage from esotericism to the new mysticism, as I try to show in Chapter 7. In both cases, the influence of Jewish traditions, direct or indirect, is apparent. Both thinkers develop a view of Christianity established upon two levels of Christianity, the upper one being secret and representing a hidden circumcision. It is in the line of Clement and Origen that Pico della Mirandola will be able to say about Kabbala that it is "non tam mosaicam quam christianam."

The transformation of esoteric traditions into mysticism is the topic of Chapter 8. It offers an analysis of the reasons for the disappearance of esotericism. It also analyzes the conditions in which interiorization, i.e., the passage from myth into mysticism, happened. Esotericism reached its end when *mustèrion* came to imply "things ineffable" rather than "hidden."

While most of the evidence produced in this book comes from Greek Patristic literature, Chapter 9 offers a sample from the same process in the west. Augustine, who had been a Manichaean *auditor* for ten years, rejects the notion of different classes of believers. The 'demotization' of religion that he incarnates entailed the necessity to fight the idea of *arcana dei*. The unending interpretation of the *mysterium* had definitively taken the place of the preservation of the *secretum*.

The last Chapter probes the paradoxical conception of a mystical 'descent' (rather than 'ascent'). I argue that 'descent' is usually conceived as a prelude to vision, and that Plotinus and Augustine reflect a paradigmatic shift which transforms religious language. This shift reflects the disappearance of esoteric traditions directly linked to the *katabasis* or descent theme in religious language.

These chapters describe the ways in which the disappearance of esotericism in late antique Christianity permitted the birth of Christian mysticism and a 'demoticization' of religion without any trivialization. In a revealed religion which acknowledges the logical implications of its own presuppositions, religious truth was no longer hidden. It remained, however, protected behind the veil of the infinite interpretation and the constant striving for *imitatio dei*.

CHAPTER ONE

MYTH AS ENIGMA:
CULTURAL HERMENEUTICS IN LATE ANTIQUITY

Must the gods mean what they say? The question runs like Ariadne's thread throughout Greek culture. Set in the context of the centuries-long reflection on the ambivalent nature of religious language, this question bears upon conceptions of truth and its expression in the ancient world. Plutarch quotes a well-known saying of Heraclitus, "to the effect that the Lord whose prophetic shrine is at Delphi neither tells nor conceals, but indicates." [1] The god's answer is not clearly expressed, but only hinted at, and its understanding requires an interpretive effort. Greek philosophers and grammarians had strived since the fifth century B.C. at least, to make sense of their religious and cultural tradition, to interpret it. Their need to interpret (*hermeneuein*) the Homeric myths stemmed from the intellectual impossibility of accepting these myths at their face value.

This effort however intensified under the Empire, when thinkers living in a world in deep transition had developed a keen and new interest in religious topics. Hence, the interpretations of myth by these thinkers and their understanding of the nature of religious language represent a major aspect of their attempt to reclaim the Hellenic legacy. Their understanding of myths as riddles (*ainigmata*) is the topic of the following pages. *Prima facie*, myth and enigma would seem to be poles apart. While the myth is a story, told in detail, usually publicly, and in words clear to all, the riddle or enigma hides as much as it reveals, alluding to the truth rather than telling it. [2]

---

[1] *oute legei, oute kruptei, alla sèmainei;* (*De Pyth. or.* 21, 404e; fragment 93 Diels). Heraclitus was known in antiquity as an obscure propounder of riddles. Indeed, some of the fragments are actually riddles. See for instance Plato, *Theethetos*, 179e; cf. G.S. Kirk and J.E. Raven, *The Presocratic Philosophers* (Cambridge: University Press, 1957), 182-184. Plutarch also refers to Pythagoras as one who makes use of riddles; see *Moralia* 12d; 672e: *De Iside et Osiride*, ch. 10, 354e.
On the god speaking in riddles, see Plato, *Apol.*, 21b (" *ti pote legei ho theos, kai ti pote ainittetai?*").
[2] Various studies have pointed out the probable original connections between myths and riddles in antiquity. See in particular A. Jolles, *Einfache Formen: Legende, Sage, Mythen, Rätsel, Spruch, Kasus, Memorabile, Märchen, Witz* (Tübingen: Niemeyer,

This traditional approach had gained added urgency from the second to the fourth centuries C.E., when the Hellenic tradition was more and more in competition with the fast-growing sophistication of Christian hermeneutics. The hermeneutics developed around the myths of old was profoundly different in its goals—although not always in its means—from the exegesis of Holy Scriptures in Judaism or in Christianity. The very concept of Holy Writings established on divine revelation is quite alien to Greek culture and religion. The hermeneutical effort of late antique thinkers has been well analyzed in various studies. Suffice it here to mention those of Jean Pépin and Robert Lamberton.[3] The key concept of *ainigma*, however, and its semantic evolution, do not seem to have received due attention.

In classical definitions, *ainigma* (the word means 'riddle' [4]) referred exclusively to a literary trope. "The very nature of a riddle (*ainigma*) is this, to describe a fact in an impossible combination of names", wrote Aristotle.[5] This definition and its literary connotations were echoed by Quintillian, when he defined *ainigma* as "*allegoria, quae est obscurior*".[6]

I shall seek here to review some of the evidence on a much broader meaning of *ainigma*. I intend to show how the identification of myth as enigma enabled late antique thinkers to see myths as early expressions of a basically ambivalent truth, which retained its essential meaning at different levels of understanding. Such a conception of truth reflects an elitist attitude whose relationships with both political power and language should also be noted.

We might begin with an important but rather underestimated text

---

1930), in the chapter on Märchen. It should be pointed out that a similar relationship between an enigmatic mode of exposition and its interpretation characterizes the first kind of dreams (out of five) in Macrobius' taxonomy. See his *Commentary on the Dream of Scipio*, I.3.2.: "By an enigmatic dream we mean one that conceals with strange shapes and veils with ambiguity the true meaning of the information being offered, and requires an interpretation for its understanding." (Transl. W.H. Stahl, *Macrobius' Commentary on the Dream of Scipio* [New York: Columbia University Press, 1952], 10).

[3] J. Pépin, *Mythe et allégorie: les origines grecques et les contestations judéo-chrétiennes* (Paris: Etudes augustiniennes, 1976), 2nd. ed.[1st. ed. 1958] ; R. Lamberton, *Homer the Theologian: Neoplatonist Allegorical Reading and the Growth of the Epic Tradition* (Berkeley: University of California Press, 1986). Both works are extremely important for our purpose.

[4] Cf. Plato, *Apology*, 27a.

[5] *Poetics*, 22, 1458a 26; cf. *Rhetoric*, 3.2.12, 1405ab; *metaphorai gar ainittontai*.

[6] *Inst.* 8.6.52; cf. Cicero, *de or.* 3.42

of Plutarch, which offers a fascinating reflection on the radical transformations of Greek culture since its early stages.[7] The text, which
covers chapters 24 to 26 of *the Oracles at Delphi*,[8] begins with consid-
erations on the nature of speech (*logos*), the value of which, like that
of currency, evolves with time. The argument, developed in Plutarch's
dialogue by Theon,[9] aims at showing that this change, willed by divine providence, has been for the better. His is an optimistic view of
cultural transformations in history. In early times, he writes,

> men used as the coinage of speech verses and tunes and songs, and
> reduced to poetic and musical form all history and philosophy and, in
> a word, every experience and action that required a mere impressive
> utterance. This aptitude for poetry, rare nowadays, was then shared by
> most people, who expressed themselves through lyre and song, using
> myths and proverbs (*muthois kai paroimiais*), and besides composed
> hymns, prayers, and paeans in honour of the gods in verse and music...
> Accordingly, the god did not begrudge to the art of prophecy adorn-
> ment and pleasing grace, even providing visions.[10]

At some point, however, "life took on a change along with the change
in men's fortunes and their natures; usage banished the superfluous
(*to peritton*)" . In a surprisingly modern fashion, Plutarch insists that the
transformation was originally of a cultural nature, reflecting a change
in ways of life and economic behavior. People began to dress, and
adorn themselves more soberly, "rating as decorative the plain and
simple rather than the ornate and elaborate." According to him, this
cultural transformation was felt also on the linguistic level:

---

[7] For the background of Plutarch as a *Kulturkritik*, the classical study remains P.
Decharme, *La critique des traditions religieuses chez les grecs, des origines au temps de Plutarque*
(Paris: A. Picard, 1904). On Plutarch's own religious thought, see Y. Vernière, *Sym-
boles et mythes dans la pensée de Plutarque: essai d'interprétation philosophique et religieuse des
Moralia* (Paris: Belles Lettres, 1977), and F.E. Brenck, S.J., *In Mist Apparelled: Religious
Themes in Plutarch's Moralia and Lives* (Mnemosyne 48; Leiden: Brill, 1977). See also
R. Flacelière, "La théologie selon Plutarque", in *Mélanges Pierre Boyancé* (Rome: Ecole
Française de Rome, 1974), 273-280. These works, however, do not deal directly with
the topic of the present study.

[8] *De Pythiae oraculis* 406b-407f. I quote the translation of F.C. Babbitt, in volume
5 of Plutarch's *Moralia* in the LCL, (Cambrigde, Mass, London, 1936), pp. 324-335.

[9] Although Theon's words might well reflect here adequately Plutarch's own
views, it is of course imposssible to claim this with certainty.

[10] Cf. *On the Fame of the Athenians*, 348a: "That poetry concerns itself with the com-
position of mythological matters Plato has also stated"(Babbitt, transl.; LCL, *Moralia*,
vol. 5, pp.506-508.

So, as language also underwent a change and put off its finery, history descended from its vehicle of versification, and went on foot in prose, whereby the truth was mostly sifted from the fabulous.[11]

In an analysis that is strongly reminiscent of Giambattista Vico's perception of the relationships between myth and poetry in the *Scienza Nuova*, Plutarch presents the mutation as entailing a change in patterns of thought: whereas the poetic style was well fitted for the telling of tales (*muthoi*), prose, leaving out all ornaments, takes away 'the mythical' or the fabulous, and retains only the kernel, unadorned truth, *a-lètheia*, which is now revealed, or dis-covered.

Philosophy, too, was transformed, when philosophers opted for the unequivocal character of common language and abandoned the vagueness and obscure quality of poetic style:

> Philosophy welcomed clearness and teachability in preference to creating amazement (*to ekplètton*), and pursued its investigations through the medium of everyday language (*dia logôn*).

The birth of a new kind of philosophy, conceived as an effort of intellectual honesty and simplicity, was directly related to the emergence of prose as the common way of expression. Language was also affected by such a dramatic change. Heralded by Apollo himself, the new age also meant the end of metaphor:

> The god put an end to having his prophetic priestess call her own citizens ' fire-blazers', the Spartans 'snake-devourers', men 'mountain-roamers', and rivers 'mountain-engorgers' ....When he had taken away from the oracles epic versification, strange words, circumlocutions, and vagueness, he had thus made them ready to talk to his consultants as the laws talk to states, or as kings meet with common people, or as pupils listen to teachers, since he adapted the language to what was intelligible and convincing.

Yet, the most important consequence of the transformation of language occurred in the field of knowledge, in particular of religious knowledge:

> The introduction of clearness was attended also by a revolution in belief, which underwent a change along with everything else.[12]

---

[11] *malista tou muthôdous apekrithè to alèthes; Ibid.*, 406e.

[12] *meta de tès saphèneias kai hè pistis houtôs estrepheto summetaballousa tois allois pragmasin. Ibid.* 407a.

Thus, according to Plutarch, the transformation of language entailed a radical change in the very conception of religion. This religious revolution meant disenchantment with all strange, uncanny or grandiloquent expressions, which had been considered in the past as so many manifestations of divine power. Now, also religious truth must also be expressed in clear and simple prose:

> As a result, people blamed the poetic language with which the oracles were clothed, not only for obstructing the understanding of these in their true meaning and for combining vagueness and obscurity with the communication, but already they were coming to look with suspicion upon metaphors, riddles and ambiguous statements,[13] feeling that these were secluded nooks of refuge devised for furtive withdrawal and retreat for him that should err in his prophecy.

In other words, Plutarch claims here that in the religious world of the early empire—and in contradistinction with early times—the deliberate use of high style and various forms of polyvalent or metonymic expressions all too often hid fraud. He mentions "the tribe of wandering soothsayers and rogues that practiced their charlatanry about the shrines of the Great Mother and of Sarapis..." It is these prophets, according to Plutarch, "that most filled the poetic art with disrepute".[14]

But religious charlatans, despite their high visibility, should not be considered the main cause of the general discontent with poetic style. This lies, rather, in the cultural changes which brought men to "banish the superfluous" and to "adorn themselves with economy", —changes, again, approved by Plutarch.

Moving to the political level, Plutarch speculates on another reason for the ambiguity of classical religious language, or, as he puts it, the "need of double entendre (*diploès tinos*), indirect statement and vagueness for the people of ancient days". Assuredly, the god at Delphi could not lie, but he did not want to reveal too much, through the oracle, to greedy rulers who would have misused knowledge of future events in their waging of unjust wars.

Hence, the obvious solution was that the god should speak through the oracle, that is to say, in a vague and ambiguous language. Only the wise leaders would understand the message precisely, while

---

[13] *all' èdè kai tas metaphoras kai ta ainigmata kai tas amphibolias*, ibid. 407a-b.
[14] *ibid.*, 407c.

it would remain opaque for the less philosophically-minded rulers. Thus the god

> is not willing to keep the truth unrevealed, but he caused the manifestation of it to be deflected, like a ray of light, in the medium of poetry, where it submits to many reflections and undergoes subdivisions, and thus he did away with its repellent harshness. There were naturally some things which it was well that despots should fail to understand and enemies should not learn beforehand. About these, therefore, he put a cloak of intimations and ambiguities which conceals the communication[15] so far as others were concerned, but did not escape the persons involved nor mislead those that had need to know and who gave their minds to the matter.

This analysis of the political reasons for the ambiguity in divine revelation points to what we would probably call esotericism: divine oracles, presented in enigmatic garb, hide as much as they reveal. We are back at the saying of Heraclitus with which we began: in the old days, the god neither told, nor concealed, but indicated. The close connections of the modes of expressing the truth with forms of political power—those analyzed by Leo Strauss and Michel Foucault—are here clearly recognizable. But those early days have passed for good, and we should not regret them, concludes Plutarch:

> Therefore anyone is very foolish who, now that conditions have become different, complains and makes unwarranted indictment if the god feels that he must no longer help us in the same way, but in a different way. Nowadays, history has found ways (through its use of prose) to sift facts ('truth') from legend ('myths'), while philosophy has learned to avoid grandiloquence and to seek precision and communicability.

Plutarch refers here to the consequences of a radical cultural transformation, which left a cognitive dissonance of sorts, a gap in the relationship of intellectuals in the Roman empire to their classical heritage. The discrepancy between two conceptual worlds is felt now in a much stronger sense than in the classical times. It is only through hermeneutics that it can be mediated. In that sense, the civilization of the empire, particularly in late antiquity, can be called a civilization of hermeneutics: the sense of distance from the cultural past is matched by the urge to relate to its fundamental classical documents,

---

[15] *toutois oun periebalen huponoias kai amphilogias apokruptousai to phrazomenon, ibid.* 407e.

that is to say, mainly, the Homeric poems and the works of the early philosophers.

For later Greek intellectuals, the writings of the wise authors must express truth, although in quite different ways from the Jewish and Christian Scriptures. If such truth is not apparent to us, it must be looked for on a deeper level: this is the task of the *homo interpres*. Attempts to speak in enigmas or other ambiguous ways are suspect today, but we must understand that in previous times these were perfectly legitimate. The role of the modern-day philosophers is precisely to interpret these pithy sayings of old, and to translate their meaning, as it were, into clear, unambiguous prose. In any case, a rational person, who understands the nature of enigmas and other kinds of indirect discourse, should not attempt to revive the old days. Both his social role and his patterns of thought are conceived of as radically different from those of the priests of old. The treatise ends with the following paragraph:

> But, just as in those days there were people who complained of the obliquity and vagueness of the oracles, so today there are people who make an unwarranted indictment against their extreme simplicity. Such an attitude of mind is altogether puerile and silly. It is a fact that children take more delight and satisfaction in seeing rainbows, haloes, and comets than in seeing moon and sun; and so these persons yearn for the riddles, allegories, and metaphors which are but reflections of the prophetic art when it acts upon a human imagination.[16]

The basic conceptions which this remarkable text develops at some length are reflected elsewhere in Plutarch's writings. For him, it is on purpose that the wise men of old used to hide their scientific knowledge under the cloak of myths. This is the reason why their writings usually appear like a mysterious theology the secret of which is protected by riddles and hidden meanings (*di' ainigmatôn kai huponoiôn epikruphos*), in which what is pronounced is clearer for the crowd than what remains unsaid, but what is kept silent is deeper than what is pronounced.[17] Such a method, of at once unveiling and veiling, Plutarch finds "in the Orphic poems, in Egyptian and Phrygian legends,

---

[16] *kai houtoi ta ainigmata kai tas allègorias kai tas metaphoras tès mantikès, anaklaseis ousas pros to thnèton kai phantastikon, epipothousi. Ibid.* 30(409c), pp.342-345 Babbitt.

[17] *Ex opere de Daedalis Plataeensibus* I (Bernardakis, vol. 7, 43. 3-13); the text is quoted by Pépin, *op. cit.*, p. 184.

and especially in the liturgies of initiation to the mysteries and the symbolic rites of sacrifices." [18]

In another passage, he insists on the purposefulness of such an esoteric theology. In the days of old, the sages, who knew the true nature of the gods and of their transformations under changing conditions, and feared this nature might be misunderstood by the people, gave different names to the god in its various forms (such as Apollo or Phoebos), "since they wanted to hide these truths from the crowd".[19] Here, the esotericism is more traditional in nature than the one refered to above. The deeper meaning of truth (be it religious or philosophical) is reserved for the elite, since its inevitable misapprehension by simple folks entails serious danger. This danger is double: both for the unprepared hearer of truth and for he who profers it. It is in this last sense that Numenius, for instance, refered to "the secrets of Plato".[20]

> Now this ancient and secret wisdom, far from having been only a Hellenic phenomenon, crossed the boundaries between Greeks and Barbarians. Among Barbarians, the Egyptians hold a place of honour: they placed sphinxes in front of their temples "to indicate that their religious teaching (*theologia*) has in it an enigmatical sort of wisdom.[21]

Similarly, the hieroglyphs retain a secret symbolism, and they deeply influenced "the wisest among the Greeks": "Pythagoras, in particular, enjoying a mutual admiration with these people, imitated their symbolism and mysterious manner, interspersing his teaching with riddles." [22] One should note that although *ainigma* is much used in this context, other words, such as *huponoia* or *allegoria* , carry a very close or even identical meaning. For, according to Plutarch,

> By the means of what the ancients called 'hidden thoughts', and which are known today under the name of 'allegories', one has tried to do violence to Homer's stories and to change their sense.[23]

---

[18] Robert Lamberton calls my attention to the fact that it is extremely unlikely that Plutarch speaks here in his own voice, refering me to F. H. Sandbach's comments in Plutarch's *Moralia*, LCL, vol. XV, 282-283.

[19] *kruptomenoi de tous pollous hoi sophôteroi*; *De E Delphico*, 9. =388F, cf. 2a, 2c, 6a.

[20] *Peri tôn Platoni aporrhètôn*; Eusebius, *Praeparatio Evangelica*, XIII.4-5. According to Numenius (Fragments 24. 57-64), it is for political reasons that Plato's writings were deliberately coded. See Lamberton, *Homer the Theologian*, 62-63; 73.

[21] *ainigmatôdè sophian*, *De Iside et Osiride*, 9. 354c.

[22] *Is. Osir.*, 10. 354e.

Plutarch's attitude, as we have seen in the long passage from the Oracles at Delphi, is one of historical optimism. The evolution of mores and the parallel transformation of patterns of thought works all for the best. In the 'disenchanted' (*entzaubert*, to use Weberian terminology) modern world [i.e. of his own days], people think more clearly, that is to say more properly than they used to in former times. This faith in the progress of reason throughout history, however, was not shared by all late antique thinkers. A strikingly different attitude to the cultural transformation is reflected by Maximus of Tyre, a second century eclectic Platonist philosopher. Like Plutarch, Maximus is deeply interested in religious questions, and shares his analysis of the drastic change that occured in modern philosophy: "As it closely examined myths and could not suffer enigmas,[24] the soul freed philosophy from the veils that adorned it and used naked speech" .

Although Maximus' diagnosis of the phenomena is identical to that of Plutarch, his evaluation of modern philosophy is strikingly different, in that it expresses much skepticism as to the value of the contemporary interpretation of myths:

> Everything is full of enigmas, with the poets as with the philosophers; the modesty with which they cover truth seems to me preferable to the direct language of modern writers. In questions unclear to human weakness, myth is indeed a more honorable interpreter.[25] If our contemporaries have reached deeper in contemplation than their predecessors, I congratulate them. If, however, without passing them in knowledge, they have exchanged the riddles of their forefathers for transparent myths, I fear lest they be accused of revealing secret discourses.[26]

Both Plutarch and Maximus, however different their reactions to cultural transformations might be, have in common the same historical consciousness, shaped by the recognition of their own belatedness. For both of them, riddles refer to traditional and esoteric ways of expressing truth.

---

[23] *De Audiendis Poetis*, 7. 419e: *palai men huponoiais, allègoriais de nun legomenais...* See Pépin, *Mythe et allégorie*, 87-88. On 'allegory' in Plutarch, see J. G. Griffiths (ed. and transl.), *Plutarch's de Iside et Osiride* (University of Wales Press: 1970), 419 (on chap. 32).

[24] *tous muthous diereunômenè kai ouk anekhimenè tôn ainigmatôn. Philosophumena*, IV.3; (44.1-7 Holbein; see Pépin, *Mythe et allégorie*, 187).

[25] *euskhèmonesteros hermeneus ho muthos*.

[26] *Ibid.* IV.5.

Various authors show a similar understanding of the cultural past. I shall refer here to some texts which appear to be paradigmatic. Strabo, around the beginning of the Christian era, reflects the Stoic attitude to myths and to their relationships with riddles:

> Every discussion of the gods is built upon the examination of opinions and myths, since the ancients hinted at (*ainittomenôn tôn palaiôn*) their physical perceptions about things and always added a mythic element to their discussions. It is not an easy thing to solve all the riddles correctly, but the whole mass of mythically expressed material is placed before you.[27]

R. Lamberton calls this 'fascinating passage' a "capsule summary of the Stoic conception of theology" that had its roots in the fourth and third centuries B.C. According to Strabo, the ancients did not express their opinions directly and openly, but clothed them in riddles and myths, i.e. in an indirect language which calls for interpretation.

The same opinion is held by Pausanias, in a revealing passage, which Paul Veyne has analyzed at length in his thought-provoking book on the belief in myths in ancient Greece:

> In the days of old those Greeks who were considered wise spoke their sayings not straight out but in enigmas...[28]

Veyne singled out Pausanias as a particularly interesting example of those late antique Greek intellectuals who combined a critical attitude to myths with the traditional respect shown towards both gods and oracles.[29]

This is best exemplified by the conception of riddles reflected in our texts. The myth is described as an *ainigma* only when it cannot be understood and believed as it is, taken at its face value. We can thus assume that while the myth looks absurd *prima facie*, it carries in fact a deep but hidden meaning, which only proper interpretation can reveal.

---

[27] *Geography* X.3.23. 474, quoted (but mistranslated) by V. Goldschmidt, "Theologia", *Revue des Etudes Grecques* 63(1950), 20-42, see 22, and Lamberton, *Homer the Theologian*, 26-27. Text in Strabo, *Geography*, vol. VII (1971), 82-83 Lasserre, cf. n.6 p. 136.

[28] *Hellènôn tous nomizomenous sophous di' ainigmatôn palai kai ouk ek tou eutheos legein tous logous... Description of Greece*, 8.8.3. Cf. P. Veyne, *Les grecs ont-ils cru à leurs mythes?* (Paris: Seuil, 1983), 24, cf. 41 and 42, n. 48 on enigmas.

[29] Ibid., 108.

According to this conception, truth (*alètheia*)[30] is to be searched for and discovered in order to be revealed, but this revelation must of necessity remain ambiguous, hiding even as it unveils. This attitude towards truth was more properly that of the prophet (*mantis*) than that of the philosopher in classical times, a fact noted anew by Michel Foucault.[31] It became commonly accepted in late antiquity by Neoplatonic philosophers, who conceived their task, in seeking the deepest levels of truth, as religious more than epistemic in nature. Like priests, they attempted to crack the enigmas in which religious truth was clothed and hidden.

For Plotinus, religious mysteries, as well as myths, allude to intellectual realities. Thus the mysteries and the myths about the gods 'say riddingly' (*ainittontai*) that Kronos, the wisest of the gods, shuts up again within himself that which he has produced before the birth of Zeus.[32] One must pierce the enigma, Plotinus tells us, just as "the wise priest understands the enigma (*to ainigma sunieis*), and, arriving there, reaches a real contemplation of the sanctuary" .[33] In a similar way, he interprets the ithyphallic Hermes as the representation of an enigma: "I believe that this is what the ancient wise wanted to say in their mysteries: representing the old Hermes with a constantly active generating member..." [34]

Porphyry, more systematically than his teacher Plotinus, devoted much effort to his search for the true, philosophical meaning of religious language. His most clearly developed statement on the matter is to be found in his *Commentary on the Cave of the Nymphs,* where he seeks to investigate Homer's 'enigma', i.e. his hidden philosophical intentions and spiritual reference when describing the cave of the nymphs in the *Odyssey.*[35] Elsewhere he writes:

---

[30] On the semantics of the word in ancient Greek literature, see for instance R. Bultmann's article in *TDNT,* vol I, 232-251.

[31] Foucault dealt with the topic in his very last lecture course. See T. Flynn, "Foucault as Parrhesiast: his Last Course at the Collège de France (1984)", in J. Bernauer and D. Rasmussen, eds., *The Final Foucault* (Cambridge, Mass.: M.I.T., 1988), 102-118, esp. 104.

[32] *Enn.* V.1.7.27ff.

[33] *Enn.* VI.9.11.25-30 and 43-45.

[34] *Enn.* III.6.19.25-41

[35] *De Antro Nympharum,* 21; I use the edition and translation of L. Westerink *et al.,* (Arethusa Monographs I; Buffalo, N.Y., 1969).

> What Homer says about Circe contains an amazing view of things that
> concern the soul. He says: (*Odyssey* 10.239-240)
> "Their heads and voices, their bristles and their bodies
> Were those of pigs, but their minds were solid, as before"
> Clearly, this myth is an enigma (*esti toinun ho muthos ainigma*), concerning
> what Pythagoras and Plato have said about the soul...[36]

Porphyry's investigations are based upon the belief that, as he states
in the *Philosophy of Oracles*, "the gods have not revealed anything about
themselves in a clear way, but only through enigmas". Hence, for Porphyry as well as for Plotinus or Plutarch, the philosopher cracks the
divine code in his interpretation of enigmas.[37] In a sense, the philosopher's role is very similar to that of the priest, but the latter also
sought to preserve the ambiguity which he was revealing. For Plutarch, as we have seen, the philosopher must strive to supress all ambiguity.

Other texts exhibit a rather different trend. The implicit identification
of the philosopher's role to that of a priest is also found among the
late Neoplatonists, who insist, more than most earlier thinkers, on the
religious context of myths. Proclus, for instance, says that "initiations
use myths so as to keep hidden the ineffable truth about the gods".[38]
He explicitly states that for him, the philosopher's task is similar to
that of the wise priest: like the latter, the philosopher is an interpreter
(*hermèneus*) in lower—and clearer, less ambiguous language—of that
which was expressed more densely in the Homeric myths. "According
to the secret doctrine (*kata tèn aporrhètôn theôrian*), he claims, the way the
gods behave in Homer's works must be interpreted, rather than understood at its face value, and hence should not be regarded as offen-
sive.[39]

---

[36] *Apud* Stobeus, *Ecl.*, 1.41.60, quoted by Lamberton, *op. cit.*, 118. Lamberton
writes on this passage: "The claim that the Homeric passage itself is an *ainigma* is
finally unimportant. Porphyry elaborates his account in the manner of Plotinus, ex-
ploiting the myths and language of Homer to communicate abstract truths.", *op. cit.*,
119.

[37] Robert Lamberton, however, calls my attention to the facts that "for Plutarch,
the hermeneutic problems he loves are essentially and necessarily insoluble", and
that "very little of Plotinus' philosophical work involved interpretation."

[38] *In Rempublicam*, II. 108 Knoll. The text is quoted by Vernière, *Symboles et mythes
dans la pensée de Plutarque*, 338, n. 2.

[39] See esp. *In Rempubl.*, I.44.14; 66.7; 73.15; 74.19; 159.15; 2.248.27. The references are given by Lamberton, *Homer the Theologian*, 169, 195, 214.

The dialectical relationship between the revealed and the hidden, which according to this conception is a main characteristic of myth, is also refered to by Sallustios, Julian's Neoplatonic mentor. A most pregnant and radical metaphor appears in his treatise *On the Gods and the World*:

> The universe itself can be called a myth (*exesti gar kai ton kosmon muthon eipein*), since bodies and material objects are apparent in it, while souls and intellects are concealed.[40]

The world is a myth: the phrase is reminiscent of another metaphor, "all the world's a stage", *skènè pas ho bios*,—a metaphor also known to Maximus of Tyre.[41] Yet the novelty of the metaphor should not be ignored. If myth has grown to take cosmic dimensions, the cosmos itself, object of the philosopher's investigations, has become identified with a myth, or rather, an enigma, to be deciphered through the help of the clues given by its revealed parts. The philosopher, according to such a conception, becomes an interpreter, an intellectual priest, or *theourgos* of sorts. It then does not come as a surprise to find similar ideas about the *arcana naturae* from the pen of Iamblichus: "Just as nature has in a way set the stamp of invisible thoughts in visible objects".[42]

> Just like myth, nature conceals in the same extent that it reveals, and just like myth, its deep kernel has to be retrieved through the correct understanding of various hints (*ainigmata*). Some of these hints are provided, for instance, by the statues of the gods.[43]

Sallustios points out that there are various kinds of myths: theological, physical, psychical, material and of mixed nature. Of all these, only the theological myths, which deal with the very essence of the gods, allude directly to the divine.[44]

---

[40] *De diis et mundo*, III; 4.9 Nock.

[41] *Dialexeis*, VII.10.

[42] *De Myst.*, VII.1 and parallel passages, quoted by A.D. Nock, ed., transl., *Sallustius, Concerning the Gods and the Universe* (Cambridge: University Press, 1926), p. XLIV and n. 29.

[43] *De diis et mundo* VI; 12.10 Nock; as is well known, the sphinxes in front of the Egyptian temples were widely perceived in this light by Greek thinkers. Clement of Alexandria, in particular, dwells on the issue in his *Stromateis*. These texts are analyzed in chapter 6 *infra*. It would be interesting to investigate the possible connections of this perception with the Augustinian concept of the 'traces' of God in the world.

[44] *De diis et mundo*, IV; 4.21-25 Nock.

In the same context, Sallustios offers a justification of esotericism not encountered before:

> Furthermore, to wish to teach all men the truth about the gods causes the foolish to despise, because they cannot learn, and the good to be slothful, whereas to conceal the truth by myths prevents the former from despising philosophy and compels the latter to study it.[45]

New is the insistence on the double character of esotericism. Whereas mythical stories satisfy the foolish, to whom philosophical truth would seem meaningless, quite the contrary is true for the good: it is precisely because myth strikes them as unconvincing or meaningless that it forces philosophical reflection upon them. In other words, it is the very absurdity of myth that triggers rational thought.

This conception is developed further by the emperor Julian. Julian's starting point is the intellectual and ethical scandal represented by so many myths about the gods. Hence, only the belief that they should be interpreted, and not understood *au pied de la lettre*, can save them:

> Accordingly, unless everyone of these legends is a myth that involves some secret interpretation (*muthos ekhôn theôrian aporrhèton*), as I indeed believe, they are filled with many blasphemous sayings about God. [46]

At once a Neoplatonist philosopher and a religious renovator, Julian seems to have been interested in myths and their interpretation.[47] If the myths are unbelievable as they stand, while they also reflect the deepest truth about the deity, their shocking character must be purposeful. Hence, we must reach the conclusion that the wise men of the past" (*hoi palaioi*), when they discovered the original meanings of things (with the help of the gods), "clothed them in paradoxical myths" (*muthois paradoxois*), "in order that, by means of the paradox and the incongruity (*hina dia tou paradoxou kai apemphainontos*), the fiction might be detected and we might be induced to search out the truth" . Indeed, it is by such riddles as these (*dia men tôn ainigmatôn*) that the wise man is reminded that he must search out their meaning.[48]

---

[45] *Ibid.* III; 4.11-15 Nock.

[46] *Against the Galileans*, 94a; vol. III, 326-327 LCL.

[47] Iamblichus, on the contrary, seems to take surprisingly little interst in myths (R. Lamberton).

[48] *Oration* V: "Hymn to the Mother of the Gods", LCL I; 170a-c.

The most impressive text dealing with the topic, however, is found in Julian's *Oration VII*: " To the Cynic Heracleios: how a Cynic ought to behave and whether it is proper for him to compose myths" . To my mind, the *Oration* constitutes one of the most interesting discussions of the relationships between myth and philosophy to have reached us from antiquity. Oddly enough, its importance does not seem to have been widely recognized.

After noting, like Plutarch, that myths seem to be originally the invention of men given to pastoral pursuits and playing both the flute and the lyre (206a), Julian asks what kinds of myths ought to be invented, and what parts of philosophy are interested in myths. Myth, he answers, can be employed or composed "only by practical philosophy, which deals with the individual man, and by that department of theology which has to do with initiation and the Mysteries." "For Nature loves to hide her secrets," adds Julian, refering to Heraclitus' saying, "and she does not suffer the hidden truth about the essential nature of the gods to be flung in naked words to the ears of the profane"(216b ff).

Myths are written for childish souls, as Plato says (Phaedrus, 251), and with the development of mythical expression, poets invented a new literary genre, the fable with a moral, or *ainos*.[49] In myth, the poet, who aims at moral exhortation and instruction, conceals this goal, by not speaking openly (*phanorôs*). He acts in this way from fear of alienating his hearers (207a).

But for those who do not belong to the multitude, and who can receive truth in its purest form, it is precisely the paradoxical and incongruous element (*apemphainon*) always present in myths that guides towards the truth (216c-d). Hence, "I mean that the more paradoxical and prodigious the enigma is, the more it seems to warn us not to believe simply the bare words but rather to study diligently the hidden truth." (217c). And later: "Whenever myths on sacred subjects are incongruous in thought, by that very fact they cry aloud, as it were, and summon us not to believe them literally (*mè pisteuein haplôs*) but to study and track down their hidden meaning" .[50]

---

[49] On the early development of the *ainos*, see G. Nagy, "Mythe et prose en Grèce archaïque: l' *ainos* ", in C. Calame ed., *Métamorphoses du mythe en Grèce antique* (Genève: Labor et Fides, 1988), 229-242.

[50] *to lelèthos*, 222c; I am quoting according to the text and translation in volume II of the LCL edition, here pp. 118-119.

Julian adds that myths expressing 'incongruous' thoughts about the gods are permitted only on the condition that their language remain "wholly dignified" (*semna khrè panu ta rhèmata einai*). It was in such strong terms that the last pagan emperor reaffirmed a long tradition of cultural hemeneutics in the Hellenic world. Thanks to this tradition, he was able to feel close to Homer and to Aesop, and to accept the Heracleitan saying as a major postulate of his epistemology.

More than any other Hellenic thinker, Julian insisted on the virtue of paradox and on its importance in the search for religious truth. Now the most famous justification of paradox in late antiquity is probably Tertullian's establishment of faith upon the rational inacceptability of its content.[51] This is not the place to analyze it. Suffice it to point out that it is set on a level quite different from Julian's own praise of absurdity. For the Christian thinker, the paradox does not hide a deeper meaning, and does by no means indicate, even in an allusive way, its own falseness. The gap between Tertullian's *absurdum* and Julian's *apemphainon* is indicative of the Christian radical break with the Hellenic hermeneutical tradition. It is not only the content of the myths, i.e. both the shocking stories themselves and their esoteric and philosophical interpretation that the Fathers rejected, but also their linguistic form, the 'high language' in which they were expressed, and which was inherent in the whole hermeneutic attitude of Hellenic thinkers.[52]

Eric Auerbach has offered a remarkable analysis of a new literary genre which appeared in Christian antiquity, the *sermo humilis*, a single popular level of expression of even the highest thought, which ought to be understood by all and sundry.[53] This *sermo humilis*, fundamentally different from the late antique Hellenic interpretation of myths (*semna rhèmata*), became an essential element of the new culture which crystallized in late antiquity and was to become the backbone of medieval Christian culture.

---

[51] Tertullian, *de Carne Christi*, 5. Tertullian does not use the lapidary formula attributed to him, "*credo, quia absurdum*".

[52] See chapter 6 *infra*.

[53] E. Auerbach, "Sacrae scripturae sermo humilis" (in French), in his *Gesammelte Aufsätze zur romanischen Philologie* (Bern, Munich: Francke, 1967); translated into English as "Sermo Humilis", in his *Literary Language and its Public in Late Latin Antiquity and in the Middle Ages* (London: Routledge and Kegan Paul, 1965).

CHAPTER TWO

PARADOSIS: ESOTERIC TRADITIONS IN EARLY CHRISTIANITY

In ancient society, where literacy was uncommon, the oral retained its essential role in cultural communication. Certain major characteristics of ancient culture result from the duality of written and oral communication, which was fundamental in the process of collective memory and in the transmission of ideas. Recently it has been emphasized that Greek myths, in their evolution and transformation, must be understood within that duality.[1] The very idea of myth necessitates a background; a myth refers to a hidden truth which it represents.[2]

The idea of a double truth, of truth with (at least) two levels, implies another consequence, that of esotericism, which is also inherent in the religious and cultural traditions of antiquity. In a society which was still largely illiterate, knowledge was primarily transmitted orally and individually, even in elite milieus where literacy was current. In various forms, this status of oral material is thus directly related to the idea of a particular and profound truth, shared only among limited circles who made it their specialty, circles ruled by those who have been called, "the masters of truth." [3] These "masters of truth," aware of their marginal position and of the danger represented by *another* truth, took precautions in expressing it: one had to know to whom and how. Truth belonged to an elite, its imprudent revelation could have unpleasant consequences for everyone; these ideas are the basis of all esotericism, particularly that which was so widely practiced in

---

[1] M. Detienne, *L'invention de la mythologie* (Paris: Gallimard, 1981), 50-86. On the place of writing in premodern societies, see for example T. R. Goody, ed., *Literacy in Traditional Societies* (Cambridge: Cambridge University Press, 1968).

[2] See in particular F. Buffière, *Les mythes d'Homère et la pensée grecque* (Paris: Belles Lettres, 1956), 33 ff. For a general view, see J. Pépin, *Mythe et Allégorie: les origines grecques et les contestations judéo-chrétiennes* (Paris: Aubier, 1958) and R. Lamberton, *Homer the Theologian: Neoplatonist Allegorical Reading and the Growth of the Epic Tradition* (Berkeley...: California University Press, 1986). The problem of attitudes toward myth in ancient society has been presented in a new manner by P. Veyne, *Les Grecs ont-ils cru à leurs mythes ?* (Paris: Seuil, 1983).

[3] M. Detienne, *Les maîtres de vérité dans la Grèce archaïque* (Paris: Maspéro, 1981[2]).

the ancient world. The ambiguous status of writing, the danger inherent in it, explains this apparent paradox of the importance of the development of oral traditions, particularly in literate circles. Education thus proceeded on two levels: while esoteric conceptions were published, esoteric traditions were only transmitted orally, from master to disciple. This tradition is preserved from Plato, who, in his *Second Epistle*, alludes to the enigmas by which he expresses himself, to Plotinus, of whom Porphyrius says that he had agreed with Herrenius and Origen (the pagan philosopher, of course,) to keep secret the doctrine taught by Ammonius Saccas.[4]

Just as much or perhaps even more than by its epistemological role, truth is identified by its soteriological function. Esotericism thus is revealed as being as much religious as intellectual in essence—to a degree the distinction is anachronistic. In *Magna Graecia*, for example, the Pythagoreans provide the most famous case of a movement which was both religious and philosophical, grounded upon an esoteric doctrine. Beyond the complexity of the traditions and the differences of opinion among scholars, it seems well established that the *akousmata* represent oral traditions, the *hieroi logoi, ipsissima verba* of the Master introduced by the famous *ephè*, "he said." It is probable that the *akousmata*, composed in dialogue form, reflect the survival or a primitive oral teaching, just as the *tetraktus* was originally an oath of secrecy.[5]

Whether or not Pythagorean influence was manifest in the formation of Essenism in Palestine is less important than to note, with Isidore Lévi, the striking similarities between the manner in which the secret traditions were developed and protected among the Jews and among the Pythagoreans—even if these similarities do not imply, as Lévi thought, direct Pythagorean influence upon Judaism. Lévi viewed the line of Jewish esotericism of the Second Temple (which he

---

[4] Porphyrius, *Life of Plotinus*, III, 24-27. For other indications regarding philosophical esotericism in Greece, see for example V. Magnien, *Les Mystères d' Eleusis* (Paris: Payot, 1950), 9 ff. Cf. W. Jaeger, *Early Christianity and Greek Paideia* (Oxford: Oxford University Press, 1961), 55-56 and 132, n. 19. See also T. Z. Szlezak, "Plotin und die geheimen Lehren des Ammonios," in A. Hulzhey, W. C. Zimmerli (eds.), *Esoterik und Exoterik der Philosopher* (Basel-Stuttgart: Schwabe, 1977), 52-69.

[5] On the esoteric and oral transmission of certain doctrines among the Pythagoreans, see above all B.L. von der Waerden, "Pythagoras," *PW*, Suppl. X, 843-863, and of course A. Delatte, *Etudes sur la littérature pythagoricienne*, (BEHE 217; Paris: Champion, 1915), in particular 10 ff., 98 ff., 265 ff. (on the *tetraktys*), 307. See also K. von Fritz, *Mathematiker und Akusmatiker bei den altern Pythagorem*, (Bayrische Akademie der Wissenschaften, Philos. Hist. Klasse 11, 1960).

identified primarily with the Essenes) as that of nascent Christianity, an esotoricism whose origins he correctly discerned in the synoptic gospels.[6]

In this chapter I wish to discuss traces of Christian esotericism and the connection between that esotericism and the idea of the apocryphal.[7] By definition esoteric traditions remain concealed, *apokrypha*, and any effort, even a prudent one, to reconstruct them risks being rejected as "speculative" by some scholars, for whom only that which is evident deserves to be stated. Nevertheless it seems that one may not only attest to their existence, but also state their origin and contents with precision. For reasons which are doubtless primarily theological, these questions have been little and rather poorly discussed. Since the term was invented in the seventeenth century by the Protestant Jean Daillé, both Catholic and Protestant scholars have repeatedly discussed, often polemically, the *disciplina arcani*, defined as the rule forbidding Christians during the first centuries to reveal the essence of their rite, their *mystery*, to pagans and catechumens. The very word *musterion* dictated an entire direction of research. Above all the Christian "mystery" was compared to the religious "mysteries" of the Hellenistic era, It was in their context or in contrast to them that one tried to discern and define the Christian mysteries. An entire literature testifies to these intense efforts, and also to their largely negative results.[8] In concentrating research on *ritual* action, *dromena*, one tended to ignore the traditions of esoteric *teaching*, the *legomena*.

---

[6] In Lévi, *La Légende de Pythagore de Grèce en Palestine*, (BEHE 250; Paris: Champion, 1927), passim, and in particular p. 307 ff. on Jesus and Pythagoras, where he analyzes Mark 4, 10-12 and 33-34 and its parallels (the distinction made by Jesus between his disciples and "those who are outside," *hoi exô*) in the context of two groups of Pythagoreans, such as those described for example in Jamblique, *Vie de Pythagore*, p. 88. On the possibility of Pythagorean influence on esoteric teachings in Judaism, see also M. Hengel, *Judaism and Hellenism* (Philadelpha: Fortress, 1974) I, 241-243. In addition to the numerous texts produced by Lévi, I would like to add one: the Pythagorean tradition occasionally refers to the master without mentioning him by name, as *ekeinos ho anèr* "that man." Similarly, though for the opposite reason, the Talmudic tradition refers to Jesus as *hahu gavra*, "that man."

[7] On the idea of the apocryphal, see, for example, Jülicher, "Apokryphen," *PW* I. 2, 2838-2841, and on the apocrypha of the New Testament, see R. McL. Wilson, "Apokryphen II," *TRE* 3, 316-362.

[8] The literature is immense. I shall merely refer as an example to A. Loisy, *Les mystères païens et le mystère chrétien* (Paris: Nourry, 1930). Against Loisy, see M.-J. Lagrange, "Les mystères d'Eleusis et le christianisme," *RB* 28, 1919, 157-217. On Loisy in the context of the study of religion in France in the first half of the century, see A.H. Jones, *Independence and Exegesis* (BGBT 26; Tübingen: Mohr [Siebeck], 1983),

The idea of a *disciplina arcani*, a law imposing silence upon Christians with respect to their rite, has been rather well studied in the past century. The major texts have been discovered and quoted; on this subject the articles in the great encyclopedias remain essential, and we shall refer to them in the presentation of this material.[9] Nevertheless it seems that some of these current conceptions should be revised.

For P. Battifol, for example, there is no doubt that "the Great Church, until the third century, knew of no law that could be termed *disciplina arcani.*" Battifol's views, presented in the beginning of this century, were taken up by O. Perler a generation ago. Gustave Bardy went further: the *arcanum* existed early, but it belonged to heretics. When an author such as Origen conceives of two categories of Christians, perfect ones and simple believers, only gnostic influence could, according to Bardy, explain such a taxonomy. He adds that there were no exact points to which the *arcana* applied. According to Battifol, Ireneus could not have composed his virulent condemnation against the *arcana* and heretics had the Church itself had mysteries and secrets.

For these authors, the fourth century and the first half of the fifth century, the era of mass conversions and the last battle of Christianity against paganism, is also the great era of the *arcana.*[10] Certainly we

---

esp. 66-77. A balanced evaluation of this issue and the byways into which research was led may be found in A. D. Nock, "Hellenist Mysteries and Christian Sacraments," in his *Essays on Religion and the Ancient World*, ed. Z. Stewart, II (Oxford: Oxford University Press, 1972), 791-820. According to E. Goodenough, Alexandrian Judaism was supposedly imbued with the influences of the mystery religions. See also the monitory ariticle by Nock, "The Question of the Jewish Mysteries," *Essays ...* I, pp. 459-468. There is a good presentation of the documentation in G. Bornkamm, *Mysterion*, *TDNT* 3, pp. 802-828. See also chapter IV for other bibliographical details.

[9] Principal references; P. Battifol, "Arcane," *DTC* 1, 2, 1923, 1738-1758. E. Vicandard, "Arcane," *DHGE* , 1924, 1417-1513. G. Bardy, "Arcane," *DDC* 1, 1935, 913-922. O. Perler, "Arkandisziplin," *RAC* 1, 1950, 667-676. D. Powell, "Arkandisziplin," *TRE* 4, 1979, 1-8. These articles also contain bibliographical repferences. I was unable to consult H. Clasen, *Die Arkandisziplin in der altern Kirche*, Diss. Heidelberg, 1956. See the review of this study in *ThLZ* 82, 1957, 153-154, according to which for Clasen the century after the Council of Nicea represents the acme of ecclesiastical arcana. In his *Histoire de l' éducation dans l' Antiquité* II, 214, n. 2, M.-I. Marrou notes that the delicate subject of the aracana has not yet been completely elucidated, and he refers to an unpublished study by G. Hocquard on this theme. For Hocquard, in the ancient church, the arcana would be less a "discipline" than a practice founded in doctrine.

[10] According to Battifol, the pagan vocabulary of the mystery religions was employed in reference to the arcana of the fourth century, "when all risk of misunderstanding had disappeared."

have more documents concerning this period than we have traces of the *arcana* before or afterward. Let us recall some of them: the *Apostolic Constitutions* mention the sending away of catechumens (the *amuètoi*) and the closing of the church doors after the homily (II, 57). Egeria, who visited Jerusalem around 400 echoes these practices, to which Cyril, the bishop of the Holy City during the second half of the fourth century, also refers several times.[11] Athanasius condemns the Arians, who are prepared to reproduce the mysteries before catechumens and pagans.[12] A similar reproach is addressed to the Marcionites by Epiphanus, for daring to show the "mysteries to the catechumens." [13]

This conception seems, however, to be more deeply anchored in a principled attitude for which pagan influences, such as allusions to the mysteries and in general the use of the vocabulary of pagan religiosity, are only conceivable if they are superficial, that is to say, appearing after the victory of Christianity over paganism. Furthermore, most scholars do not take seriously the possibility of Jewish influence at the origin of the Christian *arcana*. Battifol seems to summarize an attitude which was still current recently when he compares Judaism to Roman religion, both being cultic fossils without spiritual life. It is certainly time now to question that attitude. The importance of the secret (*raz, sod*) among the Essenes is well known, as indicated in the Qumran texts.[14] On the other hand, remarkable progress has been made during the past generation, notably by G. Scholem and his students, in the study of Jewish esotericism during the Mishnaic and Talmudic periods, a phenomenon whose importance has barely begun to be measured.[15] A priori, then, it seems legitimate to assume that there were ties between the Christian and Jewish esoteric traditions.[16]

---

[11] Egeria, *Itinerary*, XLVI, 2; XLVI, 6; XLVII, 2; Pétré, ed. (SC 21; Paris: Cerf, 1957), 256-260. Cyrille, *Catéchèses*, VI, 29; cf. *Procat.*, XII, *in fine*.

[12] Athanasius, *Apol. contra arian.*, II, PG 25, 265-269.

[13] Ephiphanius, *Panarion*, XLII, 3.3., Holl, ed. (GCS 31; Leipzig: Teubner, 1922), II, 98; cf. the critical apparatus for a parallel with Jerome. It should be noted that the division of the faithful into two classes is quite distinct in Mesopotamian Christianity, where the fourth century *Liber Graduum* speaks of the "just" and the "perfect." Of course each category of believers receives a different type of teaching.

[14] See the bibliography mentioned in chapter IV, n. 9-10.

[15] See in particular G. Scholem, *Jewish Gnosticism, Merkabah Mysticism and Talmudic Tradition* (New York: Jewish Theological Seminary Press, 1965²) and G.A. Wewers, *Geheimnis und Geheimhaltung im rabbinischen Judentum*, (RVV 35; Berlin-New York: de Gruyter, 1975), which offers a corpus of Rabbinic texts related to esotericism. See

On the other hand, the traditional interpretations of the Christian *arcana* offer only a superficial or incoherent explanation of the phenomenon which they are studying. They do not consider ancient documents such as the testimony of the pagan philosopher Celsus, who, around 170, echoes accusations levelled against the Christians and the secrecy of their rite. Similarly, Tertullian, in his book on the *Prescription of Heretics*, written around the year 200, reproaches the heretics not only with claiming that the apostles had kept certain secrets from the multitude (he uses the word *arcana*), but also for celebrating their ritual "*sine gravitate, sine auctoritate, sine disciplina*" to the extent that one cannot distinguish between the catechumens and the believers among them. Similarly Tertullian explicitly mentions that Christians, like the participants in all mysteries, were subject to the law of silence, *silentii fides*.[17]

The accusation of Celsus, quoted by Origen in the very beginning of *Contra Celsum*, does not thus seem to be entirely devoid of foundation. The very communities of Christians, their "societies," are secret, he says—and thus they are forbidden by law! Origen does not directly refute this accusation but limits himself to developing the theme of the natural right of revolt against unjust laws.[18] A bit further below he returns to the same subject, but more precisely. This time he argues that it is the *doctrine* of the Christians and not only their rite, which Celsus repeatedly asserts to be secret in character. In responding to him, Origen mentions the principal points of Christian doctrine: the virgin birth of Jesus, his crucifixion and resurrection. These dogma are public, known to all, pagans as well as Christians. Let us note that he speaks of the "mystery of the Resurrection," thus showing that the term *mustèrion* no longer necessarily had an esoteric connotation at the time. Among both Christians and Jews since the time of Philo, and perhaps for everyone since the time of Plato, this term is often no more than a figure of speech.[19] Thus it is absurd to

---

also the important work of M.N.A. Bockmuehl, *Revelation and Mystery in Ancient Judaism and Pauline Christianity* (WUNT, 2. Reihe, 136; Tübingen: Mohr [Siebeck], 1990).

[16] See *Savoir et Salut*, chapters I and II.

[17] Tertullian, *De praescriptionibus haereticorum*, XLI, PL 2, 44-47, and *Apologeticus*, VII, 6-7, Glover (trans.) (LCL; London-Cambridge, Mass.: Harvard University Press, 1931), 38-39.

[18] Origen, *C. Cels.*, I,1.

[19] On this subject see Nock, op. cit., n. 8 above, "Hellenistic Mysteries and Christian Sacraments." On the Christian *mysteries*, see also Origen, *Hom. Levit.*, IX, 10,

accuse Christian doctrine of being secret, Origen concludes. But he adds: "the existence of certain doctrines, beyond those which are exoteric and which do not reach the multitude, is not peculiar solely to Christian doctrine, but it is shared by the philosophers. For they had certain exoteric doctrines and others were esoteric." [20]

Thus discussion of Christian esotericism must concern the doctrines rather than the ritual. Not that one should ignore the esoteric aspects of Christian ritual, of course. Judaism had excluded non-Jews from the inner courts of the Temple or from private ceremonies such as the Passover Seder. Among the first Christians, mass was regarded as a private, even secret meal. At least after Nero the illegal character of the Christian religion seems to have given its rites a secret aspect. But these facts are well known and there is no reason to emphasize them. Perhaps it would be preferable to analyze doctrinal points. In effect the Christians inherited a conception of religion from the Jews which was unique in the ancient world, for *knowing*, the very process of learning the truth, was an integral part of the religiosity itself. Whereas in Greece intellectual reflection upon religion is the task of philosophers, only Jews and Christians developed the idea of religious thought, theological reflection at the very core of the religion. In the words of Arnaldo Momigliano, among the Greeks, the more one knows, the less one believes. Among the Jews, the more one knows, the more religious one is.[21]

In fact there is a manifest connection between ritual and doctrine. In one of his homilies, John Chrysostom says, for example, that the presence of the uninitiated in the audience prevents him from speaking clearly and explaining the precise meaning of Scripture.[22] Commenting on verse 4:12 in the *Song of Songs*, "A garden locked is my own, my bride, a fountain locked, a sealed-up spring," Ambrose writes:

Borret, ed. (SC 287; Paris: Cerf, 1981), 122-123. Cf. F.J. Dölger, *Der Heilige Fisch in den Antiken Religionen und im Christentum*, ICHTHYS II (Münster: Aschendorff, 1922), 516-519, where passages from the *Homilies on Leviticus* are cited in the context of an analysis of the place of Origen as a witness of the *arcana* in the first half of the third century.

[20] Origen, *C. Cels.*, I, 7. Cf. II, 60, where he mentions the doctrines revealed in private by Jesus to his true disciples.

[21] A. Momigliano, "Religion in Athens, Rome and Jerusalem in the First Century B.C.," *Annali della Scula Normale Superiore* 14 (1984), 873-892.

[22] John Chrysostom, *In I Corinth. Hom.*, LX, 1, PG 61, 348.

It signifies that the mystery must be sealed by you, ... that it must not
be divulged to those for whom it is not appropriate, that it must not be
spread among the unbelievers by vain gossip.[23]

Christian truth must not fall into pagan hands: though not universal,
this attitude was very common until the fifth century. Thus Cyril of
Jerusalem requires that the *credo* be memorized and that it not be
pronounced before the catechumens.[24] Similarly, Sozomen refuses to
reproduce the symbol of Nicea in his *Ecclesiastical History*—a scruple
not shared, moreover, by Socrates and Theodoretus.[25]

Origen's response to Celsus nevertheless indicates another level of
Christian esotericism. In the interior of the Christian community itself a line separates the initiated from the non-initiated, who are not
taught the totality of the truth. Can one state the nature of such
teaching with precision? Still in *Contra Celsum*, Origen writes that an
initiate with a purified heart can even understand the doctrines revealed by Jesus to his true disciples, that is the most secret or *mystical*
doctrines. He is referring to the verse in Mark (4:34) according to
which Jesus only revealed the meaning of the parables in private to
his authentic disciples.[26] In the same work Origen adds that the
revelations of the Master were not recorded in writing, because the
apostles

> knew better than Plato which truths should be written and how they
> should be written, what must not under any circumstance by written
> for the multitude, what must be spoken, and what was not of that na-
> ture.[27]

This text thus testifies clearly to the existence of an *oral* esoteric tradition, deriving from the apostles and having Jesus as the center of its
secret teaching. It belongs to a line of other similar testimonies, of
which I would like to mention the most striking.

---

[23] Ambrose, *De Mysteriis*, LV, Botte, ed. (SC 25 bis; Paris: Cerf, 1980), 188-189.

[24] Cyril of Jerusalem, *Catech.*, V, 12, PG 33, 521 A. According to Egeria, *Itin.*,
XLVI, 6, the catechumens could hear the doctrine of the symbol, at least at a certain
level, but they could not yet receive teaching of the more profound mystery of baptism.

[25] Sozomen, *Ecclesiastical History*, I, 20, PG 67, 921A. Cf. Socrates, *Hist. eccl.*, I, 8,
PG 67, 67A-B, and Theodoretus, *Hist. eccl.*, I, 11, PG 82, 940-941.

[26] Origen, *C. Cels.*, III, 60, Koetschau, ed. (GCS 2; Leipzig: Teubner, 1899), 244-
245.

[27] *Ibid.*, VI, 6, p. 76.

Ireneus took as his principal mission the refutation of the gnostic sects which claimed to possess hidden teachings, secrets deriving from Jesus, transmitted to his disciples and coming down to them. It is thus difficult for him openly to acknowledge the existence of secret oral traditions, deriving from the Apostles, in the Church. Nevertheless it seems that he does so, at least in veiled language:

> Now [the bishops appointed by the Apostles] neither taught nor knew anything resembling the delirious imaginations of those people. If nevertheless the Apostles did know secret mysteries which they might have taught to the "perfect," separately and unknown to the others, it was primarily those in whose care they placed the churches themselves to whom they would have transmitted these mysteries, for they wanted those whom they left as successors and to whom they transmitted their own teaching mission to be absolutely perfect and irreproachable in every respect.[28]

This text in the conditional mode might seem ambiguous. One point at least is clear. Ireneus is not categorically rejecting the existence of esoteric traditions among the bishops but rather the identity of these traditions with those popular among the gnostics. Elsewhere, quoting Papias, John's auditor, he refers to the Lord's oral teaching about the end of time, which the presbyters, "who saw John," supposedly heard from his mouth.[29]

The existence of an oral esoteric tradition deriving from the Apostles is categorically affirmed during the fourth century by Basil the Great. In a chapter of his *Treatise on the Holy Spirit* which is central to our topic, Basil writes:

> Among the doctrines (*dogmata*) and proclamations (*kerugmata*) preserved in the Church, one receives the former from written teaching and the latter have been collected, secretly transmitted from the apostolic tradition.[30]

---

[28] Ireneus, *Adversus haereses*, III, 3,1, Rousseau-Doutreleau, eds. (SC 294; Paris: Cerf, 1982), 30-31.

[29] *Ibid.*, V, 33.3-4, Rousseau-Doutreleau-Mercier, eds. (SC 153; Paris: Cerf, 1969), 410-420.

[30] Basil of Caesarea, *Sur le Saint-Esprit*, XXVII, 66, Pruche, ed. (SC 17 bis; Paris: Cerf, 1968), 478-481. Elsewhere in the same work, he again insists on the oral and secret character of these doctrines: "Is it not this teaching, kept private and secret, which our fathers kept in silence without worry or curiosity, knowing well that by keeping silent one preserves the sacred character of the mysteries; for that which the uninitiated are not permitted to contemplate, how would it be reasonable to divulge its teaching in writing?" *Ibid.*, 382-383.

Throughout the chapter, Basil names the various ritual commandments as well as their meaning (for example, if one prays toward the
east, this is to orient oneself toward Eden). The doctrines are esoteric, whereas the proclamations are public:

> This is the reason for the tradition of unwritten things: to prevent the
> high knowledge of the doctrines from becoming, for lack of serious pro-
> tection, an object of contempt for the masses.[31]

It must be recognized that Basil is somewhat disappointing with respect to the content of the oral traditions, and that he alludes only to
doctrines which are on the whole quite trivial. Could it be that he
wished to continue protecting the secret in this manner?

In any event, what counts is the clear and specific manner in
which a person quite central in the fourth century Church affirms the
existence of an oral tradition esoteric in nature. Such testimony may
not be ignored by scholars. Nevertheless, they have sought to minimize its importance, arguing that this was an isolated text in patristic
literature.[32] The facts categorically refute such an attitude.

The *Stromateis* of Clement of Alexandria, whose *leitmotiv* is the esoteric
character of true gnosis, represents a *locus classicus* on this subject.[33]

For Clement, the tradition (*paradosis*) cannot be common and public;[34] it must be hidden, "for it is dangerous to exhibit such perfectly
pure and limpid teachings regarding the true light before certain por-
cine and uncultured listeners;" [35] these teachings must not be revealed
to everyone. In brief, these are "hidden traditions concerning true
knowledge." [36] Clement develops these views in Book V. Truth must
be protected by a means of expression in veiled terms,[37] "the myster-

---

[31] *Ibid.*, 384-385.

[32] Similarly Powel, "Arkandisciplin," *TRE* 4, 7.

[33] For a recent study integrating the results of a long tradition of research, see in
particular S. R. C. Lilla, *Clement of Alexandria: a Study in Christian Platonism and Gnosticism*, (OTM; Oxford: Oxford University Press, 1971), 144-158. According to R. P.
Casey, the very desire to protect the esoteric character of the doctrines which he is
revealing is what led Clement to present his material in such an unsystematic way in
the *Stromateis*. See R.P. Casey, "Clement of Alexandria and the Beginnings of Christian Platonism," *HTR* 8 (1925), 39-101.

[34] *Strom.*, I, 12.55.1, Mondésert-Caster, eds. (SC 20; Paris: Cerf, 1951), 89.

[35] *Ibid.*, I, 12.55.4.

[36] " *Tas apocruphous tès alèthous gnôseôs paradoseis*" (*ibid.*, I, 12.56.2; 89 Mondésert-
Caster; cf. *Strom.* V, 10 66.1).

[37] *Strom.*, V, 4, 19, 3, Le Boulluec, ed. (SC 279; Paris: Cerf, 1978), 56-57.

ies are not shown freely to anyone who appears, only accompanied by certain purificatory rites and warnings." [38] More precisely, certain mysteries, which remained hidden in the Old Testament, were transmitted by the Apostles—but the content of these mysteries was revealed only to a few.[39]

These teachings, which are *hidden*, were transmitted orally, "because the God of the universe, Who transcends all words, all thought, all idea, could not be the object of written teaching." Clement quotes Plato's *Second Epistle*: "the best precaution is not to write, but to learn by heart." [40] As noted by A. Le Boulluec, the most recent editor of the *Stromateis*, "the importance of esotericism, as expressed in *Strom.* V, also shows the importance of Pythagorean Platonism at the end of the Hellenistic period and the imperial era." [41] Admittedly, however, this philosophical influence is mainly felt in the form, the presentation of Clement's texts. As for the foundation of esoteric traditions, it is not only common to Clement and heterodox gnosis, as Le Boulluec states, repeating the argument of Lilla, but it is shared by other patristic authors, as we have seen.

Another passage in Clement, from the seventh book of the *Hyptotyposes* and quoted by Eusebius, clearly sets out the chain by which that esoteric tradition was transmitted:

> After the resurrection, the Lord transmitted the tradition of gnosis to James the Just, to John, and to Peter; these transmitted it to the other apostles, and the other apostles to the Seventy, of whom Barnabas was a member.[42]

---

[38] *Ibid.*, V, 4.20.1 (58-59 Le Boulluec).

[39] *Ibid.*, V, 10.61.1 (126-127, 132-133 Le Boulluec).

[40] *Ibid.*, V, 10.75.3 (132-133 Le Boulluec). Cf. Eusebius, *Hist. eccl.*, VI, 13.9, Oulton, trans. (LCL 2; London-Cambridge, Mass.: Harvard University Press, 1932), 44-47, who refers to the *Peri Pascha* of Clement, where the author acknowledges having been forced by his companions to place in writing, for the benefit of following generations, certain doctrines which he had received orally from the old presbyters.

[41] In the introduction of his edition (SC 278; Paris: Cerf, 1981), 19. On *mysterion* in Clement, see H. G. Marsh, "The Use of *mysterion* in the Writings of Clement of Alexandria, with Special Reference to his Sacramental Doctrine," *JTS* 37 (1936), 64-88.

[42] Eusebius, *Hist. eccl.*, II, 1.4, Lake, trans. (LCL 1; London-Cambridge, Mass.: Harvard University Press, 1926), 104-105. Cf. Eusebius, *Contra Marcellam*, I, 1.36.

Moreover, Clement adds that this gnosis, coming from the Apostles and transmitted orally, had come down to a small number of men by that line of transmission.[43]

The same conception is found in numerous gnostic texts and traditions. Throughout Book I of *Adversus haereses*, Ireneus makes fun of the predilection of the gnostics of all stripes for wrapping their hidden mysteries in silence. He refers particularly to the esotericism of the Carpocratians:

> If you believe them, Jesus supposedly communicated secrets separately to his disciples and Apostles, and he supposedly told them to transmit them separately to those who were worthy and who had faith.[44]

Similarly Hippolytus mentions in his *Elenchos* that Basilides and his son Isidor claimed to have received secret doctrines from Matthias, revealed by Jesus during private conversations.[45] The same affirmation appears among the Valentinians. Clement, once again, refers to Valentine's claim that he had received the apostolic tradition from Theodas, a disciple of Paul's.[46] We find the same conception in the *Extracts of Theodotus*:

> The Savior taught the Apostles, first in figures and mysteries (*tupikos kai mustikos*), then in parables and enigmas; finally, in the third place, in clear and direct fashion, when they were alone.[47]

Moreover, Ptolemy, another disciple of Valentine's, states in his *Letter to Flora*, that the apostolic tradition, "which we too have received by way of succession," deals among other things with the principle and the birth of the demiurge and of Satan.[48]

A similar attitude, according to which the supreme truth, the secret gnosis transmitted by Adam to Seth, must not be committed to writing, appears in a way which seems at first glance paradoxical in an apocryphal gnostic book, *The Apocalypse of Adam*:

---

[43] *Strom.*, VI, 7.61.3, Stählin-Früchtel, eds. (GCS 52; reprint Berlin, 1960), 462.

[44] Ireneus, *Adv. haer.*, I, 25.5, Rousseau-Doutreleau, eds. (SC 264; Paris: Cerf, 1979), 340-343.

[45] Hyppolytus, *Elenchos*, VII, 20.1.

[46] *Strom.*, VII, 17.106.4, Stählin, ed. (GCS 17; Leipzig: Teubner, 1909), 75.

[47] *Extraits de Théodote*, LXVI, Sagnard, ed. (SC 23; reprint Paris: Cerf, 1970), 90-91.

[48] Ptolemy, *Lettre à Flora*, VII, 9, Quispel, ed. (SC 34; bis; Paris: Cerf, 1962), 72-73.

They will be known as far as the great aeons, for the words that they
have preserved, of God of the aeons, were not inscribed in a book or
written.[49]

***

Along with insistence upon the orality of the esoteric traditions, however, in several ecclesiastical authors reference is made to certain
apocryphal, that is, hidden, writings in which these traditions had
been preserved. For Tertullian, *apocryphus* is the equivalent of *falsus*.[50]
Origen and Eusebius call various apocryphal works—such as the
Kerygmes of Peter, the *Acts of Paul*, the *Shepherd of Hermas*, the *Apocalypse
of Peter*, *Barnabas*, and the *Didache—nothoi*, adulterated.[51] In *Contra
Faustum*, Augustine says of the apocryphal writings so highly prized by
the Manichaeans that they take their name from their suspicious origins rather than from their sublime content.[52] Such a negative attitude toward apocryphal literature is general among the Church
Fathers for obvious reasons—the enormous use made of them by
heretics of all stripes, Judeo-Christian, gnostic, and Manichaean.

There was an abundance of such books. The *Epistle of Peter*, itself
apocryphal, that opens the *Pseudo-Clementine Homilies* refers to apocryphal works preserved by the Judeo-Christians. Moreover one can follow the lineage of these esoteric traditions from the Elchasaites to the
Manichaeans.[53] Among the Nag Hammadi codices, on the other
hand, several texts are explicitly presented as apocryphal. The doctrines that these texts reveal are esoteric in nature. Thus we have the
Gospel of Thomas, the *Gospel of Truth*, the *Gospel of Philip*, the *Book of
Thomas the Athlete*, the *Gospel of the Egyptians*, the *Apocalypse of Adam*, the
Paraphrase of Shem, the *Three Steles of Seth*, or *Melchizedek*. It would be

---

[49] *L'Apocalypse d'Adam*, CG V, 85.1 ff. A useful English translation of all the
Coptic texts discovered at Nag Hammadi can be found in J. Robinson, ed., *The Nag
Hammadi Library* (New York-San Francisco, 1977). On *The Apocalypse of Adam*, see for
example G. Stroumsa, *Another Seed: Studies in Gnostic Mythology*, (NHS 24; Leiden: Brill,
1984), 82-88.

[50] Tertullian, *De Pudicitate*, X, PL 2, 1000B-C.

[51] Origen, *In Iohannem*, XIII, 17, Preuschen, ed. (GCS; Leipzig, 1903), 241. Eusebius, *Hist. eccl.*, III, 25.4 (I, 256-257 Lake). Cf. Ireneus, *Adv. haer.*, I, 20.1 (288-289
Rousseau-Doutreleau).

[52] Augustine, *Contra Faustum*, XI, 2, Zycha, ed. (CSEL 25; Vienna, 1891), 314-315.
On the use of the apocryphal Acts of the Apostles by the Manichaeans, see P. Nagel,
"Die apokryphen Apostelakten des 2. und 3. Jahrhunderts in der manichäischen
Literatur," in K.W. Tröger, *Gnosis und neues Testament* (Berlin, 1973), 149-182.

[53] See chapter IV *infra*.

tedious to quote these works extensively. It is sufficient to note that most of them declare their esoteric nature in the first lines: "Here are the secret words pronounced by the living Jesus and recorded by Didymus Thomas," (the *Gospel of Thomas*; cf. *Thomas the Athlete*); "That which Derdekea has revealed to me, Shem, according to the will of Majesty ... ;" or again: "The apocalypse of Dositheus regarding the three Steles of Seth ..."

In some cases the very title of the works announces their nature: *Apocryphon of John, Apocryphon of James*. Michel Tardieu suggests translating *apokruphon* uniformly as "book of secrets." Commenting on this term, he writes, "the working of the *apocryphon* into a book with a transcendent and 'silently' hidden content is peculiar to gnostic literature, distinguishing itself from the books of public and historical content of the synagogue and of the nascent church." [54] On this subject one could express certain reservations. We have seen the place given to esoteric teaching in nascent Christianity and how this teaching was generally transmitted orally, according to the "apostolic tradition." In general this is so, but not always. Clement and Origen, for example, refer to certain Jewish apocrypha as also transmitting esoteric traditions. When Clement mentions the secrets (*aporrhèta*) revealed by the angels who have fallen into women, he is alluding directly to the *Book of Enoch*.[55] In the logic of his system, the secrets or mysteries are doubtless those of which he says in the same book of the *Stromateis* that they had remained hidden in the Old Testament.[56] Elsewhere he quotes the words of Jesus in an apocryphal Gospel.[57] Since the discovery of a letter of Clement referring explicitly to a secret Gospel of Mark preserved by the church of Alexandria and its masterful interpretation by M. Smith, it may not longer be doubted that esoteric writings existed in the church during the first centuries nor that Clement was familiar with them. In this letter, Clement insists on the secrecy which must surround the secret Gospel of Mark: its very ex-

---

[54] M. Tardieu, *Ecrits gnostiques*, " *Codex de Berlin* '' (Paris: Cerf, 1984), 239-240. See H.-C. Puech, *En quête de la gnose* II (Paris: Gallimard, 1978), 97-98, on the esotericism of the *Gospel of Thomas* and on the word *apokruphon*, that is "a compilation of the hidden words of Jesus, issued and transmitted in secret."

[55] *Strom*, V, 1.10.2, Stählin-Früchtel, eds. (GCS 52; Leipzig: Hinrichs, 1903), p. 332. Cf. Origen, *In Rom*. II, 4.

[56] *Ibid.*, X, 61.1 (126-127 Le Boulluec).

[57] *Ibid.*, X, 63.7 (130-131 Le Boulluec).

istence must be denied in presence of the Carpocratian heretics, who will make bad use of it.[58]

Origen for his part affirms that the Jews knew of *aporrhèta* such as the transmigration of souls before the advent of the Lord.[59] Elsewhere he refers explicitly to the books of Enoch.[60] Without mentioning apocryphal books, Ireneus recounts the opinions of the presbyters regarding the celestial abduction of Enoch, Elijah, and Paul, "thus introducing incorruptibility."[61] Here again the context suggests that he is alluding to esoteric traditions about mystical ascent. Origen contrasts apocryphal books (*biblia apokrupha*) to common and popular books (*biblia koina kai dedèmeunena*), though he regards both kinds as transmitting the truth, but on different levels.[62] As he notes several times, in effect the Bible has a hidden meaning for him, which only the exegetical traditions are capable of making explicit.[63]

***

Whether oral or recorded in apocryphal works, the esoteric traditions transmitted within Christianity during the first centuries often seem to be of Jewish origin. R.P.C. Hanson noted that in two thirds of the cases where Origen uses the word *paradosis* (approximately thirty out of forty-five cases), it denotes an ancient Jewish or rabbinic tradition.[64] In commenting on Proverbs 1,8, "My son, heed the discipline of your father, and do not forsake the instruction of your mother," Origen identifies "your father" with the written tradition and "your mother" with the oral tradition.[65] Does not this conception of the oral and esoteric tradition seem strangely close to that of the rabbis,

---

[58] Text, translation, and an ample introduction and commentary in M. Smith, *Clement of Alexandria and a Secret Gospel of Mark* (Cambridge, Mass.: Harvard University Press, 1973). The authenticity of the letter has been questioned from various directions. On the subject of the controversies aroused by the publication of the document, see M. Smith, "Clement of Alexandria and Secret Mark: the Score at the End of the First Decade," *HTR* 75 (1982), 440-461. In the present context it is sufficient to note that even if the letter were apocryphal, it would retain its value.

[59] Origen, *In Ioh.*, VI, 13.76 (122 Preuschen).

[60] *Hom. in Num.*, XXVIII, 2, quoted by A. von Harnack, *Der kirchengeschichtliche Ertrag der exegetischen Arbeiten des Origenes* I (TU 42.3; Leipzig: Teubner, 1918), 17.

[61] Ireneus, *Adv. haer.*, V, 5.1 (60-67 Rousseau-Doutreleau-Mercier).

[62] Origen, *In Mattheum*, XIII, 53.18, Klostermann, ed. (GCS 40; Leipzig: Teubner, 1935), 24.

[63] For example, *C. Cels*, I, 18; I, 42; Koetschau, ed. (GCS 2; Leipzig: Teubner, 1899), 69-70, 95.

[64] R.P.C. Hanson, *Origen's Doctrine of Tradition* (London: SPCK, 1954), 73.

[65] *Fragmenta e catenis in Proverbia*, PG 17, 157A.

for whom the *Mishna,* the oral law, was the *mistorin* (the transcription of *mystery*), the secret, the esoteric tradition of Israel?[66] Is not the word *paradosis* itself the exact equivalent of the Hebrew *kabbala,* which in Talmudic Judaism, even before becoming a technical term referring to mystical and theosophical literature during the Middle Ages, designated the oral transmission of the esoteric tradition beginning with Moses?[67]

The importance of Jewish traditions in Origen is well known. In Alexandria and later in Caesaria, he had many occasions, to which he often alludes, to converse with Jews, whether or not they had converted, and to discuss the ways of interpreting Scripture with them.[68] Before him, Clement also mentions having had a Jew, "a Hebrew from Palestine," among his teachers.[69] Clement's intellectual environment was certainly profoundly different from that of Origen, and one does not find Midrashic traditions in his work. One passage, however, deserves mention in our context. Describing " natural philosophy and the gnostic tradition of the canon of truth, or rather illumination (*epopteia*)," Clement writes that it began with the creation of the world, and only later bacame the subject of theology.[70] One cannot refrain from comparing this description to that of mystical science which was current in Hebrew literature from the Mishnaic period.

The two stages of this science are first of all the study of *ma'asse bereshit,* that is, cosmogony, *and then* that of *ma'asseh merkavah,* Ezekiel's vision of the chariot, or, in other words, contemplation of divine glory.[71] Even if it is not possible to push further with precise arguments regarding Jewish influence on Clement on this subject, the par-

---

[66] In *Ps. Rabba* 5 (14b), R. Judah ben Shalom (active c. 370) calls the *Mishna* the *mistorin* of God. See also the texts cited by H. Strack and P. Billerbeck, *Kommentar zum Neuen Testament aus Talmud und Midrasch* I (Munich: Beck, 1922), 659-660.

[67] See G. Scholem, "Kabbalah," *Encyclopedia Judaica* 10, 489 ff., particularly pp. 490, 494. Scholem notes that in the Talmud the word is used for the books of the Bible other than the Pentateuch, and the oral law is called *kabbala* in post-Talmudic literature.

[68] See N. De Lange, *Origen and the Jews: Studies in Jewish-Christian Relations in Third Century Palestine* (COP 25; Cambridge: Cambridge University Press, 1976); cf. my "The Hidden Relationship: on the Church Fathers and Judaism," *Mehqarei Yerushalayim be-Mahshevet Israel* II (1982), pp. 170-175 (in Hebrew).

[69] *Strom.,* I, 1.10.2 (II, 8 Stählin).

[70] *Strom.,* IV, 1.3.2 (II, 249 Stählin).

[71] See for example *Mishna Hagiga* II, 1 and parallel texts. For a description of mystical and esoteric currents in rabbinic Judaism, see G. Scholem, *Major Trends in Jewish Mysticism* (New York: Schocken, 1944), 40-79, also his *Jewish Gnosticism, Merk-*

allel seems striking enough to be noted, at least indicating the plausibility of such an influence.

At the end of a study of the "secret traditions of the Apostles," Jean Daniélou concluded that the secret doctrines attributed to the Apostles by the Apocrypha and the traditions of the presbyters referred primarily to the theme of the celestial voyage.[72] Rather than return to the texts cited by Daniélou, I chose to review other texts here—doubtless too briefly—which at least have the advantage of showing the existence of other themes alongside individual eschatology in the framework of esoteric traditions. Daniélou concluded that the "esoteric traditions of the Apostles are the continuation within Christianity of a Jewish esotericism that existed at the time of the Apostles." [73] We can support this conclusion with arguments and texts to which Daniélou did not refer. Finally, the esotericism whose outlines we have been attempting to discern seems to have developed first in Judeo-Christian milieus. These milieus are also where we must seek the origin of esoteric traditions such as those developed by the gnostics in the second century. As the gnostic writings placed under the name of James the Just permit us to surmise, a close study of the elements shared by gnosticism and Judeo-Christianity would doubtless clarify major problems regarding the nature of the relations between these two movements and their evolution. Therefore it is within this framework, I believe, that one must explain the importance of Jewish esoteric traditions among the gnostics—such as one finds in the *Apocryphon of John*, the *Gospel of Philip*, or in Mark the Gnostic, according to the testimony of Ireneus.[74]

***

---

abah Mysticism and Talmudic Tradition (second ed.; New York: Jewish Theological Seminary Press, 1965).

[72] J. Daniélou, "Les traditions secrètes des Apôtres," *ErJb* 31, 1962, pp. 199-215. In his argumentation Daniélou uses in particular the *Apocryphon of James* discovered at Nag Hammadi and the *Epistula Apostolorum*.

[73] *Ibid.*, p. 211. One should remember that for Daniélou, Jewish Christianity was a phenomenon far more widespread than is conceded by most scholars. It seems nevertheless that in this context, he is referring to Jewish Christianity in the proper sense of the word, meaning a movement of Jews who recognized Jesus as the messiah without abandoning the Law.

[74] I have dealt with these issues in the first three chapters of *Savoir et Salut*.

In conclusion, one cannot avoid wondering about the disappearance of Christian esotericism, whose traces are lost in our period. Whereas the facts seem to disappear, the words remain. The vocabulary of Christian esotericism had itself been based on that of the pagan mysteries. One finds this vocabulary among the mystical authors, who even occasionally develop it in a new direction, such as Gregory of Nyssa or Pseudo-Dionysius the Aeropagite. Thus Gregory, in his *Life of Moses*, presents his hero as having been initiated in divine things, "hidden mysteries," in the sanctuary, though his vocabulary reveals traces neither of epistemic contents nor of esoteric doctrine.[75] Similarly, in his *Mystic Theology*, Dionysius speaks of the *logia mystika* without seeming to refer to any specific writings.[76] But these writings still remain in some measure objective analyses of the divine. It is only later, when the experiential and subjective element becomes predominant, that one will be dealing with a purely mystical literature.

How are we to understand this phenomenon? The legal prohibition against any secret gathering, the violence of the gnostic challenge, and finally the tension between the very idea of esotericism and the catholic ethos inherent in the logic of Christianity—these three causes combine from the second to fifth centuries to void Christian esotericism of its contents, and then to transform its vocabulary and to use it to express purely personal and inner experiences of illumination. Beginning in the fourth century, in fact, the very status of the *epistemè* becomes problematic. Dangerous or disquieting in nature, knowledge often becomes the object of prohibitions, as Carlo Ginzburg has shown. "*Noli altum sapere, sed time*" is how the Vulgate translates Romans 11:20, doubtless in a very idiosyncratic manner.[77]

Late antiquity is no longer as interested in *the truth to teach* as in *the example to give*. Augustine presents *curiositas* as sinful, being interested in hidden things, endeavoring to discover them.[78] The living ethical example is the saint or the monk, he whom Max Weber called the religious virtuoso in his typology, no longer the "Master of Truth." [79]

---

[75] Gregory of Nyssa, *Vie de Moïse*, II, 160.164, Daniélou, ed. (SC 1ter; Paris: Cerf, 1968), 208-209, 212-213: "*ho en autôi adutôi muètheis ta aporrhèta;*" cf. I, 56, where Moses is described as having acquired secret doctrines.

[76] Dionysius the Aeropagite, *Mystika theologia*, I, 1, PG I, 997A.

[77] C. Ginzburg, "High and Low: the Theme of Forbidden Knowledge in the Sixteenth and Seventeenth Centuries," *Past and Present* 73, (1976), 28-41.

[78] See H. Blumenberg, "*Curiositas* und *veritas*: zur Ideengeschichte von Augustin, *Confessiones* X. 35," *StPatr* 6, (TU 81; Berlin: Akademie Verlag, 1962), 294-302.

Rather than upon knowledge, the accent is now placed on soteriology. The saint offers a model of behavior to everyone (the stylite, a living monument on top of a column, is like a symbol of an entire movement, an entire epoch), an *exemplum* which anyone may imitate rather than secret traditions.[80]

Nothing less than a new religious sensibility develops in late antiquity, and Peter Brown in particular has contributed masterfully to shedding light upon it.[81] With this new development, the need or desire to retain esoteric traditions is extinguished within Christianity, so that these traditions were taken over by isolated groups of persecuted heretics. But this is an entirely different conception of esotericism. During the Middle Ages it is actually among Jewish and Muslim thinkers that one may find certain characteristics of ancient Christian esotericism—though this esotericism is then different in essence, for it exists to protect the philosopher from dangers of a political nature.[82]

---

[79] From a typological point of view, the absence of an ethical moment in gnosis, as noted by Plotinus, doubtless presents one of the major differences between gnostic encratism and Christian asceticism. This difference between the *religious* value of ethics among the gnostics and among Christians must be viewed as one of the causes of the eventual defeat of gnosis. See *Savoir et Salut,* ch. 8 and 9, pp. 145-181.

[80] See in particular P. Brown, *The Cult of the Saints* (Chicago: Chicago University Press, 1981), and his "The Saint as Exemplar in Late Antiquity," *Representations* 1 (1983), 1-25.

[81] For example, P. Brown, *The Making of Late Antiquity* (Cambridge, Mass.: Harvard University Press, 1978).

[82] L. Strauss in particular has produced numerous analyses of intellectual esotericism and medieval philosophy. See for example, *Philosophie und Gesetz* (Berlin: Schocken Verlag, 1935) and *Persecution and the Art of Writing* (Glencoe, Ill.: Free Press, 1952).

CHAPTER THREE

GNOSTIC SECRET MYTHS

The esoteric character of gnostic mythology seems to have elicited little attention.[1] To be sure, an esoteric sense inherited from the early Christian heresiologists has been attached to the word 'gnosticism' since the sixteenth century. Most of the esoteric uses of 'gnosticism', however, have remained rather vague; much has been qualified 'gnostic' which obviously belongs to other intellectual trends of ancient thought and religion, in particular to the occult and to what we call today 'magic'.[2] A better understanding of gnostic esoteric mythology may shed some light on the nature of the deep religious transformations in the Eastern Mediterranean under the early empire, and on one of the reasons for the ultimate disappearance of gnosticism.

1. The Thunder

Both in its content and literary genre *The Thunder—Perfect Intellect*—is one of the most puzzling—and poetical—texts discovered at Nag Hammadi. George MacRae was the first to call attention to the similarities between the 'I am' (*egô eimi*) statements in our text and Isis aretalogies.[3] *The Thunder* (*hè brontè*) is described by Bentley Layton as "a riddlesome monologue spoken by the immanent savior, here rep-

---

[1] See for instance the following important contributions on gnostic mythology, which all lack a real discussion of the esoteric character of this mythology: H. Jonas, *The Gnostic Religion* (Boston: Beacon, 1958), M. Tardieu, *Trois mythes gnostiques* (Paris, Etudes augustiniennes, 1974), G. Filoramo, *L' attesa della fine: storia della gnosi* (Roma, Bari: Laterza, 1983), K. Rudolph, *Die Gnosis* (Göttingen: Vandenhoeck & Ruprecht, 1980), I. Culiano, *Les mythes du dualisme occidental* (Paris: Payot, 1989). On the Gnostic esoteric traditions, see now K. Rudolph, "Geheimnis und Geheimhaltung in der antiken Gnosis und im Manichäismus", in *Secrecy and Concealment*, 265-288.

[2] M. Tardieu and J.-D. Dubois, *Introduction à la littérature gnostique*, I (Paris, Cerf, CNRS: 1986), 30- 34

[3] G. W. McRae, S. J., "Discourses of the Gnostic Revealer", in G. Widengren and D. Hellholm, eds., *Proceedings of the International Colloquium on Gnosticism, Stockholm, Aug. 20-25, 1973* (Stockholm and Leiden: Kungl. Vitterhets Historie och Antikvitets Akademiens. Handlingar. Filol.-filos. Serien 17, 1977), 111-122.

resented as a female character and identifiable as 'afterthought', a manifestation of wisdom and Barbelo in gnostic myth." [4]

Layton has dedicated an important study to the self-descriptive passages, which he defines as 'identity riddles', and the speaker's paradoxical assertions about her kinship and ethical relations.[5] He shows that our text retains some of the features of the Greek and Hellenistic riddles, which formed a literary genre of itself, while noting that the literary framework of our text is quite different from that of known examples of Hellenistic riddles. Such texts are usually only a few lines long. Their nature is that of social games. According to Layton, the peculiar character of *The Thunder* stems from "the blending of three ordinarily unrelated literary modes: the Isis/Wisdom proclamation, ...the philosophical sermon...and the riddle".[6] One should add that *The Thunder* is not a short enigma with a single solution, which one is supposed to guess. Moreover, Greek riddles, despite the original mythical context of riddles, were of a public, exoteric character.[7]

Comparing *The Thunder* to other Gnostic texts such as the *Gospel of Thomas* and in particular to the known fragments of the *Gospel of Eve*,

---

[4] B. Layton, *The Gnostic Scriptures: A New Translation with Annotations and Introductions* (Garden City, N. Y.: Doubleday, 1987), 77, in the introduction to his translation of the text, which appears on pp. 80-85. See also McRae's translation, in J. M. Robinson, ed., *The Nag Hammadi Library in English* (San Francisco: Harper and Row, 1977), 271-277. The Coptic text has been edited by G. W. McRae, in *Nag Hammadi Codices V, 2-5 and VI with Papyrus Berolinensis 8502, 1 and 4* (D. M. Parrot, ed.; NHS 11; Leiden: Brill, 1979), 231-255.

[5] B. Layton, "The Riddle of the Thunder (CG VI, 2): the Function of Paradox in a Gnostic Text from Nag Hammadi" [henceforth "Riddle"], in Ch. Hedrick and R. Hodgson, Jr., eds., *Nag Hammadi, Gnosticism, and Early Christianity* (Peabody, Mass.: Hendrickson, 1986), 37-54. This article has also appeared in a French translation in *RTP* 119 (1987), 261-280. See also G. Quispel, "Jewish Gnosis and Mandean Gnosticism: Some Reflections on the Writing *Brontè*", in J.-É. Ménard, ed., *Les textes de Nag Hammadi* (NHS 7; Leiden: Brill, 1975), 82-122. For a similar pardoxical 'coincidentia opppositorum', see Clement of Alexandria, *Paedagogus* I. 6. 42. 1 (in H.I. Marrou and M. Harl, transl.; SC 70; Paris: Cerf, 1960), 186-187, on the "wondrous mystery of the Virgin Mother, figure of the Church.

[6] Layton, "Riddle", 44.

[7] See C. Ohlert, *Rätsel und Gesellschaftspiele der alten Griechen* (Berlin, 1912, second ed.), quoted by Layton, "Riddle", 44, n. 30. On riddles as a literary genre in early Christian literature, and on its relationships with myth, see further H. Leroy, *Rätsel und Misverständnis: ein Beitrag sur Formgeschichte des Johannesevangeliums* (Tübingen: [Imprimerie orientale, Louvain], 1967), and A. Jolles, *Einfache Formen: Legende, Sage, Mythos, Rätsel, Spruch, Kasus, Memorabile, Märche, Witz* (Tübingen: Niemeyer, 1965, third ed.).

Layton identifies the genre of our text as a " "riddle gospel", in which
"the voice of Dame Wisdom", in his terms, is a voice of riddle. According to him, therefore, it is a mythic *huponoia,* or 'buried meaning.'
Layton insists on the mythic framework of our text, the myth of the
soul's descent into the body, its incarnations, and the descent of the
Savior. For him, the Thunder represents Eve, who relates in the cryptic language of the riddle the Gnostics' own myth of the origin and
fate of the soul, her salvation by a heavenly teacher, and her ultimate
return to her home.[8] Without denying the resonnances of Wisdom
literature on the formation of our text, Layton concludes his study by
insisting, after McRae and Quispel, on the Isiac character of the person of the Thunder and by calling attention to the well-known puns
on Eve and the Serpent [*Hawwa-Hiwwya*] in some Gnostic "Sethian"
texts. In his words, "The *Thunder* is gnostic and Sethian to the same
degree that the Hawwa puns in the gnostic Sethian *Hypostasis of the
Archons* are gnostic and Sethian." [9] Following McRae, Layton points
out a very important quotation of a lost *Gospel of Eve* made by
Epiphanius in his account of the sect of the *gnôstikoi* .[10] In this text,
"the speaker, presumably the fleshy Eve, hears a *phônè brontès,* a voice
of thunder, who says:

> I am thou, and thou art I... [11]

Layton concludes that "there is some chance that the Gospel of Eve
stands behind... the Nag Hammadi *Thunder.*" His analysis however
leaves unclear the origin of the identification between Eve and the
thunder. He only mentions that the riddle gospel "is set in Paradise
atop a high mountain, where reference to thunder (*brontè*) is at
home" . [12] Layton's identification of the close literary affinities of our
text to the riddle genre is convincing. Yet, his solution, in its turn,
leaves open some questions.

1. Neither Layton nor other scholars seem to have addressed directly the question of the destination of *The Thunder.* Was the text

---

[8] McRae had been unable to detect in the text traces or echoes of the gnostic
myth; see his short introduction to his translation of the text.

[9] Layton, "Riddle", 52.

[10] Epiphanius, *Panarion* 26. 2. 3 (K. Holl, ed. [GCS; Leipzig: Hinrichs, 1915], 278);
Layton, "Riddle", 48-49.

[11] See below, section 5 *in finem,* for similar identifications in gnostic and
Manichaean texts.

[12] Layton, "Riddle", 49.

written for gnostics, insiders who would have understood the allusions
to the myth in the riddles, or rather to sympathisers, like the uninitiated lady to whom the Valentinian Ptolemaeus adressed his *Letter to
Flora*, who would not have picked up these allusions?[13] In other
words, is our text esoteric or exoteric? The dearth of evidence makes
a clear answer this question very difficult. A way to approach it, perhaps, is through asking about the function of the riddle in each of
these two possibilities.

2. In the hypothesis that the text was esoteric, another question
arises. Why would the gnostic writer wish to hide the myth from the
initiated through the *huponoia*, and what purpose would be achieved
by alluding to the myth, rather than presenting a de-mythologized
version of gnostic teaching, like, say, the *Letter to Flora*?

A tentative answer to these two questions will be offered below.

Noting that nowhere else was the thunder found as a title in ancient
religious literature, McRae sought to provide parallels and references
to the thunder in hierophanic contexts, from the Old and New Testaments (Job 26: 14; John 12: 29, where the voice from heaven is
related to either the thunder of an angel; Rev. 6: 1) to the figure of
Jupiter tonans in Isis aretalogical inscriptions and Greek magical formu-
las. Other references, which, oddly enough, were not adduced by
either McRae nor Layton, would seem to indicate more precisely the
significance of thunder in early Christian context.

In *Revelation* 10: 3-4, the thunder is connected to a heavenly revelation:

> And when [the mighty angel] had cried, seven thunders uttered their
> voices. And when the seven thunders had uttered their voices, I was
> about to write: and I heard a voice from heaven saying to me, Seal up
> those things which the seven thunders uttered, and write them not.

This reference is more detailed than the one in *Rev.* 6. 1,[14] since the
seven thunders "utter their voices" in the context of the revelation of
words to be sealed, but not written. The thunder thus seems to represent an *oral* revelation of divine secrets.

---

[13] See G. Quispel, ed., transl., Ptolémée, *Lettre à Flora* (SC 24; Paris: Cerf, 1949
[1966]).

[14] "And I saw when the Lamb opened one of the seals, and I heard, as it were
the noise of thunder, one of the four beasts saying, Come and see."

In *Mark* 3: 16-17, some of Jesus' apostles are called 'the sons of the thunder':

> And Simon he surnamed Peter; and James, the son of Zebedee, and John, the brother of James; and he surnamed them *Boanèrges*, which is, the sons of thunder (*huioi brontès*).

The New Testament references to the thunder in hierophanic context were picked up in Patristic literature. I shall refer here only to two texts.

In his *Contra Celsum*, Origen writes:

> And again, John teaches us the difference between matters that may and may not be written down when he says that he heard seven thunders teaching him about certain subjects, and forbidding him to commit their words to writing.[15]

The voice of the thunder is here specifically related to esoteric teachings, which should not be committed to writing. For Origen, therefore, the thunder reveals secret teachings, directly from heaven.

Eusebius, on his side, understands the thunder as a veiled, or 'enigmatic' reference to the evangelical *kerygma*, since the apostles, who are *claiming* Christ's message to the world, are called by the Gospel *Boanèrges*, i. e. "sons of the thunder".[16] Unfortunately there do not seem to be many such references to 'thunder' in Patristic literature. Our few examples may, none the less, be enough to argue that when *brontè* was refered to, the immediate associations were to the New Testament, and in particular to the Gospel references. These references were clearly hierophanic in character.

If such references reflect the common metaphorical meaning of thunder in early Christian literature, then it is perhaps legitimate to try and read *The Brontè: Perfect Mind* in the light of this meaning. The

---

[15] Origen, *Contra Celsum*, VI. 6, *in finem;* (I quote H. Chadwick's translation [Cambridge: Cambridge University Press, 1953]). See also his *Com. on Mat.*, 12. 32, and his *Com. on Apoc.*, 36, where he says that the sons of *Brontè* were called so because of the elevation of their thoughts and religious conceptions. Cf. Lampe, *A Patristic Greek Lexicon*, 305 A. Bauer, *Greek English Lexicon of the New Testament*, 147 B, notes that the seven thunders are thought by some to be the thunders of the seven planetary spheres.

[16] " *brontè... to kèrugma to euaggelikon ainittetai...dio kai tous apostolous...boanèrges ônomazen.*" Eusebius, *in Psalmos*, 76.18; *P.G.* 23, 897c.

bronte may represent Eve, but it may also have a broader meaning, refering to the heavenly [oral] revelation of divine secrets. These two meanings are not necessarily mutually exclusive.

A more precise understanding of the nature of secret myths may shed some light on the function of the paradoxical statements in our text.

2. Esoteric and exoteric myths in antiquity

We know of the existence in the Greek cultural orbit of some *secret* myths. Most famous among them probably is the myth of the dismemberment of Dionysos, or of Dionysos Zagreus. Relatively old and well known among the Greeks, it was consciously kept secret as a doctrine of mysteries, mainly in specific and marginal social contexts, such as Orphic and Bacchic milieus, and perhaps also in Pythagorean communities.[17] Did the various mysteries, such as those at Eleusis, also make use of esoteric myths? The lack of sources makes any categorical answer impossible. What happened in the mysteries was kept secret, and very little has reached us. As Walter Burkert has pointed out, however, "there is not the slightest evidence" to support Reitzenstein's assertion that there was some esoteric theology behind the secret rituals.[18]

In the Greek world, secret myths remained something of an anomaly. Most myths were exoteric by nature, since they were telling stories in simple terms, to be understood, remembered, and repeated by everyone. The Greek grammarians and philosophers had developed hermeneutical tools to interpret traditional mythology. Various interpretations were offered of the myths of old, which were thus rationalized, and presented as carrying a deep spiritual meaning, hid under the veil of the story, meant for the simple ones (since it was dangerous to reveal the deeper truth to all). The philosophical interpretation of myths, a method developed, in particular, by the Neoplatonic philosophers, stems from this paradox: on the face of it, myths are incredible, stupid or scandalous. But since they are transmitted by a

---

[17] W. Burkert, *Greek Religion* (Cambridge, Mass: Harvard, 1985), 298. (= *Griechische Religion der archaischen und klassischen Epoche* [Stuttgart: Kohlhammer, 1977]). For Plato's proposal to keep some myths secret in the ideal city, see *Resp.* II, 377- 378.

[18] W. Burkert, *Ancient Mystery Cults* (Cambridge and London: Harvard, 1987), 46.

venerable tradition, a deep truth must be hiding behind their literal meaning. Hence, their interpretation, rather than the myths themselves, is esoteric.[19] In ancient religious thought, therefore, myths were considered to express in popular fashion a *philosophia perennis* of sorts, known by the wise of all nations since the dawn of civilization, but kept hidden through the veil of the popular story. It was the task of philosophers to decode such myths and express their message in rational discourse. For these philosophers, indeed, myths were riddles to be deciphered. In Porphyry's words, at the penultimate stage of a long tradition: "This myth is a riddle".[20]

Riddles, or *ainigmata*, had kept a place of their own among literary genres in Greek and other ancient literatures. With the rise, and then the establishment, of Christianity, however, even literary genres were transformed. Myths, obviously—or at least conscious myths about the divinities—disappeared. So did riddles, which were replaced by the Christian *mysterium*.[21] The interpretation of myths, on its side, was replaced by the exegesis of holy texts, but these texts had been revealed, and were perfect expressions of the whole truth. For the Hellenic philosophers, only a 'high' language was deemed fit to reflect the lofty nature of the divinity. According to the Christian ethos, on the other hand, it was a matter of pride that the deepest truths of the Gospels had been redacted in a simple, popular language, thus being available, like redemption itself, to all, and not only to a thin layer of the educated class. From Origen to Augustine, even the more intellectually minded among the Fathers reflect this attitude.[22]

---

[19] See R. Lamberton, *Homer the Theologian: Neoplatonist Allegorical Reading and the Growth of the Epic Tradition* (The Transformation of the Classical Heritage, 9; Berkeley, Los Angeles, London: California University Press, 1986).

[20] " *esti toinun ho muthos ainigma*", Porphyry, *de antro nympharum*, 21. I use the edition and translation of L. Westerink *et al.* (Arethusa Monographs, 1; Buffalo, N. Y., 1969). For a discussion of the relationships between myth and riddle in late antique thought, see chapter 1 *supra*.

[21] On the transformation of *musterion* in early Christianity, see for instance C. Colpe, "Mysterienkult und Liturgie: zum Vergleich heidnischer Rituale und christlicher Sakramente", in C. Colpe, L. Honnefelder, M. Lutz-Bachmann, eds., *Spätantike und Christentum* (Berlin: Akademie Verlag, 1992), 203- 228.

[22] For the sake of brevity, I refer only to the discussion and texts in chapter 6 *infra*.

3. The belatedness of gnostic mythology

In gnostic texts, the myths are presented under various garbs. In the *Hymn of the Pearl* the myth appears in the guise of a folk-tale, in the *Apocalypse of Adam*, it is presented as a revisionist *sive* antinomian biblical history, Irenaeus presents Ptolemaeus' version of the myth as a full-fledged system, while in the *Brontè*, the myth is hidden under the enigmas. Although the idiosyncratic nature of gnostic mythology has often been noticed, the precise identification of this nature remains an arduous task. Karl Kérényi spoke of a "only midway mythology (nur halbwegs Mythologie)", while Paul Ricoeur has insisted on "the Aufhebung of myth into Gnosis". Michel Tardieu, on his side, could write that "the mythical thought at work in Gnosticism has rationalized and systematized myth".[23]

The three views quoted here are respectively those of a student of Greek religion, of a philosopher, and of a specialist of gnostic thought. Each in his own way insists on the novelty of gnostic mythology, as compared to Greek mythology, and on the limitations of this mythology. For the historian of religious thought, the peculiar interest of gnostic mythology lies in what can be called its 'artificial' character. There, probably better than anywhere else, we can observe mythology in the making. One of the main peculiarities of Gnostic mythology seems to lie in its *belatedness*, in the fact that it was created as a re-mythologisation process, in a religious and intellectual world dominated by the two great reactions to archaic mythologies, Hebrew prophecy and Greek philosophy. Hence the self-conscious hybrid character of gnostic mythology.

Mythopoiesis has long been recognized as an essential element of the gnostic mind. The gnostics, however, did not invent their myths *ex nihilo*. These myths were built from stones reassembled from the debris of previous monuments, mainly from a few texts and themes in the Hebrew Bible and the New Testament, as well as from Greek mythology. Gnosticism is usually seen as a radical religious and intellectual movement of revolt against traditional (monotheistic) paterns of thought.[24] Layton, after Pagels, prefers to speak, in milder fashion,

---

[23] References in G.G. Stroumsa, *Another Seed: Studies in Gnostic Mythology* (NHS 23; Leiden, Brill, 1984), 1, n. 3-5.

[24] see for instance B.A. Pearson, "Some Observations on Gnostic Hermeneutics", in W. Doniger O'Flaherty, ed., *The Critical Study of Sacred Texts* (Berkeley Religious Studies Series; Berkeley: University of California Press, 1979), 243-256.

of a 'revision' of monotheism: "Much of gnosticism can be seen not
as a revolt against, but as a revision of, traditional religions, especially
in their textual manifestations." [25] This is a rather odd statement. The
gnostic attitude toward Judaism and the Old Testament is not identical to that shown towards Christianity. And it is doubtful that the
gnostics had a clear theological attitude toward pagan religions,
which they would have intended to 'revise'. As far as I can see, it is
only Christianity that the gnostics intended to 'revise'.

The 'revisionist' view of gnosticism leaves unexplained the drastic
passage, the 'mutation', from monotheism to dualism, and the creation of a dualist mythology. The demonization of the cosmos and of
the forces of evil is no innocent 'revision'. It creates a major break in
the self-peception of culture and religion—a break to this day unexplained.

For our present purposes, however, the fact remains that we witness with gnosticism a fundamental transformation of patterns of
thought. What did such a transformation entail? Rather than on the
passage from monotheism to dualism, we might focus on the meaning
of the new kind of mythology invented by the gnostics. In these pages
we are asking, in a sense, the question of what happens in a culture
when the mythic mode becomes self-conscious.[26]

The self-conscious re-mythologisation shown by the Gnostic writers was no doubt indicative of an intellectual revolution. Robert
Grant once speculated about the origins of gnosticism: were they
mythological (as Hans Jonas had argued), or rather philosophical?[27] It
seems that one should reject the implicit opposition between two contradictory options. All signs point to gnostic origins as a *hermeneutical*
revolt against Jewish and Christian *Weltanschauung*, and the creation of
an alternative mythology, offering a provocative reinterpretation of
cosmogony and of salvation history.

---

[25] Layton, "Riddle", 54. On E. Pagels, *The Gnostic Gospels* (New York: Random
House, 1979), see G.G. Stroumsa, "The Gnostic Temptation", *Numen* 27 (1980), 278-
286.
[26] On this question, see C. Bennett, *God as Form: Essays in Greek Theology* (Albany:
SUNY Press, 1976), esp. 144.
[27] R. Grant, "Review of Hans Jonas, *Gnosis und spätantiker Geist*, II, in *JTS*, N. S. 7
(1956), 313.

4. Gnostic esotericism

Since gnostic mythology was conceived as hermeneutical by nature, it also inherited the esoteric character typical of Greek philosophical interpretations of myth. Precisely at the time when the success of Christianity was bringing both mythologies and esoteric traditions to an end in the Mediterranean world, we can witness the development of an esoteric mythology.

Like mythology, esotericism is an essential feature of Gnostic patterns of thought and behavior. Gnostic soteriological doctrines that were to remain esoteric stayed hidden from outsiders and from allies of the evil rulers of this world, the archons. The Gnostics claimed that they had received their secret traditions through apostolic tradition. They were the depositories of secrets revealed by Jesus to his disciples, secrets transmitted only to those worthy of it. This was the basic conception of the Valentinians, as we know from Irenaeus of Lyon, who pokes fun at them on this issue, as well as from Clement of Alexandria. Irenaeus reports similar conceptions about the Carpocratians.[28]

The Alexandrian gnostic theologian Basilides, "the first Christian philosopher," [29] shows similar thought patterns. Hippolytus tells us that Basilides and his son Isidore claimed to have received from Matthias secret doctrines of Jesus.[30] Clement tells us that Valentinus derived his teachings from Theodas, a follower of Paul. According to Epiphanius, Basilides claims that

> [they may] not reveal anything at all to anyone about the Father, and about his own mystery, but [must] keep it secret and reveal it to one out of thousands and two out of ten thousands. He advises his disciples: "Know all yourself, but let none know you." When questioned, he and his followers claim that they are "no longer Jews and have not yet become Christians, but that they always deny [their true religious identity], keep the faith secret within themselves, and tell it to no one.[31]

---

[28] Irenaeus, *Adv. Haer.*, I.25.5 (A. Rousseau, L. Doutreleau, eds., transl.; [SC 264; Paris: Cerf, 1979], 340-343).

[29] Layton, "The Significance of Basilides in Ancient Christian Thought", *Representations* 28 (1989), 135-151, esp. 136. Layton points out Basilides' antisemitism, plausibly arguing that it reflects the "innate" antisemitism of Alexandrian gentiles of the time (p. 144).

[30] Hippolytus, *Elenchos*, VII.20.1 (P. Wendland, ed. [GCS; Leipzig: Hinrichs, 1916], p. 195).

[31] Epiphanius, *Panarion*, 24.5.4 (262 Holl).

Similarly, various Gnostic texts discovered at Nag Hammadi describe the efforts put into protecting the doctrines from being revealed outside the inner group. In this, they are of course following a literary pattern inherited from Jewish apocalyptic literature. For the *Apocalypse of Adam*, for instance, "The words which they hid, of the God of the Eons, were neither inscribed in a book, nor were they written". These words represent "the secret gnosis of Adam, that he delivered unto Seth." [32] There is reason to believe that such attitudes stem from Jewish-Christian traditions. Jewish-Christian texts, such as the *Kerygmata Petrou*, reflect similar attitudes toward esoteric traditions. Such traditions also became part of gnosticizing Jewish-Christian baptist sects such as the Elchasaites, and from there formed the background of Mani's doctrine.[33] Those trends of gnosticism which we have become accustomed in the last generation to qualify as 'Sethian' seem to stem from a radical reinterpretation, or inverted reading, of early Biblical history. Gnostic mythology is here presented in the form of Biblical esoteric exegesis.[34] As other examples of Gnostic texts refering to secret knowledge, one can refer to the *Gospel of Mary*, where Peter asks Mary to share her secret gnosis, or to the *Acts of John*, where Jesus states: "I have been considered for what I am not, since I am not what I am for the multitude." A docetic attitude entails esotericism, since the true nature of the Savior cannot be revealed to the masses. "I shall tell you in veiled fashion what it is about, since I know that you will understand." [35]

More generally, the Gnostic texts claim to reveal "the secret words of Jesus." So we read in the Gospel of Thomas: "These are the secret

---

[32] CG V, 85, 3-24.

[33] On the Jewish Christian origin of early Christian esoteric traditions, see chapter 2 *supra*. On the esoteric background of Mani's doctrines, see chapter 4 *infra*.

[34] On gnostic and Manichaean Biblical exegesis, see J.-D. Dubois, "L'exégèse des gnostiques et le canon des Ecritures" and M. Tardieu, "Principes de l'exégèse manichéenne du Nouveau Testament", both in M. Tardieu, ed., *Les règles de l'interprétation* (Patrimoines; Paris: Le Cerf, 1987), respectively pp. 89- 97 and 123- 146. Dubois points out that the gnostics had developed an esoteric exegesis of the fourth Gospel. In this respect, Irenaeus accused them of "breaking apart the members of Truth (*aletheia*)". See Irenaeus, *Adv. Haer.*, I.3.1 on Valentinian esoteric scriptural hermeneutics. In general, gnostic myth is presented as biblical exegesis; see for instance Irenaeus, *Adv. Haer.*, I.3.1, establishing itself on Mat. 19:11: the Savior's parables (they don't want to call him Lord) are indications, in mysteries, of the secret gnosis, for those able to understand (cf. I.3.6: the Valentinians interpret not only the New Testament, but also the Torah and the Prophets.

[35] *Acta Johannis*, 99, 101, in E. Junod, J.-D. Kaestli, eds., *Actes de Jean: Acta Johannis* (Corpus Christianorum, Ser. Apocryphorum 1; Turnhout: Brepols, 1983), 210, 212.

words which the living Jesus spoke and Didymus Judas Thomas wrote." [36]

In the Naassene Hymn, a gnostic psalm preserved by Hippolytus, and a gem of gnostic literature, Jesus asks his Father to send him to earth in order to save the Soul, who is unable by herself to escape 'the bitter Chaos' . The main task of Jesus in order to offer salvation will be to reveal the esoteric knowledge:

> For that reason send me, Father.
> Bearing the seals I will descend;
> I will pass through all the Aeons;
> I will reveal all the mysteries
> and show the forms of the gods:
> I will transmit the secrets of the holy way,
> calling them Gnosis [37]

Although it is very difficult to extrapolate from theological doctrine to the sociological background of texts, esoteric theology seems to reflect a particular social organization and *Sitz im Leben*. The Gnostics probably lived as small, isolated groups, *ecclesiolae*, which we could call secret societies. Stephen Gero, for instance, has shown that the Borborites, a later Gnostic group in the East, led a clandestine existence within other Christian groups. [38]

All these different texts and traditions, chosen almost at random from our sources, and which I have brought here only as a few instances, show clearly that esoteric attitudes, revelations, exegesis, were rife in Gnostic milieus. What they don't reflect, however, is the existence of esoteric Gnostic *myths*.

---

[36] See Puech, *En quête de la gnose* (Paris: Gallimard, 1977) 93-284, and H. Koester, *Ancient Christian Gospels: their History and Development* (Philadelphia, London: Trinity, SCM, 1990), 124-128, on the *Gospel of Thomas*.

[37] On *musteria panta*, see M. Marcovich, "The Naassene Psalm in Hippolytus (*Haer.* 5. 10. 2)", in B. Layton, ed., *The Rediscovery of Gnsoticism, II* (Supplements to *Numen* 41; Leiden: Brill, 1981), 775: "probably a concrete thing: a secret password, sign or symbol, different for each of the archons (aeons)."

[38] S. Gero, "With Walter Bauer on the Tigris: Encratite Orthodoxy and Libertine Heresy in Syro-Mesopotamian Christianity", in Ch. Hedrick and R. Hodgson, Jr., eds., *Nag Hammadi, Gnosticism, & Early Christianity* (Peabody, Mass.: Hendrickson, 1986), 287-307, esp. 306.

5. Gnostic esoteric mythology

The complex cosmogonical myth developed by the Valentinian teacher Ptolemaeus is one of the best known gnostic texts.[39] In his *Letter to Flora*, the same Ptolemaeus presents the exoteric version of Valentinian doctrine to a sympathizer, still belonging to the Catholic Christian church. What must be emphasized here is the fact that in this work, Ptolemaeus presents gnostic doctrine as a higher, more spiritual exegesis of the Bible (both Old and New Testaments), but is very careful not to reveal the cosmogonic myth. From a reading of the *Letter to Flora* alone, one would remain unable to guess the existence of a gnostic myth.

That means, then, that the myth itself must remain secret and be told only to the initiates. And indeed, some allusions to this secret nature of the myth can be found in Irenaeus' report, where mention is made of the 'secret of the apostle', of the 'mystery of gnosis', of the 'great mystery of the pit'.[40] Ptolemaeus insists that only the spiritual ones, who have been initiated to the mysteries of Wisdom, possess the perfect gnosis of God.[41] Showing the exoteric character of the Valentinian *Gospel of Truth*, Harold Attridge has offered a demonstration of the esoteric character of Valentinian mythology. According to Attridge, the *Gospel of Truth* cannot be understood without postulating the Valentinian myth of Sophia, a myth which however is not revealed in the text. "If there is a cosmogonic myth of the Sophia variety behind our text, it is well concealed." [42]

A particularly baroque and syncretistic myth is the one propounded by the book *Baruch*, of a certain Justin.[43] There is no need to retell here the juicy love story of Edem, Elohim, and Naas, the Serpent of old (*nahash*). Let us only point out the esoteric character of

---

[39] The myth is related by Irenaeus, *Adv. Haer.*, I.1-8. On this text, the most thorough study is F. Sagnard, *La gnose valentinienne et le témoignage de saint Irénée* (Etudes de philosophie médiévale 36; Paris: Vrin, 1947).

[40] " *to mega musterion tou buthou*", Iren., *Adv. Haer.*, I.19.2; cf. Sagnard, *La gnose valentinienne*, 426.

[41] Irenaeus, *Adv. Haer.*, I.6.1.

[42] H. Attridge, "The Gospel of Truth as an Exoteric Text", in Hedrick & Hodgson, eds., *Nag Hammadi, Gnosticism and Early Christianity*, 252. One should note that Attridge is not particularly interested in the question of an esoteric *myth*.

[43] The content of the book is preserved by Hippolytus, *Elenchos* V. 23-27 [= 18-22]; cf. X. 15. 1-7.

the myth, which Justin asks his followers not to reveal to anybody, by swearing to "preserve the secrets... the unspeakable mysteries" .[44]

It thus seems that since the gnostics formed exclusive groups, cherishing their secret soteriological knowledge, their mythopoieic thought, too, was endowed with an esoteric character.

Let us now come back to *the Thunder*. If the text was esoteric, written for the gnostics themselves, why should the myth remain hidden under enigmatic hints? *Prima facie*, one would think that in micro-societies such as the gnostic communities, the myth would have been told *in toto*, and clearly, to the initiates, since it is their knowledge, precisely, which defined the identity of the gnostics in opposition to the rest of mankind. Or should this text rather be perceived as exoteric, meant to be read by 'fellow travellers', such as Flora, rather than by the gnostics themselves?[45]

According to our identification of the references to *brontè* in early Christian literature, there is some probability that the text expresses the heavenly revelation of divine secrets. *The Thunder* thus appears to be an esoteric text, adressed to the initiated, who alone are deemed fit to receive the revelation of secrets which cannot be committed to writing.

The Thunder is not the only gnostic text with riddles. Layton himself refers to the *Apocryphon of John*, the *Hypostasis of the Archons* and the *Apocalypse of Adam*.[46] In Gnostic and Manichaean literature, we know of other enigmas, which reflect a paradoxical identity between two entities.

The enigmatic figure at the beginning of the *Apocryphon of John* is a famous riddle. The figure appears under three different forms, and then it declares: "I am the Father, the Mother, the Son." [47] The iden-

---

[44] Hippolytus, *Elenchos*, 24 (M. Marcovich, ed., Hippolytus, *Refutatio omnium haeresium* [PTS 25; Berlin: De Gruyter, 1986], 199); cf. *Elenchos*, 23, 198 Marcovich. Cf. M. Marcovich, "Justin's *Baruch*: A Showcase of Gnostic Syncretism", in his *Studies on Graeco-Roman Religions and Gnosticism* (Studies on Greek and Roman Religions 4; Leiden: Brill, 1988), 93-119.

[45] Another question, which cannot be dealt with here, is that of the possible cultic role of our text, and of the mythic riddles that it contains, within the gnostic communities.

[46] Layton, "Riddles", 44ff.

[47] This passage is adequately identified by Michel Tardieu, as an 'enigma', though the commentary is disappointing; see M. Tardieu, *Ecrits gnostiques; Codex de Berlin*

tity between the various figures is obtained through a transformation of the Revealer.

Another transformation is also reported in the *Gospel of Thomas*, logion 108:

> Jesus said: "Whoever drinks from my mouth will become like me; I, too, will become that man, and to that man the obscure things will be shown forth."

This text, however, does not describe the transformation of the Revealer, but rather the identification of the believer and his god. A similar process is described in the Pistis Sophia:

> "That man is me, and I am that man." [48]

Thanks to this revelation, the man in question will be able to be absorbed into Jesus, and, as it were, to become equal to him, i. e. to become king with him.

Various Manichaean texts preserve similar patterns of paradoxical expression. In the Coptic Manichaean *Psalms*, the Kingdom of God is said to be at once "within and without us." On Jesus, the same text says:

> You are inside and you are outside. You are above and you are beneath. You are close and far away. You are hidden and manifest. You are silent and also speak.[49]

It is to such statements that the identification between Eve and the thunder, as reported by the Gospel of Eve, should be compared. Such an identification, which explains the paradoxical statements in the text, may be called *theosis*, or *unio mystica*, or even be related to a shamanistic trance of sorts. It should be pointed out here that such

---

(Sources gnostiques et manichéennes 1; Paris: Cerf, 1984), 84- 86. Cf. *Savoir et salut*, ch. 3.

[48] C. Schmidt, V. MacDermot, ed., transl., *Pistis Sophia* (Nag Hammadi Studies 13; Leiden: Brill, 1978), 231.

[49] C. R. C. Allberry, ed., transl., *A Manichaean Psalm-Book, Part II* (Stuttgart: Kohlhammer, 1938), 160, 20- 23 and 155, 34- 38. See C. H. Puech, *En quête de la gnose* II, 271- 274, who concludes :" En conséquence, et somme toute, il est apparu qu"intériorité' et 'extériorité' représentent deux aspects simultanés d'une même réalité susceptible d'être, dans le même temps, cachée aux uns, révélée aux autres..."

transformations of the religious hero into a divine person are found also in Jewish texts of the Rabbinic period. These texts probably reflect experiences dating back to the first or second Christian centuries.[50]

6. The disappearance of gnosticism

In an important article, George McRae has sought to analyse the reasons for the Church's opposition to Gnosticism.[51] But why did Gnosticism lose the grand battle, and disappear from the map? Is the disappearance of gnosticism related to causes similar to those which brought to the eradication of the mystery cults a few centuries later? Walter Burkert has pointed out the complexity of their organization as a main reason for their losing to Christianity.[52] Our attempt to analyze the esotericism of the Gnostic myths may bring us closer to an understanding of what happened to the dualist movement. We know very little of gnostic cultic practices and of the way the communities were organized.[53] But the instance of *the Thunder* emphasizes the intellectual complexity of gnostic traditions.

The abstract character of the gnostic myths points to their lack of liveliness. Their esotericism is another trait hinting at their inability to survive. An esoteric myth cannot be interpreted. Gnosticism offered a new kind of doctrine, in which myth was the highest level of truth. The secrets were revealed in myths; the nature of truth itself was mythical.[54] The fact that there was no possibility of an interpretation of myth entailed the need to find new ways of representing myth, of telling it without revealing it completely, even within the gnostic community. It is this "esoteric urge", this need to protect the myth, as it were, to present it as the highest level of truth, that brought to hiding it under the cloak of enigmas. This esoteric character of gnostic myth,

---

[50] For a strong argument about the early dating of these traditions, see C.R.A. Morray-Jones, "Transformation Mysticism in the Apocalyptic Merkabah Tradition", JJS 43 (1992), 1- 31, esp. 24.

[51] G. McRae, "Why the Church Rejected Gnosticism", in E.P. Sanders, *Jewish and Christian Self-Definition, I* (London: SCM Press, 1980), 126- 133 and 236- 238.

[52] W. Burkert, *Homo Necans* (Berkeley, Los Angeles, London: University of California, 1983 [original ed. Berlin: De Gruyter, 1972]), 248- 256.

[53] See Rudolph, *Die Gnosis*, 221- 261.

[54] See for instance the mythical figure of *alètheia* in the conceptions of Mark the gnostic, as reported by Irenaeus, *Adv. Haer.*, I, 13.

again, reflects its innate weakness, and its inability to be transformed, reinterpreted, a constant and imperative need for religious messages if they want to survive cognitive dissonances.[55]

Both myths and secret traditions or cults were essential elements of religion in various cultures of the ancient world. Both disappeared, for all practical purposes, in the radical religious transformations of late antiquity. Gnosticism lost in the grand spiritual battle of the first Christian centuries because it tried to revive old patterns of thought in a changing world. The esoteric doctrines in the earliest strata of Christianity eventually disappeared, since they were running against the grain of the new religious sensitivity. The vocabulary of ancient esotericism was transformed into esoteric *metaphors*, and these in their turn formed the basis of Christian mysticism.[56]

---

[55] This is what happened later to Augustine with Manichaean mythology. Once he could not believe it anymore, there was no possibility within the system to offer a higher, subtler, more spiritual interpretation. The system was total, and thus closed to any hermeneutics. See esp. *Confessions*, V.

[56] See chapter 9 *infra*.

CHAPTER FOUR

ESOTERICISM IN MANI'S THOUGHT
AND BACKGROUND

Mani is the only known Antique thinker to have established, quite intentionally, a world religion. With the notable exception of Judaism, all major religious traditions had a place in his highly syncretistic system and were integrated into his conception of *Heilsgeschichte*. One well-known aspect of this attitude was the systematic translation, or rather adaptation, of Manichaean mythology into various languages and cultures. Mani considered himself as being the last of a series of prophets sent to mankind, and among whom stood prominent Buddha, Zarathustra and Jesus. As the last prophet, Mani would reveal Truth, for the first time, in its entirety, and to all peoples. Previous prophets had each revealed only one side of Truth to their own people. Now, no aspect of Truth would remain hidden or partially understood.[1]

Prima facie, such an attitude would appear to rule out the existence of any esoteric trend in Manichaean teachings. Indeed, students of Manichaeism do not seem to have noticed yet any allusion to esotericism in Manichaen texts and traditions. The purpose of this chapter is to argue that a closer look at Mani's *Umwelt* and early development, as it is revealed to us mainly in the Cologne Mani Codex (= CMC), should bring to a revision of the *opinio communis*.

One of the points most worthy of our attention in the CMC is the description of the sectarian background from which Mani's very conscious and eclectic universalism emerged. For the historian of religion, this is puzzling only in appearance. The propensity of small and radically exclusive sects to devote intense theological attention to the destiny of the whole of humankind is a well-known fact—one need think only of Qumrân in this respect. Indeed, Mani's interest in the fate of humankind might have been partly inherited from the baptist sects against whose beliefs and practices he revolted.

---

[1] For a recent presentation of Mani's conception of prophecy, see M. Tardieu, *Le Manichéisme* (Paris, 1981), 19-27. For a more detailed discussion, with references, see H.-C. Puech, *Le Manichéisme, son fondateur, sa doctrine* (Paris, 1949), 61-63 and notes.

The new text offers a glimpse at the very passage from sect to world religion, from a basically monotheistic theology to the most radically dualistic system ever devised.[2] As a radical reformer, Mani exploded theological as well as sociological patterns. Early in his career, he claimed to go back to the original heritage of the baptists, to the truth that had once been their portion, and which they had forgotten with time. Mani's revolt, which appears to be primarily of a cultic character (rejection of the Elchasaites' way of life, and in particular of their baptismal rites and food-tabus) is accomplished in the name of a truer interpretation of their own tradition.[3] Mani knew how to appeal to Elchasai's doctrinal authority while arguing with the baptist leaders about the soteriological value of cultic practices.[4] It should be noted that his attitude did not arouse only suspicion, and that to some of the baptists he seems to have appeared as a prophet and a teacher, as the holder of a secret revelation who should be listened to, or even as the expected Messiah (CMC 85, 13 - 87, 6).

Mani, who claimed that "in no way would (he) destroy the commandments of the Savior" (CMC 91, 20-22), also boasted to have "destroyed and put to nought [the baptists'] words and mysteries" (CMC 80, 6-8), on the strength of the "mysteries" revealed to him by his heavenly Twin. This would imply that the baptists had become in time alienated from the Truth once imparted to them. But to what do the *mustèria* refer in the context of the CMC? The word has obviously a very broad semantic spectrum in late antiquity, and is more often that not amphibological, or used in a metaphoric or at least a rather loose sense.

Yet, it seems to be used also in the stricter sense of *Glaubensgeheimnisse* in the CMC, as the editors have noted.[5] I shall first analyze the main passages where *mustèrion/a* and connected words appear in the

---

[2] On Manichaean dualism, see *Savoir et Salut* 243-258.

[3] See in particular A. Henrichs, "Mani and the Babylonian Baptists: a Historical Confrontation", *HSCP* 77 (1973), 23-59, and J. J. Buckley, "Mani's Opposition to the Elchasaites: a Question of Ritual", in P. Slater and D. Wiebe, eds., *Traditions in Contact and Change* (Waterloo, Ont., 1983), 323-36.

[4] CMC 94, 1 - 97, 17. The text, edited by A. Henrichs and L. Koenen, is published in the *Zeitschrift für Papyrologie und Epigraphik* (= *ZPE* 19 (1975), 1-85 (pages 1-72); 32 (1978), 87-199 (pages 72, 8 - 99,9); 44 (1981), 201-318 (pp. 99,10-120); 48 (1982), 1-59 (pp. 121-192). Page 1 to 99, 9 of the CMC have been translated into English by R. Cameron and A. J. Dewey in their *The Cologne Mani Codex* (P. Colon. inv. nr. 4780) "Concerning the Origin of his Body" (SBL, Texts and Translations, 15; Missoula: Scholars Press, 1979). It is this translation which is quoted here.

Codex. Only later shall I turn to the broader context and attempt to show the roots of Mani's conception of esotericism.

Salmaios the ascetic tells of a baptist who intended to fell a date-palm tree. When the endangered tree pleaded with Mani for its life, the confounded baptist fell at Mani's feet, saying "I did not know that this secret mystery (*touto to aporrhèton mustèrion*) is with you. Whence was [the agony of the palm-tree] revealed to you?" When Mani lets him know that all plants speak to him, he says in his bewilderment: "guard this mystery (*to mustèrion touto*), tell it to no one, lest someone become envious and destroy you" (CMC 8, 11-13). The "mystery" is here conceived as a supernatural power, or ability, possessed by Mani alone and ignored by everyone else. It appears as a *mana* of sorts, through which Mani retains a contact with the vegetal world, he alone knowing that it is ensouled. This "mystery", moreover, should remain hidden, since it could evoke jealousy, with immediately dangerous consequences for its possessor.

What is the origin of this "mystery" bestowed upon the young Mani? Another passage gives us the answer: "When, then, that all-glorious and all-blessed one (i.e. the Twin) disclosed to me these exceedingly great secrets (*ta aporrhèta tauta kai megista*), he began to say to me: 'This mystery (*tode to mustè[rion]*) I have revealed to you [...] to reveal...'" (CMC 26, 7-15). It is his heavenly Twin, then, who reveals the mystery to Mani. The Twin is thus functionally similar to those angels who had revealed "very great mysteries of majesty" (*megista mustèria tès megalôsunès*) to Mani's prophetic precursors, such as Sethel (i.e. Seth), Enosh, Shem, Enoch, or Paul, who had been snatched up to heavens for the occasion.[6] Secrets (*aporrhèta*) is then an exact equivalent of "mystery", a term which also appears in the plural with a similar meaning: "Now he revealed to me (*apekalupse de moi*) the mysteries (*ta mustèria*) hidden to the world, which are not permitted for anyone to see or hear" (CMC 43, 3-7). Here again, the esoteric character of the knowledge imparted to the prophet by his revelatory angel is quite explicit. This knowledge—the mystery, or mysteries—is hidden and should remain so. The social consequences of the revelation of the mystery are thus obvious: the prophet can no longer be

---

[5] *ZPE* 32 (1978), 136, n. 183 on CMC 80, 8; *cf. ZPE* 44 (1981), 278, n. 398 on CMC, 112, 10-11.

[6] On Enoch's rapture, CMC 52, 5-7.

part of his community, his blessing directly entails a curse: "Then immediately I separated myself from the ordinances of that teaching in which I was reared, and became like a stranger and a solitary in their midst..." (CMC 44, 2-8). Or again: "Little by little, I detached myself from the midst of that Law [in] which I was reared, marvelling beyond all measure at [those] mysteries..." (CMC 30, 4-7).

To be sure, the mystery is eventually to be revealed, but the prophet is unable to do so while it is still he alone who knows the Truth in the midst of Error: "How then shall I, alone against all, be able to reveal this mystery in the midst of the multitude, [entangled in] error..." (CMC 31, 3-9). In order to proclaim the Truth of which he has been made the bearer by angelic revelation, the prophet reaches the ultimate social conclusion: he must leave the community of his youth.

The first and obvious level of esotericism, then, is that forced by social circumstances: the proclamation of Truth among devotees of false dogmas is immediately and physically dangerous for the prophet. Thus, he must keep silent until these circumstances are changed: "... I went about in that Law, preserving this hope (*tènde tèn elpida*, an equivalent of *mustèrion*) in my heart; no one perceived who it was that was with me, and I myself revealed nothing to anyone during that great period of time" (CMC 25, 2-13). Esotericism is thus shown to be of a circumstantial character: it seeks to hide doctrines since their revelation could have adverse consequences in a given situation. One may speculate as to whether all doctrines of esotericism eventually partake of a circumstantial character. In any case, it may be noted here that the ultimate transformation of this doctrine, which justifies *lying* in order not to reveal one's true doctrines under duress—a phenomenon known as *taqiyya* in Shi'ite Islam—was also known to the Manichaeans, as attested by a Sogdian text.[7]

The fundamentally ambivalent character of esoteric doc-

---

[7] I refer to the parable of the child who pretends to be deaf and dumb. One of the fragments contains the *epimuthion*:: "Lord Mar Mani said to the magus: I, together with my disciples and Electi, and like that child who was silent as an expedient (...) (who) did not speak and did not hear... So we are silent (*swkw*) and we speak with no one and perform good deeds and pious actions as an expedient, (but) that time will come at last when I shall *speak* before all, like that child (*z' kw*), and we *shall* demand justice for ourselves..." The fragment is edited and translated by N. Sims-Williams, "The Sogdian Fragments from Leningrad", BSOAS 44 (1981), 231-240, esp. 238. On other aspects of secretive attitudes among Manichaeans, see *Savoir et Salut*, 299-314.

trines—which should be kept secret from most, at least for a time, but eventually meant to be revealed to those able to recognize their truth—this character is admirably described in the CMC.

Esoteric doctrines can be transmitted in two ways: either orally or in writing. Both ways were known in late antiquity, although the second is obviously much more easily documented than the first. The CMC provides clear evidence of the fact that at least some of Mani's writings transmitted esoteric doctrines. Two epistles of Mani are quoted in our text. The quotation from the first, sent to Edessa, begins thus: "The truth and the secrets (*ta aporrhèta*) which I speak about... not from men have I received it nor from fleshy creatures, not even from studies in the Scriptures" (CMC 64, 8-15). Mani goes on acknowledging his heavenly Twin's grace for having pulled him "from the council of the many who do not recognize the truth and revealed to me his secrets (*ta te autou aporrhèta*) and those of his undefiled Father and of all the cosmos. He disclosed to me how I was before the foundation of the world, and how the groundwork of all the works, both good and evil, was laid, and how everything of [this] aggregation was engendered..." (CMC 65, 3-22). The point of the revelation of these secrets—which seem to encompass the most part of Manichaean mythology—was to save Mani, and "those prepared to be chosen by him (i.e. by Mani's Twin) from the sects," from death. These are Mani's "fellow-travellers", as he calls them (*tois emois xunemporois*), in his Gospel quoted a little further in the CMC (67, 2).

It is to these "children of peace", to this "immortal race", to his Elect (*eklogèn*)—and only to them—that Mani's Gospel is adressed, which includes "these eminent mysteries (*tauta ta tès huper[o]chès orgia*, CMC 67, 16-18). Mani here states most explicitly the esoteric character of his doctrines: "All the secrets (*panta ta aporrhèta*) which my Father has given to me, while I have hidden and covered (them) from the sects and the heathen, and still more from the world, to you I have revealed according to the pleasure of my most blessed Father" (CMC 68, 6-15).

In order to understand more precisely the meaning of words such as *mustèrion, aporrhèta, apokalupsis* in Mani's parlance, we should turn to the broader context of Jewish, Christian and Gnostic literatures, and in particular to the Jewish Christian background of the Elchasaites. We shall see that these various literary traditions all keep rather precise traces of esotericism. The best way to protect the secrecy of doctrines in antiquity was, of course, to keep them oral, to refrain from

committing them to writing. Individual by nature, oral transmission
permitted the careful selection of those worthy of having imparted to
them the secret knowledge. Another way of protecting secret doctrines from falling into unworthy hands was to strongly limit access to
secret writings, and to punish severely revelation of their content outside the group of elect, the sect. Both methods were known among
Jews in the first Christian centuries.

The Essenes had secret writings: Josephus tells us that a new member of the sect had to swear "terrible oaths" to protect its secret teachings from outsiders, s.to keep secret the names of the angels, and to
guard the sect's secret writings.[8] The *Damascus Document* as well as the
Manual of Discipline reiterate this insistence on protecting the esoteric
character of Essene teachings.[9] Moreover, reference should be made
to the importance of the word *raz* in the Qumran texts—a word
whose semantic range is as broad as that of its Greek equivalent,
mustèrion.[10] The texts refer to various kinds of "mysteries": together
with cosmic mysteries (which include the calendar) there are historical
mysteries—for instance the fate of mankind and the future reserved
for the elect. The Master of Justice, in particular, is the bearer of a
great mystery, and has been sent by God to communicate it to his
disciples.[11] Mention should also be made of a *scriptural* mystery, hidden in the Scriptures and destined to be revealed at the end of
times.[12]

The semantic spectrum of *raz* in the Qumran texts is not unlike
that of *mustèrion* in the Pauline epistles. In particular, there is a close
parallelism between the connection of *raz* to da'at in one corpus and
mustèrion to *gnosis* in the other (see for instance I Cor. 13:2). For Paul
as for the Covenanters, the knowledge of the mysteries clearly retains
an esoteric character, reserved for a handful of the perfect.
Apocalyptic literature, too, knows of esoteric knowledge: the author
of IV Ezra for instance (a work written towards the end of the first

---

[8] Bell 2.141 ff. see " *kruptô* [...]" in *TDNT* III, 957-1000.

[9] *Damascus Doc.* 15.10 f.; see C. Rabin, *The Zadokite Documents* (Oxford, 1958), 73.
Man" *Disc.* 1 Qs 9.17; *cf.* 5.16 f., 8.11 f.

[10] On the semantic spectrum of *raz* and cognate words in Qumrân texts, see J.
Coppers, "Le 'Mystère' dans la théologie paulinienne et ses parallèles Qumrâniens",
in A. Descamps *et al.*, *Littérature et théologie pauliniennes* (Recherches Bibliques 5; Paris,
1960), 142-151, esp. 142-I46 and 144, n. I. see also E. Vogt, " 'Mysteria' in textibus
Qumrân", *Biblica* 37 (1956), 247-257.

[11] 1 QH 5.25; 8.11.

[12] 1 Qp Hab. 7.5.

century C.E.) tell us only the 24 Biblical books were made public by Ezra, while the remaning 70—the apocalypses—were given only to the wise among the people.

The very language of the Hellenistic mystery cults is borrowed by Philo, who refers to the "holy mysteries" hidden in the Biblical text and revealed only to the initiated,[13] while a similar use of the word *mustèrion* is made by the Rabbis in reference to biblical exegesis. Besides *raz* and *sod* Rabbinic literature knows the loan word *mîsterîn, mîstorîn*.[14] The *Mishna*, the oral tradition, is referred to as God's *mîstorîn* (R. Judah b. Shalom, around 370, in *Ps. Rab.* 5 [14b]); he who knows my *mîstorîn*, says God "is my Son". Further, the Messianic times are called *mîstorîn* while the calendar count is referred to as a *sod*. The exegetical rules of the Torah (*ta' amei Torah*) moreover, are called *razei Torah,,* while the teachings about cosmogony (*ma' asse bereshîth*) and the mystical vision of God (Ezechiel's charriot, *ma' asse merkavah*) are identified by a semantic parallel, *sitrei Torah*. To be sure, it is very difficult to date rabbinic sources with precision, but the antiquity of these esoteric conceptions is not to be doubted. They go back at least to the first century C.E., as Gershom Scholem and others have conclusively argued.[15] Indeed, the Rabbis are the heirs of the esoteric doctrines of the Pharisees. One further point should be noted. The polyvalence of *mustèrion, raz* or *sod,* does not lie only in the various kinds of doctrines they refer to, but also in that they can also stand for rites of initiation, such as circumcision or baptism. This fact has been recently emphasized by Morton Smith, who has argued convincingly that both Paul and the rabbis "took over the word

[13] See for instance *De Cherub.* 48 f., cited by J. Jeremias, *The Eucharistic Words of Jesus* (London, 1966), 129. Jeremias devotes an entire section to esoteric trends in Judaism and in early Christianity. See also A.D. Nock, "Hellenistic Mysteries and Christian Sacraments", in his *Essays on Religion and the Ancient World*, ed. Z. Stewart, II (Oxford, 1972), esp. 801-803.

[14] See the texts cited by Strack and Billerbeck, *Kommentar zum neuen Testament aus Talmud und Midrash*, I (München, 1922), 659-660, from which the following examples are taken. See also G.A. Wewers, *Geheimnis und Geheimhaltung in rabbinischen Judentum* (Berlin-New York, 1975).

[15] G.G. Scholem, *Jewish Gnosticism, Merkabah Mysticism and Talmudic Tradition* (New York,1965²), 36-42; M. Smith, "Observations on Hekhalot Rabbati", in A. Altmann, ed., *Biblical and Other Studies* (Cambridge, Ma., 1963), 142-160, esp. 152. See also J.M. Baumgarten, "The Book of Elkesai and Merkabah Mysticism", in *Proceedings of the Eighth World Congress of Jewish Studies, Section C* (Jerusalem, 1983), 13-18. Cf. *Savoir et Salut*, 65-84.

mustèrion with the full range of its Greco-Roman meanings." [16] Thus, in the Hekhalot writings, which stem from the circles of the Merkavah mystics, the "Great Secret" (*ha-sod ha-nora*) is not only to be revealed to the fit, but also practised by them. This act is to be preceded by a propaideutic ascetical behavior, which involves the mystic's fasting, baking his own bread, and taking ablutions. [17]

There is little doubt that esoteric doctrines existed in Christianity too, from its earliest strata. Documentation is here very sparse, but by no means nonexistent. Joachim Jeremias has insisted on the role played by esotericism already in the teaching of Jesus. Jesus's self description as "son of man" is for Jeremias the key element for understanding his messiahship as being of an esoteric character. [18] Various references are also made in the Gospels of esoteric teachings of Jesus, either on particular topics, such as the eschatological prophecies, or in general terms. Paul, too, alludes to the divine "wisdom" which can be imparted only to the "perfect" or "spiritual" ones (II Cor. 2:6, 13). Similarly, the secrets of Christology are not to be taught to everybody, as *Hebrews* makes clear: repentance from dead works, faith and baptism are taught to all Christians, but not Christology, which is reserved for those mature in faith (Heb. 5:11 - 6:8; *ibid.* 7:1 - 10:18).

Finally, and most importantly, Paul knows that the secrets of the divine nature belong to the *Arkandisziplin*, of which it undoubtedly forms the center. Indeed, Paul's ascension to Paradise, of which he speaks only in the most allusive terms, has often been compared to the mystical ascent—or rather descent—of the Merkavah mystics. [19]

How far these secret teachings were preserved later on, and how far the very idea of esotericism was retained in a later period, is very difficult to evaluate. It stands to reason that the combination of the Roman view of Christianity as a "secret society" —with the implica-

---

[16] M. Smith, *Clement of Alexandria and a Secret Gospel of Mark* (Cambridge, Ma., 1973), 181. For the broad spectrum of meanings in the Greek Magical Papyri, see A.-J. Festugière, *L' idéal religieux des Grecs et l' Evangile*, (Paris, 1981 [reprint]), 304 and esp. n. 1.

[17] I. Gruenwald, "Manichaeism and Judaism in Light of the Cologne Mani Codex", *ZPE* 50 (1983), 29-45, esp. 38.

[18] *The Eucharistic Words of Jesus*, 129-130. See now F. Dreyfus, *Jésus savait-il qu' il était Dieu?* (Paris, 1984), 45-55.

[19] See for instance Scholem, *Jewish Gnosticism*, 14-19. But see the serious reservation expressed by P. Schäfer, "New Testament and Hekhalot Literature: The Journey into Heaven in Paul and in Merkavah Mysticism", *JJS* 35 (1984), 18-35.

tions of such a perception[20]—and the proliferation of esoteric groups in the second century (I am referring mainly to the various Christianizing Gnostic trends) encouraged the Church Fathers to insist on the universal character of Christianity, and on the exoteric nature and universal claims of its soteriological doctrine.

In Alexandria, however, clear traces survive of esoteric doctrines transmitted only among a religious élite. Clement of Alexandria, in particular, does not only make liberal use of the language of the mystery cults; he also refers to a body of secret traditions derived from Peter.[21] In a fragment preserved only by Eusebius (*HE* II.1.4. f.) he mentions the *gnosis* given by the Lord, after his Resurrection, to James the Just. In the *Eclogae Propheticae*, Clement refers to certain books kept secret by the Christian *gnostikoi* in Alexandria. Morton Smith, who has analyzed all these references at great length, notes that in Clement's works, the *presbuteroi*—who would seem to keep traditions originating in the Jerusalem church—are the bearers of secret traditions. finally, mention should be made of Clement's now famous letter to Theodore, discovered by Smith at the Mar Saba monastery, and stating in no ambiguous terms the existence of esoteric doctrines, relating to the teachings of Jesus, in the Alexandrian church. In particular, Clement speaks of *ta megala mustèria* a term which is for us of special interest since it is also used by Hippolytus in his description of Elchasaite doctrine and practice.[22]

It is very difficult to find further traces of esoteric doctrines in later Patristic literature. In Early Byzantine spiritual literature *mustèrion/a* seems to have been used mainly—besides its cultic and christological meanings—in reference to mystical contemplation.[23] Yet, it should be noted that in the Syrian Orient, in Mani's *Umwelt*, the idea of esoteric doctrine survives a little longer. The Syriac *Liber Graduum*, for instance, dated from the fourth century, insists on the two classes of

---

[20] On this see R.L. Wilken, *The Christians as the Romans saw them* (New Haven, 1984), 31-47.

[21] See M. Smith, *Clement of Alexandria*, 30. Origen, too, refers to esoteric doctrines; see J. Daniélou, *Message Évangélique et culture hellénistique* (Paris, 1961), 427-430. See also R.P.C. Hanson, *Origen's Doctrine of Tradition* (London, 1954), 53-72 on Clement's and 73-90 on Origen's doctrine of secret Tradition. On the preservation of esoteric doctrines in early Christianity, see D. Powell, "Arkandisziplin" in *TRE* 4(1979), 1-8.

[22] Hippolytus, *Elenchos* IX, 15.1, pp. 116-117 in A.F.J. Klijn and G.J. Reinink, *Patristic Evidence for Jewish Christian Sects* (suppl. to N.T. 36; Leiden, 1973).

[23] See references in Lampe's *Patristic Greek Lexicon, s.v.*

Christians, the *just* and the *perfect* ones to whom different teachings must be imparted.[24]

Texts usually qualified as "Gnostic" by modern scholarship vary greatly in their cultural background and cultic implications. Yet, we can detect esoteric doctrines in various Gnostic trends. Among Gnostic texts, the "Naassene Hymn" seems to stand particularly close to those trends in Hellenistic religiosity commonly referred to as "Mystery religions". The Hymn purports to reveal a mystical doctrine (*logos mustikos*) about anthropogony. This doctrine—actually a myth of the Primal Man—is also called *mustèrion*, and has been known to various peoples, such as the Egyptians or the Samothracians, under various garbs. About the latter, for instance, the text adds that this "great and unspeakable mystery" is *known* only by the perfect ones (*tout' esti to mega kai arrhèton samothrakeôn, mustèrion, ho monois exestin eidenai tois teleiois*) a phrasing which implies that the *mustèrion* is *a secret doctrine*.[25]

Other texts, Christianized in a less tangential way, confirm the importance of secret traditions in Gnostic trends. The *Gospel of Truth* knows of esoteric speculations on the Divine Name, when it calls the Name "the mystery of the invisible which comes to ears that are completely filled with it".[26] Esoteric traditions about the true meaning of scriptural passages were preserved in the Valentinian school. In his *Letter to Flora*, Ptolemaeus claims that the apostolic tradition alone, transmitted through succession only to those deemed worthy, knows about the origin and birth of both demiurge and devil.[27] According to Clement of Alexandria, Valentinus would have inherited this tradition from Theudas, a disciple of Paul—hence its *apostolicity*.[28] Irenaeus confirms the existence of such a conception: "The Valentinians forge an accusation against the Holy Writ when they say that some passages are not correct, and have no authority or contradict each other,

---

[24] On the *Liber Graduum* see M. Kmosko's detailed introduction to his edition, in *Patrologia Syriaca*, III.

[25] See J. Frickel, *Hellenistiche Erlösung in christlicher Deutung: die gnostische Naassenerschrift* (NHS 19; Leiden, 1984), Hymn, 10.9, p. 222; cf. 218 (about the Egyptians).

[26] CG I, 36, 17-21. See also the *proemium* of the *Apocryphon of John*, CG II, 1, 1-4. On which see now M. Tardieu, *Ecrits gnostiques; Codex de Berlin* (Paris: 1984), 239-240. On *mustèrion* in Gnostic literature see A. Böhlig, "Mysterion und Wahrheit", in his *Mysterion und Wahrheit: Gesammelte Aufsäzte zur spätantiken Religionsgeschichte* (Leiden, 1968), esp. 31-40.

[27] *Letter to Flora*, 7.9, in G. Quispel, ed., trans., Ptolémée, *Lettre à Flora* (SC 24bis; Paris, 1964), 72-73.

[28] Clement, *Stromateis*, VII. 106, quoted by Quispel, *op. cit.* 15 and 104.

so that it is impossible for those who do not know the secret tradition to find Truth in the Bible" .[29] As to Clement himself it would seem, particularly in the light of his recently discovered letter, that he was in agreement with the Gnostics about the existence of an esoteric oral doctrine, of apostolic origin,[30] but thought that they had got their knowledge of it in an illegal way and then corrupted its content.[31]

For the *Apocalypse of Adam*, a text whose background is to be found in the Baptist milieus of Syria-Palestine, Adam's revelations to Seth are a "hidden knowledge", identical to "the holy baptism of those who know the eternal knowledge" . As was the case for various Apocrypha, these revelations could not be committed to writing—which would have destroyed their esoteric character—but were to remain protected "on a high mountain, upon a rock of truth" .[32] Indeed, some Gnostic teachers counted on private revelations in order to impart their teaching. Thus did Cerinthus, whose Christology retains some very close affinities to that of the Ebionites, "preach the *agnooumenon theon*" by means of revelations.[33]

W.B. Henning had already noted that the Aramaic word for mystery, *raza*, was "nearly as multivocal" in the Manichaean as in the Mandaean texts.[34] Kurt Rudolph has confirmed the polyvalence of the term in Mandaean parlance: "For the Mandaeans, the World is full of Mysteries", he states, insisting that the whole content of the soteriological teaching is called "mystery" .[35] Such are, too, cultic practices or magical incantations. One of Rudolph's references is particularly noteworthy in our context: In the Ginza, the foreign (or false) religions are called "fallen mysteries", *raze naple*,[36] which is closely parallel to Mani's saying in the CMC that he has destroyed

[29] Irenaeus, *Adversus Haereses*, III.2.1.

[30] See *Strom.*, VI.7.61. The passage is discussed by Quispel, *op. cit.*, 17-20.

[31] This is at least W. Jaeger's opinion, as quoted in M. Smith, *Clement of Alexandria*, 38.

[32] CG V, 85 passim.

[33] Eusebius, *Hist. Eccles.*, III.28.1.

[34] Henning, "Two Manichaean Magical Texts, with an Excursus on the Parthian Ending—*êndêh*" in his *Selected Papers* III (Acta Iranica 15; Téhéran-Liège-Leiden, 1977), 45-46. See already Albirûnî's testimony; "By mystery Plato means a special kind of devotion. The word is much used among the Sâbians of Harrân, the dualistic Manichaeans, and the theologians of the Hindus" . In E. Sachau, *Alberuni's India* (London, 1910), I, 123.

[35] Rudolph, *Die Mandäer*, II, *Der Kult* (FRLANT 75, N.F. 57; Göttingen, 1961), 254-259.

[36] *Ginza R.* 320, 31; Rudolph, op.cit., 255 n. 11.

all the Baptists' mysteries—a testimony to the use of the term *in malam partem* (CMC 80, 6-8).[37]

Yet, the most interesting traditions for a better understanding of Mani's background are found among the Elchasaites and other Jewish Christian groups. According to Patristic tradition, the very name of Elchasai reflects a strong propensity to esotericism. Epiphanius knows that the name means, in Aramaic, "secret power" (*hail kasay*),[38] an etymology which draws immediate associations with Simon Magus's self appellation as "the Great power" of God (Acts 8:10). It is Hippolytus, however, who is most explicit about the existence of esoteric doctrines among the Elchasaites. A candidate to baptism had the Book containing the secret doctrine read to him before being baptised a second time "in the name of the great and most high God (*hupsistos* = '*elyôn*) and in the name of his son, the mighty king". He would then purify himself through immersion, while invoking the names of "seven witnesses", heaven, water, the holy spirits, the angels of prayer, oil, salt and the earth. Hippolytus concludes: "these are the marvellous, ineffable and great mysteries of Elchasai, which he transmits to worthy disciples.[39] It is thus clear that by these "great mysteries" Hyppolytus does not only refer to baptism, but also to the esoteric doctrines revealed, during that *rite de passage*, to those deemed worthy of it. Unfortunately, however, Hippolytus does not tell us anything else about the nature of these doctrines. It stands to reason to assume, among the Baptists of Mani's youth, a rather similar relationship between baptism and esoteric doctrines. Our direct sources, however, remain very scant, and do not permit a clear identification of the content of such doctrines. Yet, we might at least get a clue to the patterns which these doctrines might have followed if we turn to traditions about Jewish Christian groups whose theology stood close to that of the Elchasaites.

The Ebionites, for instance, are known to have invoked the Book of Elchasai, as well as some apocryphal Acts of the Apostles.[40] These Ebionites also conceived of themselves as the bearers of secret revelations: according to Eusebius, it is due to such a revelation, adressed

---

[37] The amphibological use of *mustèrion/a* is noted by the editors, ZPE 44 (1981), 278, n. 398.

[38] Epiphanius, *Panarion*, 19.2.2; 156-157 Klijn-Reinink.

[39] " *tauta ta thaumasia mustèria tou Elchasai ta aporrhèta kai megala ha paradidôsi tois axiois mathètais.*" Hippolytus, *Elenchos*, IX.15.1; 116-117 Klijn-Reinink.

[40] Epiphanius, *Panarion*, 30.16.6 and 20.17.4; 184-185 Kliin-Reinink.

to the worthy ones and prophesying the destruction of Jerusalem, that they had decided to leave the holy city.[41] They also boasted of direct revelations from Christ on the existence and the nature of false pericopes in the Pentateuch. "Because Christ has revealed it to me", *hoti christos moi apekalupse*, answers Ebion to a question on his knowledge of the false pericopes.[42]

The most interesting testimony, however, comes from the *Kerygmata Petrou*, fragments of an early Jewish Christian writing later incorporated into the Pseudo Clementinian novel, which preserve many major aspects of Jewish-Christian theology. Scholarship on the *Kerygmata Petrou* has insisted on the gnosticizing tendency of the work, in which baptismal terminology in particular is strongly coloured by gnostic traits.[43] The baptism described in the letter of Peter which introduces the Clementine writings is of special interest, and has been described as an "act of initiation".[44] Georg Strecker has duly noted the close parallelism between the *Kerygmata Petrou* and the Book of Elchasai, which both represent diverse aspects of a gnosticizing Jewish-Christianity.[45]

Yet the importance of the esoteric element in the *Kerygmata Petrou* does not seem to be emphasized enough in current research.[46] On various occasions, the *Kerygmata Petrou* refer to "the mysteries" which Jesus taught his disciples, insisting that this knowledge was to remain private: "And Peter said: we remember that our Lord and Teacher, commanding us, said: 'Keep the mysteries (*ta mustèria*) for me and the sons of my house...' ". The text goes on: "for it is impious to tell the secrets").[47] What are these mysteries which must be kept secret by the Jewish-Christians? In the singular, *mustèrion* appears in two main different contexts in the *Homilies*.

---

[41] Eusebius, *Hist. Eccles.*, III.5.2 ff.

[42] Epiphanius, *Panarion*, 30.18.9; 188-189 Klijn-Reinink.

[43] See for instance G. Strecker, *Das Judenchristentum in den Pseudoklementinen* (TU 70*; Berlin, 1981), 209. On the Pseudo Clementine littrature, see also F.S. Jones, "The Pseudo-Clementines: a History of Research", *Second Century* 2 (1982), 1-34 and 63-96. On Jewish Christianity, see esp. pp. 84-96.

[44] Rudolph, *Die Mandäer*, II, 396; cf. H.-J. Schoeps, *Jewish Christianity* (Philadelphia, 1969), 17.

[45] Strecker, *Das Judenchristentum*, 214.

[46] The existence of this element had already been noted by O. Cullmann, *Le problème littéraire et historique du roman pseudo-clémentin* (Paris, 1930), 190.

[47] *ta aporrhèta legein asebein estin, Ps. Clem. Hom.*, 19.20.1, 263 Rehm. See also *Hom.*, 3.19.1 (63 Rehm): *ta apo aiônos en kruptôi axiois paradidomena*.

On the one hand, reference is made to the "mystery of the books which are able to deceive".[48] This refers no doubt to the Ebionite conception of the false pericopes. In other words, the mystery here is the secret hermeneutical principle given by Jesus to his worthy disciples and then transmitted orally. *Mustèrion* is also used in relation to the doctrine of God. "This is the mystery of the *Hebdomas* ,"[49] do we read in the section which deals with the physical—but incorporeal—aspect of God, his "most beautiful form" . The Hebdomad remains a cryptic reference to the nature of God, who is said to be both infinite, thus extending in the six dimensions, reflected in the six days of creation, and identified with Rest, *anapausis*, i.e. the Sabbath, the seventh day. It remains unclear whether this Hebdomad is somehow related to the seven cosmic witnesses of Elchasaite baptism, or to the seven spirits of Mani's *Book of Mysteries*, to which we shall come back.

One of the most important texts in the Pseudo Clementine *Homilies* for our present purpose is the introductory letter of Peter to James. In this document, Peter makes clear that the doctrines which he is about to reveal in his *Preachings* should not be made public. They should only be revealed to those deemed worthy of them, who must have spent at least six years in probation before they are led to baptism in "living water" —"according to the initiation of Moses" . During the ceremony, the new initiate, taking to witness heaven, earth, water and air, swears not to communicate in any way the secret books to any one. This ceremony offers the most obvious similarities with that of the Elchasaites as described by Hippolytus. The secret books contain the true Gospel, which must be transmitted only esoterically since the destruction of the Temple.[50] According to the same passage this true Gospel tells about the false prophet, the deceiver, who must come before the true prophet, Antichrist before Christ.

The purpose of the tactical concealment of the "mystery of the Scriptures" (*Hom.*, II.40) is made clear by Peter in his response to Simon's intention to speak publicly about the false pericopes. The text is very revealing and is worth quoting at length:

---

[48] *tôn apatan dunamenôn biblôn to mustèrion*, Hom., 3.4, 58 Rehm, cf. *Hom.*, 2.40: *to mustèrion tôn graphôn mathôn.*

[49] *touto estin hebdomados mustèrion*, Hom., 17.10.1; 234 Rehm.

[50] *houtôs meta kathairesin tou hagiou topou euaggelion alèthes krupha- diapemphthènai, Hom.*, 2.17.4; 42 Rehm.

For we do not wish to say in public that these chapters are added to the Bible, since we should thereby perplex the unlearned multitudes... For they not having yet the power of discerning, would flee from us as impious..

Wherefore, we are under a necessity of assenting to the false chapters, and putting questions in return to him concerning them, and... to give in private an explanation of the chapters that are spoken against God to the well-disposed after a trial of their faith...[51]

It is interesting to note that a similar accusation is made later by Simon against Peter. When the latter lays bare Simon's conception during the open *disputatio*, Simon accuses him angrily of revealing plainly the secret doctrines (*ta aporrhèta*) before the unlearned multitudes (*ep ochlôn amathôn*).

Elsewhere Peter explains to Simon the nature of revelation. Interpreting *Mat.* 11:27 (= *Lc.* 10:22 "the Son will reveal Him to those whom he wishes"), Peter says: "not by instruction, but by revelation only".[52]

These quotations have sufficiently established the existence and the importance of esoteric traditions among the Jewish-Christians. They also have made clear that the central theme of these traditions was the proper exegesis of the Biblical text, and in particular, the correct understanding of the nature of God. For Peter, these parts of the Scriptures in which God appears to be ignorant and to rejoice in murder, where he accepts sacrifices or behaves unjustly, are false, and are written only in order to try men. Those who know the truth will not err and slander God.[53] Indeed, the major problem of Biblical exegesis was, for the Ebionites, the problem of God's nature. This problem also appears to have been the central preoccupation of the Gnostics. Only their conclusions were radically different.

For the Ebionites, therefore, baptism sealed the catechumen's passage from his first birth, derived from sexual lust, to knowledge and salvation.[54] This conception seems very close to that known to Mani in his childhood, and which he rejected.

The background which I have attempted to map here might help

---

[51] *Hom.*, 2.39; 51 Rehm. I quote according to the translation in the *Ante Nicene Christian Library*, vol. 17 (Edinburgh, 1870).

[52] *ou didaskaliai tina toiouton mathein legei, alla apokalupsei monon, Hom.*, 18.6.1; 244 Rehm. Cf. *Hom.*, 18.14, where Simon reveals to the evil ones "the secrets which he would not reveal to the just."

[53] *Hom.*, 18 19-20; 249-250 Rehm.

[54] See for instance *Hom.*, 11.24.

us in understanding the context and meaning of the word *mustèrion/a*
in the CMC as well as in other Manichaean texts, and in raising—although not answering—the question of the existence of esoteric doctrines, to be imparted only to the elect, in Manichaeism.

In the piety of the newly established religious community, Mani
himself is the "noble holy image of the mysteries of God" (*Manichaean
Psalms* 16:28), in whom all the mysteries have been fulfilled by the
Churches (*ibid.* 18:3; 21:8-9). The members of the new community
know that "the mysteries that were before the foundation, thou didst
reveal them to [thy] faithful, that there was Light" (*ibid.* 3:22). They
also "know the mystery, to whom there has been revealed the knowledge of the secret of the Most High through the holy wisdom,
wherein there is no error, of the holy church of the Paraclete, our
Father" (*ibid.* 8:22-25).

The Baptist leaders accused Mani, in front of his father, of wishing
"to go into the world" (CMC 89, 11-14). The accusation was quite
founded. As we have seen, his revelation forced Mani into a radical
conflict with the Baptists. Eventually, he had to make public the private revelation he had received, and open up to his followers the secret knowledge imparted to him.

Hence he even wrote a *Book of Mysteries*. Unfortunately, the contents of this book have remained sealed for us. The book is lost, and
the only trustworthy testimony we have about it is that of Ibn Al
Nadîm, in the long chapters of his *Fihrist* devoted to the
Manichaeans.[55] Ibn Al Nadîm gives a list of 19 chapters of this *Kitab
sifr al-asrâr*. Three of the chapters, at least, were devoted to polemics
against Bardaisan. Otherwise, the book would appear to have been
particularly concerned with Judaism and Christianity (in particular
prophecy) as Prosper Alfaric noted in his analysis of the various traditions about the *Book of Mysteries*.[56] What appears clearly, in any case,
is that the Book was widely read. Both Heraclion of Chalcedon and
Photius, Râzî and al Ya'akûbî refer to it.[57] Mani did succeed in revealing the secrets. But his success was that of his religion, and it
eventually drowned with it.

---

[55] See G. Flügel, *Mani, seine Lehre und seine Schriften* (Leipzig, 1862), (text) 102-103
(translation) and 356-361 (notes).

[56] P. Alfaric, *Les Ecritures Manichéennes*, II (Paris, 1919), 17-21.

[57] On Râzî's testimony, see J. Ruska, "Al-Birûni als Quelle für das Leben und die
Schriften al-Râzî's", *Isis* 5 (1923), 26-50, esp. 30-32, where Birûnî notes his decep-
tion when finally able to peruse the *kitâb sifr al-asrâr*.

CHAPTER FIVE

THE BODY OF TRUTH AND ITS MEASURES: NEW TESTAMENT CANONIZATION IN CONTEXT

For the last hundred years or so, the canonization of the New Testament has remained one of the most notoriously vexing problems in Early Christian studies. Today, the main debate is still between those followers of Adolph von Harnack, like Hans Freiherr von Campenhausen, who insist on the paramount importance of Marcion,[1] and those for whom the canonization process should mainly be seen as an internal development in the early Church; Werner Georg Kümmel, following Theodor Zahn, is probably the main representant of this line of thought, at least within German Protestant scholarship.[2]

The canonization process during the second century had been directly connected by Harnack to Marcion's bold attempt to establish the new religion upon a new corpus of texts, and his rejection of the Septuagint and of the majority of Christian writings known to him, Gospels included. As is well known, Zahn argued, against Harnack, that the complex process through which the canon of the New Testament, as we know it now, had emerged, during the second century, was mainly the product of inner developments within the Christian Church, rather than reflecting a reaction to Marcion's highly selective choice. The broader religious context of the canonization process, in particular the Jewish and the Gnostic dimensions of early Christianity, seem to have remained understudied.

---

[1] See mainly his epoch-making *Die Entstehung der christlichen Bibel* (BHTh 39; 1968). See also his "Marcion et les origines du canon néotestamentaire", *Revue d' Histoire et de Philosophie Religieuses* 46 (1966), 213-226.

[2] See for instance his *Einleitung in das Neue Testament* (Quelle & Meyer, 1973), §35: "The Formation of the Canon of the New Testament", (475 ff). Kümmel's book includes very thorough bibliographies on all aspects of the problems treated. For a recent thorough work, see B. M. Metzger, *The Canon of the New Testament: its Origin, Development, and Significance* (Oxford: Clarendon, 1987). See also W. Schneemelcher, "Bibel III: Die Entstehung des Kanons des Neuen Testaments und der christlichen Bibel", *TRE* 6, 22-48, and W. Künneth, "Kanon", *TRE* 17, 562-570, both with detailed bibliographies.

1. Canonization

Some preliminary remarks ought to be made on the concept of canonization, which does not seem to have been studied enough from a comparative perspective.[3] The study of the canonization of the Hebrew Bible and that of the New Testament have advanced together in the last hundred years or so, progress in one field often being usefully applied to the other.[4] Such a pattern, however natural it may seem, also involves certain dangers. It has not been noted clearly enough, for instance, that the two canonization processes are not quite comparable on all terms.

One major difference is that the Tanakh may be called a primary canon, while the New Testament reflects a secondary canonization, established upon the existence of another, primary body of texts. One should never forget the obvious fact that the first Holy Writ of the early Christians was the Septuagint, and that the texts of the New Testament were added, not substituted to it. As a secondary process, the canonization of the New Testament cannot be quite similar to that of the Tanakh. The secondary religious text stands in a complex relationship with the primary text. The nature of this relationship is first and foremost hermeneutical. The new text constantly refers to the old one, explicitly and implicitly. In a sense, it is conceived as the key to the proper understanding, or interpretation, of the primary text.

One should stress the existence of different kinds of canonization

---

[3] For a pionneer attempt to analyse the phenomenon in the broadest comparative perspective, see C. Colpe, "Sakralisierung von Texten und Filiationen von Kanons", in A. and J. Assmann, eds., *Kanon und Zensur* (Archäologie der literarischen Kommunikation, 2; Munich: Fink, 1987), 80-92.

[4] I shall not deal here at all with the canonization of the Hebrew Scripture (Tanakh). See for instance F. Crüsemann, " 'Das portative Vaterland' . Struktur und Genese des alttestamentliche Kanons", in Assmann, eds., *op. cit.*, 63-79, with bibliography. Crüsemann points out that the closure of the canon of the Tanakh was part of the transformation of Israel after the catastrophe of 70. One must note, however, that contrary to received opinion, there is no reason to believe that the final canon was decided upon at the "council of Jamnia" . See esp. P. Schäfer, "Die sogenannte Synode von Jabne. Zur Trennung von Juden und Christen im 1./2. Jh. n. Chr.", in his *Studien zur Geschichte und Theologie des rabbinischen Judentums* (Leiden: Brill, 1978), 45-64. See also D. Stern, "Sacred Text and Canon", in A. Cohen and P. Mendes-Flohr, eds., *Contemporary Jewish Religious Thought* (New York: Scribner's, 1987), 841-847. Cf. S.Z. Leiman, "Inspiration and Canonicity: Reflections on the Formation of the Biblical Canon", in E.P. Sanders *et al.*, eds., *Jewish and Christian Self-Definition, II* (Philadelphia: Fortress, 1981), 56-63 and notes.

processes. *Religious* canonization is not the same as a *cultural* canonization, i. e. the process through which a text becomes established as foundational, or esssential to a culture (rather than to a religious community). The canonization of the Greek classics, since the fourth century B. C. and in particular by the Alexandrian lexicographers and scholars in their *pinakes*, for instance, is obviously a *cultural* (and not a religious) canonization. As to the Christian Bible, one can speak of two canonization processes. The first, religious, in the second century, and the second, cultural, during the fourth century, when the biblical text became part and parcel of the education of the leading classes in Roman society. The Bible, including the Old Testament, was then integrated to the *res maiorum* of the cultural elites, and became a main source for political *exempla*, from late antiquity up to Spinoza.

Finally, one should also mention a correlate question: when (and how) do texts cease to be canonical? We can follow the process through which texts, in various historical contexts, lose their former canonical character. There are at least two ways through which a text can cease being perceived as canonical. It can be rejected (usually by a radical or antinomian movement of revolt against the tradition), or it can fall into "benign" oblivion, when it is removed from the religious realm to that of culture. A major instance of such a relativisation of canonical texts is what has happened to the Bible in the modern and contemporary world.

The case of Marcion shows that canonization and de-canonization processes are often closely connected. The canonization of a new, or secondary text can be established upon the de-canonization of a primary text.

2. Kanôn

It is only in the fourth century that *kanôn* received the meaning of a list of the Scriptural texts.[5] The first use of *kanôn* in this sense seems to be in a letter of Athanasius. In earlier Christian literature, *kanôn* has a significantly different meaning.

In his *Adversus Haereses*, Irenaeus accuses the Valentinians of trans-

---

[5] For a survey of the literature and the evidence, see Metzger, *The Canon of the New Testament*, Appendix I, 289-293: "History of the word *kanôn*." For a thorough discussion of the term in classical sources, see H. Oppel, *KANÔN* (Philologus, Suppl. 30; Leipzig, 1937).

forming the "body of Truth" and dismembering it (*luontes ta melè tès alètheias, soluentes membra veritatis*), when they add spurious or plainly false books to it.[6] These heretics also misinterpret the texts of the Scriptures. This they do because they do not possess the 'rule of faith' (*kanôn tès pisteôs* or *regula fidei*). Irenaeus is the first writer to use this concept, fundamental in the development of Christian doctrine.[7] He also refers to a synonymous term, the *kanôn tès alètheias*, or "rule of truth". Only he who keeps faithfully this "rule of truth" which he received at baptism will be able to place the words of revelation in context and to adjust them to the "body of Truth", and thus unveil the heretics' fiction. Doing so, the faithful will not mistake the shape of a fox for the portrait of the king.[8] The expression "body of truth" reflects Irenaeus's insistence upon an organic and systematic unity. In the same vein, Origen speaks of a *corpus* (*sôma*) to describe the evolution of Christian doctrine until his days.[9]

Behind Irenaeus' metaphors hides a very interesting, mythical, conception of truth. The "body of Truth" stands here for the collection of the Scriptures. Which books belong to the Scriptures, which don't, and how can one identify falsifications and other perverse alterations in the text of the books of Scripture used by the heretics? The criterion permitting an answer to these questions is the *regula veritatis*. Only this rule permits one to tell what belongs with and what fits into the holy *corpus* of writings written with divine inspiration and which we call, simply, the "canon". Indeed, the collection of writings is called a "body", the body of the true writings, or "the body of Truth". There are two criteria defining the canonicity of a writing, its

---

[6] Irenaeus, *Adv. Haer.*, I. 8. 1 (112-117 Rousseau-Doutreleau; vol. II; SC 264; Paris: Cerf, 1979).

[7] See E. Lanne, " 'La règle de la Vérité': aux sources d'une expression de saint Irénée", in *Lex Orandi, Lex Credendi: Miscellania in onore di P. Cipriano Vagaggini* (Studia Anselmiana 79; Rome: 1980), 57-70, with bibliography. The expression, first used by Irenaeus, is found nine times in *Adv. Haer.*, while Irenaeus uses 'rule of faith' in the *Demonstration of the Apostolic Predication*. Dom Lanne shows that the origin of the concept is to be found in Philo, who speaks three times about "the rules of truth" in the plural (*Det.*, 125; *Conf.*, 2; *Ios.*, 145), and once in the singular (*Leg. All.*, 233). See further A. Faivre, *Ordonner la fraternité* (Paris: Cerf, 1992), 315-321. See further G. Florovsky, "The Function of Tradition in the Ancient Church", in his *Bible, Church, Tradition: an Eastern Orthodox View* (Belmont, Mass.: Northland, 1972), 73-92. For the Greek background of the concept, see G. Stricker, " *kritèrion tès alètheias*", Nach. Akad. Wiss. Göttingen (1974), 2; Philol.-hist. Klasse, 47-110.

[8] *Adv. Haer.*, I. 9. 4, *in finem* (150-151 Rousseau-Doutreleau).

[9] See Origen, *Peri Archôn*, I, Praef. 10 (98-99 Görgemanns-Karpp; see there n. 34, refering also to Origen, *Com. Ioh.* 13. 46 and to Eusebius, *Praep. Evang.*, 11. 2. 2).

belonging to the *corpus*. The first is its apostolic origin, the second is the 'rule of faith'. A work which contradicts the rule of faith cannot be apostolic.

Corpus is used already in classical Latin in a metonymic sense, representing a whole composed of parts united, and hence refering to a collection of books. Examples of such a meaning are found in Cicero, Seneca, Suetonius, as well as, of course, in the expression *corpus iuris*, refering to a collection of laws and legal texts.[10] The expression, "the body of Truth", is not used by Irenaeus alone. According to him, a certain Mark, whom he calls a magician, and who seems to have been a disciple of Valentinus, claimed to have received a revelation by the Tetrad. The Tetrad showed him Truth, who had come down from the heavenly abode in order for Mark to see her naked and to be impressed by her beauty. The body of Truth (*sôma tès Alètheias*; *corpus Veritatis*) is very impressive indeed: her limbs are not made of flesh, but of the letters of the Greek alphabet.[11] Irenaeus's report on the speculations on letters of Marcus Gnosticus, as he is called in scholarly literature, has been known to students of early Jewish mysticism since Moses Gaster called attention, a century ago, to its parallelism with the bizarre Hebrew texts from late antiquity which describe the dimensions of the cosmic body of God, the *Shi'ur Qomah*, or "measurements of the Body.'"[12] More recently, Moshe Idel has analyzed some early Jewish traditions which describe the Torah as a body made of letters in infinite permutations.[13]

From Irenaeus's testimony, it would seem that the conception of the Scriptures as a body made of letters was partaken by Jewish and

---

[10] See Lewis and Short, *Latin Dictionary*, s. v. It is to be noted, however, that *sôma* seems to have the same meaning only in later, Christian Greek; see for instance Lampe, *Patristic Greek Lexicon*, s. v., which gives instances from Procopius of Gaza and John Moschos.

[11] Irenaeus, *Adv. Haer.*, I. 14. 3 (214-217 Rousseau-Doutreleau); cf. the following paragraphs, to I. 16. 3 (274-275 Rousseau-Doutreleau), where Irenaeus develops Mark's cogitations on the letters of the alphabet. On the many speculations on the letters in Antiquity, see F. Dornseif, *Das Alphabet in Mystik und Magie* (Stoicheia 7; Leipzig, 1925). For a detailed analysis of Mark's thought as presented in *Adv. Haer.* (our single source), see F. Sagnard, *La gnose valentinienne selon le témoignage de saint Irénée* (Paris: Vrin, 1947).

[12] See for instance G. Scholem, *Major Trends in Jewish Mysticism* (New York: Schocken, 1944), 46 and notes. See further G.G. Stroumsa, "Form(s) of God: Some Notes on Metatron and Christ", *HTR* 76 (1984), 269-288 (= *Savoir et Salut*, 65-84).

[13] M. Idel, "The Conception of the Torah in *Heikhalot* Literature", *Jerusalem Studies in Jewish Thought* 1 (1981), 23-84 (Hebrew).

Christian (and Gnostic) intellectuals. The body of the Scriptures, or
"Body of Truth", can be measured by the "rule of Truth", i. e., the
criterion of the true faith, that permits one to know what belongs and
what does not belong to this body. The image appears to imply a
profound mythicisation of the concept of truth: a (naked) body is being measured by a yardstick. In the words of Jean-Daniel Dubois,
"...le principe régulateur devient pour Irénée une sorte de corps du
Sauveur incarné dans un corpus d'Ecritures." [14]

This early meaning of *kanôn, regula* was retained in later Patristic
literature. Augustine, for instance, presents in his *de Genesi ad litteram*
the dialectical relationships between the *regula pietatis* and the body of
the Scriptures. The latter can be interpreted correctly only according
to the former. But the *regula pietatis*, in its turn, is defined through its
fidelity to the Scriptures.[15] In a sense, one can speak here of a double
canon, written and oral, in a way which recalls the duality of the oral
and the written Torah in Rabbinic Judaism.

It has often been pointed out that the Greek word *kanôn* seems to
be etymologically related to Hebrew *qaneh*, a 'rod'. By means of a
rod, one can take the measurements, check the dimensions of a body.
It might also be worth recalling that the hermeneutical rules for interpreting the Torah developed by the Rabbis are called the *middot*,
i. e., literally, 'dimensions', through which the Torah is to be
exegeted.[16]

According to this understanding, Irenaeus claims that the heretics
dismember the body of truth because they do not possess the proper
measures, which alone permit the correct measuring of the Scriptures. In other words, the canon is what measures, not what is measured.

[14] J.-D. Dubois, "L'exégèse des gnostiques et l'histoire du canon des Ecritures",
in M. Tardieu, ed., *Les règles de l' interprétation* (Patrimoines; Paris: Cerf, 1987), 89-97.
[15] Augustine, *De Genesi ad litteram*, I. 21. 41, *in finem*, in P. Agaësse and A. Solignac,
eds., transl., (Bibliothèque Augustinienne 48; Paris: Desclée, 1972), 142-144: "Aliud
est enim, quid potissimum scriptor senserit, non dinoscere, aliud autem a regula pietatis errare. Si utrumque uidetur, perfecte se habet fructus legentis; si uero utrumque
uitari non potest, etiam si uoluntas scriptoris incerta sit, sanae fidei congruam non
inutile est eruisse sententiam."
[16] "*middot she-ha-torah nidreshet bahen*" (*Sifra*, intr., beginning). See M. Jastrow, *Dictionary of the Talmud*, 732 b. Aramaic *mekhilta* is the equivalent of the Hebrew *middah*.

3. Oral traditions

It looks as if, in the discussion of the problem at hand, the importance of Marcion had obliterated other dualist trends in Early Christianity. Jean-Daniel Dubois has called attention to this fact, insisting on the potential contribution of the Nag Hammadi writings to the history of the canon.[17] As Dubois points out, one can observe in the second century Church a devaluation of oral traditions. This devaluation was apparently the result of a conscious effort to prevent the exploitation of secret traditions, which could hardly be controlled by the hierarchy.

Oral traditions, *paradoseis*, were known in the Church since its early days. The "sayings of the Lord" had been thus received from the ancients (*para tôn presbuterôn*), and their origin inspired confidence in their truth (*alêtheia*). This is how the Jewish Christian writer Papias of Hieropolis, who may well have influenced Irenaeus, describes the oral tradition, adding: "For I did not suppose that information from books would help me so much as the word of the living and surviving voice." [18]

The central role of the oral transmission of doctrines in earliest Christianity entails the decisive importance of memory. Terms such as *mnèmoneuein*, *apomnèmoneuein*, are capital for the preservation of testimonies from the apostolic times. Christian memory is first and foremost a cultic memory: the central act is the *anamnèsis* of the sacrifice of Christ.[19]

Such oral traditions are often directly related to secrecy: what was said orally and not committed to writing was usually said privately, often secretly. Thus a Gnostic text found at Nag Hammadi, the *Apocryphon of James*, describes how the twelve disciples were sitting together, remembering what the Lord had said to each of them, in secret or openly.[20]

---

[17] See art. cit., n. 14 *supra*.

[18] Papias probably published his *Explanations of the Lord's Sentences* (*Logiôn kuriakôn exegèseôs*) in the thirties of the second century. The work is not extant, but the tradition is preserved by Eusebius, *H. E.* III. 39. 1-4 (I. 290-293 Loeb Classical Library). See further W. Kelber, *The Oral and the Written Gospel* (Philadelphia: Fortress, 1983).

[19] See for instance J.-C. Basset, "L'anamnèse: aux sources de la tradition chrétienne", in Ph. Borgeaud, ed., *La mémoire des religions* (Genève: Labor et Fides, 1988), 91-104.

[20] *Apocryphon of James*, CG V . Cf. H. Koester, *Ancient Christian Gospels: their History and Development* (Philadelphia, London: Trinity, SCM, 1990)31-43.

The question of esoteric traditions in early Christianity is directly connected to the role of Gnosticicsm in the progressive self-definition of the new religion during the second century. The Gnostics claimed that they possessed secret traditions coming direcly from the apostolic times. They also offered esoteric interpretations of texts known to all. For instance, the Valentinian Heracleon had developed in the early second century the first known written interpretation of the Gospel, an esoteric exegesis of the *Gospel of John*,.[21]

Now the Gnostics possessed writings of their own, which preserved the deepest tradition. Can these texts be perceived as representing an alternative canon? Although the question is rarely asked in such terms, it seems to be often assumed that this was indeed to case. Thus, for instance, Bentley Layton's comprehensive anthology of Gnostic and cognate texts in translation bears the title *The Gnostic Scriptures*.[22] Layton himself, in his introduction, deals with the question in rather ambiguous terms, which may lead the reader to assume that there was a canon of gnostic writings, an 'Alternative Scripture', as it were.[23] Actually, the questions should be answered in the negative: by definition, a corpus of texts is a closed, limited list of texts. The apocryphal Gospels and other writings proliferating in Gnostic circles during the second century, and then among the Manichaeans, do not amount to such a corpus, and hence cannot be defined as a canonical corpus.

The negative answer to the question of a Gnostic canon is actually twofold. On the one hand, the Gnostic texts do not form a canon because they are not a closed corpus. On the other hand, they do not belong to a defined community, a church, or even to a group still engaged in a self-definition process. Among the various dualist trends which we call Gnostic, one cannot identify a clear striving for political or ecclesiastical unity, something which is quite obvious in contemporaneous mainstream Christianity.[24]

---

[21] See E. Pagels, *The Johanine Gospel in Gnostic Exegesis* (Society of Biblical Literature Monograph Series, 17; Nashville, New York: Abingdon,1973).

[22] *The Gnostic Scriptures* (Garden City, N. Y.: 1987), esp. XVII-XXI, where Layton speaks of Gnostic Scripture "as a kind of Christian Scripture."

[23] On this concept, in a different cultural and religious context, see Sarah Stroumsa, "Ecritures alternatives", in A. Le Boulluec and E. Patlagean, eds., *Retours aux Ecritures* (Bibliothèque de l'EPHE, Sciences Religieuses; Turnhout: Brepols, 1993).

[24] This is the main argument of E. Pagels, *The Gnostic Gospels* (New York: Random House, 1979).

Most scholars agree that there occured a change toward the mid-second century. Tatian's *Diatessaron* shows that the Gospels which were later to become canonical had already begun to achieve growing significance and authority as a source of the tradition. Ecclesiastical writers, however, continued to widely use apocryphal Gospels and oral Jesus traditions. The most famous example of such a text is probably the *Secret Gospel of Mark* mentioned by Clement of Alexandria in a letter discovered by Morton Smith.[25] According to Justin Martyr, use was made in the Sunday worship of apostolic testimonies (*apomnèmoneumata tôn apostolôn*). These were probably oral traditions, rather than the Gospels as we have them.

Marcion himself, who came to Rome in 144, rejected all writings belonging to the Old Testament. He also rejected most Christian writings, except Luke and ten letters of Paul, and even these he submitted to a strict censorship. It is not known whether Marcion himself, when he established the canonical authority of Paul, knew the four Gospels and the Pastoral letters. There is little doubt that Marcion's establishment of a strictly limitative canon provided an impetus for a "counter-canon," and hence for the canonization of the New Testament. But above all, Marcion's challenge forced mainstream Christian intellectuals into defending the threatened Septuagint and reaffirming the self-definition of the Church as *Verus Israel*.

The threat of the Montanist movement strengthened the need to close the canon. The followers of Montanus, who were particularly strong in Phrygia in 155-160, refused to see an end to prophecy. Montanism was, first and foremost, a movement of religious enthusiasts. Such movements tend to be active at the early stages of the development of a new religion, when the ecclesiastical structures are not yet quite fixed.[26] Emerging hierarchies find it to be one of their most pressing duties to fight against such trends, which threaten their power.

---

[25] See M. Smith, *Clement of Alexandria and a Secret Gospel of Mark* (Cambridge, Mass.: Harvard, 1973). About the heated discussion over the authenticity of the letter, see M. Smith, "Clement of Alexandria and Secret Mark: the Score at the End of the First Decade", *HTR* 78(1982), 449-461.

[26] A somewhat similar trend has been detected, for instance, at the early stages of Islam: according to this trend, Muhammad was not the last prophet, and the expression *ḫâtem al-nabyyîn* meant "Confirmation of the prophets". It is only later, and as a reaction to such views, that it came to mean "the closure of prophecy." See Y. Friedmann, " Finality of Prophethood in Sunni Islam", *Jerusalem Studies in Arabic and Islam* 7 (1986), 177-215.

It seems that the need to fight Montanism and to prevent freedom of interpretation, in order to strengthen central authority in the Church, served as a catalyst for closing the canon of the New Testament. An anti-Montanist tract written around 192 refers to "the wording of the New Testament of the Gospel (*ho tès tou euaggeliou kainès diathèkès logos*) from which nothing may be added or taken away."

Although Apostolic writings such as II Clement and Barnabas could refer to sayings of Jesus as *graphè*, or *hôs gegraptai*, it was only in the last two decades of the second century that the concept of a New Testament came to emerge. When Melito of Sardis had spoken of an Old Testament (*palaia diathèkè*), the phrase implied the idea of a New Testament, but this last expression seems to appear for the first time in Irenaeus's *Adversus Haereses*.[27] This does not mean, of course, that the canon of the New Testament as we know it was fixed. There was still in the end of the second century considerable hesitation about writings such as *Hebrews, Revelation*, or the Catholic letters. But the idea of an *euaggelion tetramorphon* was established. In any case, it is also from the end of the second century that dates the Muratorian canon, the first list of the New Testament books.[28]

4. Mishnah and New Testament

The canonization of the New Testament was a process, which happened over time, rather than the result of a single decision. There is no conciliar decision about the canon, for instance, before the fourth century. Canonization processes should be understood as part and parcel of religious and social processes of identification. Such processes deal mainly with boundaries, and hence, direclty, with the exclusion of those movements which cross these boundaries and thus threaten the search for an identity.

Throughout the second century, Christianity underwent a series of crises which brought to the crystallisation of its specific identity. The most serious of these crises was brought neither by Marcion nor by Montanus. For monotheist Christianity, the world—and man—had been created by a benevolent divine power; it is this basic perception

---

[27] Irenaeus, *Adv. Haer.*, IV. 9. 1.

[28] The document, discovered in 1740 in the Ambrosiana, bears the name of its founder, the librarian Muratori. It is extant in a poor Latin translation of a late second-century original Greek document.

that the dualist Gnostic movement threatened. Modern research has shown that the Gnostics did not completely reject the Old Testament, or rather, that they did not quite ignore it. In rather peculiar fashion, the Gnostics, who despised or hated the creator god, the "ruler (*archôn*) of this world," offered interpretations of those few Old Testament texts which interested them most.[29]

The canonization of the New Testament must thus be seen in direct connection with the fight for the correct interpretation of the Scriptures. Now this fight was fiercest between the Christians and the Jews, who argued about the same corpus, the Old Testament. Their argument was essentially of a hermeneutical nature. The two religious communities disputed with one another the same heritage and its correct interpretation. Each religion claimed the Bible as its own, and each believed that it alone knew and applied the hermeneutical rules that reveal the deeper sense of the texts. Jews and Christians confronted each other while they strove to define themselves. Indeed, after the series of traumatic events during the first century and in the early second century, the Jewish communities had to seek a new identity, after the main components of the traditional national and religious identity of Israel had disappeared or been put in great jeopardy. The religion of Israel, after it had lost its Temple and all it entailed, became deeply changed. In a sense, therefore, Judaism and Christianity in the second century can be perceived to be sister religions, rather than standing in a filial relationship.

The Jewish communities underwent in the second century a series of traumatic events (the Bar Kokhba war and its terrible consequences for the Palestinian Jew, revolts, their repression, and also epidemics, for the Jews of Egypt and Cyrenaica). Although the Rabbinic sources are rather opaque on that matter, one can guess the internal argument against various attempts to break the communal and theological unity in the making. In Rabbinic Hebrew, all the various kinds of heretics and schismatics who offered alternative interpretations were designated by a generic term of opprobrium: *minim*.[30]

The Christians, on their side, fought their own radical heresies at a time when they themselves lived under the constant threat of per-

---

[29] See for instance B.A. Pearson, "Biblical Exegesis in Gnostic Literature", in M. E. Stone, ed., *Armenian and Biblical Studies* (Jerusalem: St. James Press, 1977), 70-80.

[30] See for instance A.F. Segal, *Two Powers in Heaven* (Studies in Judaism in Antiquity 25; Leiden: Brill, 1977).

secution. Thus, throughout the second century, both the Jewish and the Christian communities were simultaneously engaged in different polemical activities, from within and from without. They were striving to define themselves and were confronting each other, directly and indirectly. Both communities were engaged in a dramatic process of 'orthodoxisation', which entailed the censorship of many of the oral traditions which had been so important in the past. For the Jews as well as for the Christians, the oral traditions granted a prominent place to esoteric traditions. The censorship process went together with a strong effort to establish precise and competing rules of interpretation for the Biblical texts common to both religions.

I suggest that the clearest result of these efforts was the establishment of a *secondary* holy text, which embodied the key to the correct interpretation of the Bible. For the Christian community, this text was the New Testament, which provided the code to the real meaning of the Septuagint, by seeing it as the *praeparatio evangelica*. For the Jewish community, a similar code was embodied in the Mishnah, which reflected, through a set of complex hermeneutical rules, the proper way to understand the meaning of the Tanakh: the law of a living community. It is through the prisms of these two interpretive, secondary texts that the Jewish Tanakh and the Christian Old Testament came to be perceived as two deeply different texts. It is in this context that one must undertand Buber's paradoxical formulation, according to which the holy book of the Jews was "neither old nor testament." [31]

Both texts, then , the New Testament and the Mishnah, can be considered as two kinds of "meta-Tanakh", as it were, two parallel works coming after the Tanakh, deeply different in content but rather similar in function. It is a remarkable fact that both texts became cristallized and canonized more or less at the same period, toward the end of the second century, or at the latest in the early third century. The closure of the Mishnah, the *ḥatimat ha-Mishnah*, by Rabbi Judah the Prince, dates at the latest from the early years of the third century.

Oddly enough, this striking synchronism does not seem to have been noticed by either New Testament or Rabbinical scholarship. It is only to the Roman juridical *corpora*, for instance to the *Digest* of

---

[31] On the transformation of the Hebrew Scripture in the process of formation of the Christian Bible, see R. Greer in J.L. Kugel and R.A. Greer, *Early Biblical Interpretation* (Philadelphia: Westminster, 1986), 126-154.

Justinian (533) that the Mishnah has been compared, not to the New Testament.[32] I began these pages with the remark that the study of canonization processes of the Tanakh and of the New Testament have at once often benefited from insights and progress made in either discipline, and sometimes suffered from questions framed in a different context. I hope to have at least made a tentative case for a new approach, which would recognize the secondariness of the New Testament (as well as that of the Mishnah) and seek the implications of this fact for the canonization process.[33] Only the discussion of this suggestion by both New Testament and Rabbinic scholars will permit one to evaluate its significance.

---

[32] For a bibliography of earlier studies, see B.S. Jackson, "On the Problem of Roman Influence on the Halakah and Normative Self-Definition in Judaism", in Sanders et al., eds., Jewish and Christian Self-Definition, 157-203 and notes; Jackson points out that the results of centuries of research on the issue "may be thought to be inconclusive" (157).

[33] See A.M. Ritter, "Die Entstehung des neutestamentlichen Kanons: Selbstdurchsetzung oder autoritative Entscheidung?", in A. and J. Assmann, eds., Kanon und Censur, 93-99. Ritter points to the same direction when he argues that Christianity and Judaism did not become "religions of the book" despite the canonization process, by calling attention to the paramount importance for the two religions of, respectively, the Talmud and the New Testament together with the regula fidei.

CHAPTER SIX

MOSES' RIDDLES: ESOTERIC TRENDS
IN PATRISTIC HERMENEUTICS

Christianity provided a new kind of discourse in late antiquity. Its canon of revealed writings implied a hermeneutical attitude radically different from the one developed by the Hellenic intellectuals and philosophers towards the Homeric corpus. This fundamental difference is well documented, and has been emphasized in various studies.[1] The primary purpose of this chapter will be to insist on a less well known correlate of this fact. As we shall see, early Christian thinkers developed, as part of their hermeneutical attitude to the Holy Writ, a particular conception of esotericism. The analysis of this conception and its context may throw some light on aspects of the religious and intellectual *Auseinandersetzung* between them and Hellenic thinkers.

It should be pointed out from the outset that various religious or intellectual systems, from the Eastern Mediterranean and the Near East, very different from one another, had all developed esoteric trends during the later stages of antiquity. The distance from the early, classical stages of culture was felt then to have reached a dangerous level, and to threaten the sense of continued identification with the great classical texts and conceptions, which one may perhaps call 'foundational', in the sense that the whole later Greek culture was established upon them. Hence the need, felt by intellectuals, to overcome that 'cognitive dissonance' of sorts by developing two-tiered systems of interpretation of the lore and wisdom of old.

Christianity made a bold claim: it offered salvation to all and sundry. Despite this claim, however, esoteric traditions inherited from Palestinian and Hellenistic Judaism formed the basis of secret oral traditions in the earliest stages of the new religion. These traditions, some of which can be detected already in Jesus' teaching, remained in existence during the first Christian centuries. Although these tradi-

---

[1] Jean Pépin, in particular, has devoted a lifetime to the study of this problem. See for instance the two volumes of his collected essays on the topic, *La tradition de l' allégorie de Philon d' Alexandrie à Dante* (Paris: Etudes Augustiniennes, 1987).

tions, oral by nature, became blurred in the following period, it is still possible to retrace them.[2] They formed the nucleus of what came to be called in the fourth century, at a time when they were already in an advanced process of disintegration, the *disciplina arcani*. These traditions reflected older trends, embodied in the apocryphal writings, and they can also be shown to form the background of both Jewish-Christian and Gnostic conceptions. It stands to reason that one of the main causes of their progressive disappearance from what came to be known as 'mainstream', or 'orthodox' Christianity is directly related to their use and abuse by Gnostics and other 'heretics' .

In his seventh *Oration*, Julian, the last pagan emperor, quoted Heraclitus as saying that nature loved to hide her secrets.[3] Different cultural and religious systems entail different kinds of esotericism. Hellenic esotericism was one of *arcana naturae*. In Greek culture there was no concept of divine revelation in history, and hence no chronological dimension of the revelatory process of truth. There was, however, a clear linguistic hierarchy: by definition, the language of myths was popular and simple, whereas the language of the philosophical attempts at decoding them had to remain lofty and as close as possible to the sublimity of its subject.

The history of philosophical interpretation of Greek mythology is a very long one indeed. The myth was thus conceived as alluding *(ainittetai)* to some truth that could be spelled out more precisely and more fully in other terms.[4] The myth, then, had turned into an *ainigma*, a riddle, protecting the truth, which it revealed only through a veil, from the misunderstanding of the multitude and its dangerous consequences.[5] Late antique thinkers remained in this regard in the wake of an honored tradition, the early stages of which can be exemplified by the saying of Heraclitus about the god at Delphi: he neither reveals nor hides the truth, but rather indicates it (*oute legei, oute kruptei, alla semainei*).[6]

---

[2] See chapter 2 *supra*.

[3] *Philei gar hè phusis kruptesthai*, fragment 123 Diels, cf. Themsitius 69b; Julian's *7th Oration*, 216b, in volume II in LCL.

[4] See in particular J. Pépin, *Mythe et allégorie : les origines grecques et les contestations judéo-chrétiennes* (Paris: Études augustiniennes, 1976, 2nd. ed. [1st. ed., 1958], and to the volume of his collected essays, quoted in note 1 *supra* . Robert Lamberton has recently devoted a major study to one particularly important aspect of this topic; see his *Homer the Theologian : Neoplatonist Allegorical Reading and the Growth of the Epic Tradition* (Berkeley: University of California Press, 1986).

[5] See chapter 1 *supra*.

[6] Heraclitus, fragment 93 Diels, in Plutarch, *de Pyth. or.* 21, 404e.

On various counts, the Christian attitude was at odds with this conception. The secrets to be decoded were those of God (*arcana dei*), and were written in the Great Book of God, not of Nature. The interpretation or this book was *ipso facto* to become literary exegesis. So far, this position is identical to that in Judaism. But the specific religious structure of Christianity added some new elements. First and foremost, revelation had come in stages. Divine scripture was now composed of two 'testaments'. Jesus had completed the revelation given to Israel, in fact had interpreted the Law and the Prophets, had explained what had remained until then an enigma of sorts. Thus Irenaeus could write:

> Every prophecy, before its accomplishment, is enigma and contradiction for men (*ainigma esti kai antilogia*). But when came the moment that the prediction was accomplished, it found its correct interpretation. This is why the Law, when read by the Jews in our times, is similar to a myth (*muthôi eoiken*), since they do not possess what is the explanation of it all, namely the coming of the Son of God as a man.[7]

In this striking text, Biblical prophecy is seemingly identified to Greek *mantis* and called an enigma, an ambiguous expression of divine will. By referring to the Jewish reading of the Bible as similar to that of pagan mythology, Irenaeus does not mean, of course, that it is false, but that it does not possess within itself the criterion of its own truth.[8] This was not a new position. The semantics of *muthos* in classical literature is notoriously complex; yet, a common understanding of the word had been already expressed by Aristotle, for whom myth, although not necessarily false, was in no way proven truth. Ireneus conceives of the coming of Christ—and hence of the text of the New Testament—as the key to the proper understanding of the Hebrew Bible. This key is the very opposite of esotericism, since it is offered to all. But those who refuse it are unable to open the treasures of

---

[7] Ireneus, *Adversus Haereses*, IV.26.1., 714-715 Rousseau, (SC 100; Paris: Cerf, 1965).

[8] On the opposition between *muthos* and *alètheia* in early Christianity, see 2Tim. 4:4; "and they shall turn away their ears from the truth (*alètheias*), and shall be turned unto fables (*muthous*)". On the Greek and Hellenistic background of the meaning of *muthos* in early Christian writings, see Stählin," *muthos*", in *TDNT* IV, 762-795 . On *mythos* and *ainigma* in early Christian literature, see further M.J. Hollerick, "Myth and History in Eusebius's *De Vita Constantini*: *Vit. Const.* in its Contemporary Setting", *HTR* 82 (1989), 421-445, esp. 427-439.

divine revelation, which remain sealed for them even when they read the Old Testament.

From this attitude, two important implications follow. First, in contradistinction with the Hellenic conception, the chronological element is here essential. Divine revelation was carried out in a double "economy". Hence the Holy Writ itself is two-tiered by nature, since it includes its own interpretation: the New Testament is perceived as explicitating the true meaning of the Old. This development of the perception of religious truth in the course of history, or *Heilsgeschichte*, is rooted in the earliest strata of Christianity, a fact exemplified by the famous verse of I Corinthians 13:12: "For we now see through a glass, darkly *(blèpomen gar arti di' esoprou en ainigmati)*: but then face to face". These words, enigmatic enough in themselves, were often reflected upon in Patristic literature, where they served to justify the use of allegory as the obscure and figurative expression of truth.[9]

The second implication, which seems to have escaped notice, is that, from a literary point of view, this interpretation of "Biblical myth" is held at the same level, simple and "low", at which the earlier text was written. It is indeed a matter of pride in the writings of the Church Fathers that the language of Christian revelation is characterized by its simplicity, its *euteleia*, and this is actually one of the criteria that distinguish their "barbarian philosophy" from the misleading elegance of Hellenic thought. This mean style of Scripture, as defended by Origen against Celsus' mockery, is anti-elitist on purpose. Yet Origen makes a point of arguing that this fact does not entail the negation of esotericism. It simply means that the same text can be understood at different levels of truth. Christianity thus offers, according to Origen:

> a method of teaching which not only contains the truth but is also able to win the multitude. After conversion and entrance into the Church each individual according to his capacity can ascend to the hidden truths in the words which seem to have a mean style *(euteleia)*.[10]

One must note here that for Christian intellectuals, the Bible's 'mean style' despised by Hellenic intellectuals is not simply a literary char-

---

[9] See for instance R. Mortley, "Mirror and I Cor 13:12 in the Epistemology of Clement of Alexandria", *VC* 30 (1976), 109-120.

[10] Origen, *Contra Celsum*, VI.2. I am quoting H. Chadwick's translation (Cambridge: University Press, 1953), p. 316.

acter of their writings but is directly related to the human nature of
the Son of God. It reflects the humility of Jesus Christ, who voluntar-
ily lowered Himself until the cross. This 'lowliness' is thus an inherent
character of Christian soteriology,[11] except, of course, in milieus
influenced by Docetic trends of thought.

It was Erich Auerbach's intuition that this low style, typical of
early Christian literature, and so different from the sublime register
of discourse on the divine in pagan literature, permitted the subsequent development of Western literature along radically new lines.
This intuition stands at the basis of his *Mimesis*. Auerbach also analyzed the phenomenon at length in his seminal study ' *Sermo humilis* ' .[12]
A text of Tertullian may exemplify this conception:

> This wisdom which he says was kept secret [Tertullian refers here to I
> Cor. 2-3] is that which has been in things foolish and little and dishon-
> ourable, which has also been hidden under figures, both allegories and
> enigmas (*quae latuerit etiam sub figuris, allegoriis et aenigmatibus*), but was af-
> terwards to be revealed in Christ who was set for a light of the gen-
> tiles...[13]

Together with the text of Irenaeus quoted above, this passage emphasizes the nature of the structural change from Hellenic to Christian
hermeneutics. Greek myths could express religious truths in a language understandable to all. But they were also hiding a higher level
of truth. Only the philosophers could reach this level, and then express it in proper terms, i.e., in a language fit for the expression of
sublime truths. For Christian intellectuals, in contradistinction, the
enigmas were to be deciphered in simple and 'low' language. The two
linguistic levels of the dis-covery of total truth (*a-lètheia*) had been replaced by the two chronological levels of *Heilsgeschichte* as expressed in
the Old and New Testaments.

---

[11] For the implications of this conception, see G.G. Stroumsa, " *Caro salutis cardo*:
Shaping the Person in Early Christian Thought", *HR* 30 (1990), 25-50.

[12] E. Auerbach, *Mimesis: The Representation of Reality in Western Literature* (Princeton:
Princeton Univ. Press, 1953); see esp. chapters 1 and 3. ' *Sermo Humilis* ' is reprinted
in Auerbach, *Literary Language and its Public in Late Latin Antiquity and in the Middle Ages*
(London: Routledge and Kegan Paul, 1965). Cf. p. 26 *supra*.

[13] Tertullian, *Adversus Marcionem*, V.1. I follow the text and translation of E. Evans
(Oxford, 1972) II, 540-541.

The analysis of the texts quoted above has shown a distinctive pattern of Patristic thought, according to which *ainigma* was endowed with a new meaning, unknown in Hellenic literature. More than any other Christian writers, the two Alexandrian Fathers Clement and Origen struggled with the issues raised by the contact of early Christian thought with philosophical esotericism. Hence the legitimacy of a focus on their views. The conception of the riddle developed at length by Clement of Alexandria, particularly in the fifth book of his *Stromateis* would seem *prima facie* to be somewhat different from the one exemplified above. Raoul Mortley's short study of the concept of enigma in Clement's writings emphasizes its similarity with contemporaneous usage. (This usage is well reflected in Quintillian's definition: "*Haec allegoria, quae est obscurior, aenigma dicitur*"). Mortley concludes that the riddle, or enigma, is for Clement a category of the symbol, which joins the two opposite notions of revelation and of dissimulation. The enigma, in this sense, refers to the symbol's ambiguity.[14]

For Clement, the ancient Hebrews possessed enigmas, which expressed their deepest religious truths. These enigmas, which are referred to in the Bible, are of the same nature as those of other nations, such as the Egyptians. Dealing with the esoteric character of Egyptian mysteries, Clement writes: "It is thus that their riddles (*ainigmata*) are similar to those of the Hebrews in their concealment method (*kata ge tèn apokrupsin*)."[15] He also considers the sphinxes standing in front of the Egyptian temples as marking the enigmatic and obscure character of religious discourse. The sphinxes propound

---

[14] R. Mortley, *Connaissance religieuse et herméneutique chez Clément d'Alexandrie* (Leiden: Brill, 1973), appendice 1: "la notion de l'énigme", 229-232. See also R. Mortley, *From Words to Silence, I: The Way of Negation, Christian and Greek* (Theophania 31; Bonn: Hanstein, 1986), 38: "Clement's major interest is not to promote a secret body of esoteric teaching, but to offer a view of language which is consistent with both Christianity and Platonism". Quintillian's words are quoted from his *Inst. Orat.*, II.1. VI.6.52.

[15] Clement, *Strom.*, V.8.41.1. I am using the edition (with French translation and commentary) of A. Le Boulluec (SC 278; Paris: le Cerf, 1981), 76-77. In his commentary, (S.C. 279, p. 134), Le Boulluec points out that no idea of mystery or riddle was related to the sphinx in ancient Egypt. Such an idea appears only in Greek Theban legends; cf. J. G. Griffiths (ed. and transl.), *Plutarch's de Iside et Osiride* (Cardiff: University of Wales Press, 1970), commentary on IX.354.b-c. See further R. Merkelbach, "Un petit *ainigma* dans le prologue du *Proteptique*", in *Alexandrina: Mélanges Claude Mondésert* (Paris: Cerf, 1987), 191-194. Merkelbach points out the Platonic background of Clement's approach to esotericism.

enigmatic, i.e. obscure and ambivalent doctrines, such as love and fear of God, because they are themselves ambivalent figures, being half beasts and half human.[16] This conception has nothing original, but reflects a tradition found in Plutarch, for whom Egyptian philosophy is for the most part

> veiled in myths and in words containing dim reflexions and adumbrations of the truth, as they themselves intimate beyond question by appropriately placing sphinxes before their shrines to indicate that their religious teaching has in it an enigmatical sort of wisdom.[17]

Clement consciously uses the vocabulary developed for the description of pagan mysteries and applies it to the Biblical text: "Prophecies and oracles speak through riddles, and mysteries are not shown freely to anyone, but are accompanied by some purificatory rites and caveats".[18] Elsewhere, he speaks about the oracles of the divine plan.[19] Doing so, he actually follows Philo, for whom the many riddles in the scriptures were so many examples of its oracles.[20] But in a much more systematic way than Philo, Clement integrates this conception into a coherent theory. He points out that all heavenly manifestations are obscure "so that research seeks to crack the riddles and thus spring towards the discovery of truth".[21] Here again, he is following a Hellenic tradition, stated, for instance, by Sallustios in the fourth century: "to conceal the truth by myth prevents the contempt of the foolish, and compels the good to practice philosophy".[22]

To sum up, Clement recognizes that riddles, as well as other similar or roughly identical techniques of religious revelation, are to be found in the religious traditions of all nations:

> Thus one can say that both the Barbarians and the Greeks who have dealt with God have hidden the principles of things, and have transmitted truth through riddles, symbols, allegories, metaphors and other similar figures, for instance divination among the Greeks...[23]

---

[16] *Strom.*, V.5.31.5.
[17] Plutarch, *Isis and Osiris*, 9. 354b-c. (in *Moralia* V; F.C. Babbitt, transl.; Loeb Classical Library), 22-25.
[18] *Strom.*, V.4.20.1,
[19] *Strom.*, V .8.55.1.
[20] *De Mundo*, 3.
[21] *Strom.*, V.4.24.1.
[22] *De Diis et Mundo*, 3; 4.11-15 Nock.
[23] *Strom.*, V.4.21.4.

But a presentation of Clement's discourse as applying pagan vocabulary to the religious experience of the Hebrews (something which is often done) would reflect a radical misunderstanding of his enterprise. I think that it is precisely in this context that his famous theory of "theft" —a theory borrowed from him by Origen—should be located.[24] As is well known, Clement claims that what is best in Greek thought finds its ultimate roots among the Hebrews. In his words:

> But the poets, on their side, who learned theology from the prophets, give many philosophical teachings in an indirect way; I refer to Orpheus, Linos, Museos, Homer, Hesiod and similar wise men. For them, the veil that separates them from the crowd is the charm of poetry. As to dreams and symbols, they all have some darkness for men, not because of any jealousy (it is not permitted to suppose passions in God) but so that research seek to crack the riddles, and thus spring towards the discovery of truth.[25]

Hence, it becomes clear that Greek religious vocabulary is not itself primary, but directly dependent upon God's prophetical revelation in the Bible. There is indeed a *philosophia perennis*, but it is identical to the *praeparatio evangelica*.

Clement agrees with Irenaeus and Tertullian that there is a progressive revelation throughout history, or to borrow the title of Lessing's famous essay, an *Erziehung des Menschengeschlechts*. In this conception, it is not the philosophers but Jesus Christ whose task it is to crack the riddles:

> The action of the Savior on us is immediate, and comes through the presence, hidden until then under the riddle of prophecy. He has shown the prophecies through direct vision, who has manifested the coming of this presence, advancing from so far towards full light. He has really 'detached' and brought to their end the oracles of the divine scheme by revealing the sense of the symbols." [26]

---

[24] On this theory see esp. K. Thraede, "Erfinder II", *RAC* 5, 1191-1278.. Cf. H. Chadwick, *Early Christian Thought and the Classical Tradition*, (Oxford: Clarendon, 1966), 141 (= n. 52 on p.43); Chadwick notes that the theme of plagiarism is recurrent in the *Stromateis*. For Origen cf. for instance *Contra Celsum*, III.39, where it is speculated that Plato may have learned the myth of the *Symposium* from Jewish teachers during his stay in Egypt.

[25] *Strom.*, V.4.24.1-2. For Clement, this veil is primarily symbolized by the *katapetasma*, which stood in front of the Holy of Holies in the Temple and protected the supreme religious secret from impure eyes; see for instance *Strom.*, II. 1.1.2.

[26] *Strom.*, V.8.55.3.

The oracles, or prophetic riddles, which appear here in all their
power, are the deepest religious truths of mankind. They were revealed by God to the Hebrews (and first expressed by Moses) in a
cryptic way. They were then borrowed, or rather stolen, by the pagans—but this was no doubt a *felix culpa* of sorts, since it permitted the
propagation of truth, albeit distorted to some extent, among the gentiles. It thus prepared them in a way for the future aknowlegment of
Christ. Yet, although philosophers claim to reveal the hidden sense of
these riddles, and the Jews read the Bible as if they understand it,
only the Christians can possess a total knowledge of this truth at its
highest level. Indeed, the *philosophia barbarum* of the Christians, so despised by the Hellenic intellectuals, is the only true philosophy.[27]

In this context, however, Clement's esotericism appears to rest on
rather shaky grounds. If Jesus revealed to the whole world the meaning of Moses' riddles and of those of the other Hebrew prophets, then
it is hard to understand the need for a secret teaching, a need on
which Clement insists so much. The solution given by Clement to this
apparent contradiction is that Jesus himself took pains to express his
own revelation of religious truth in a veiled fashion. Thus, it would
be within the reach of all, understandable at every level. Similar
efforts were taken by his disciples, who transmitted an oral, esoteric
tradition (*paradosis*) side by side with their public teaching.[28]

The borrowing of Greek hermeneutical vocabulary by the Christian
intellectuals created ambiguities of a new kind. These ambiguities re-
sulted in a fundamental misunderstanding between philosophical and
Christian hemeneutics in late antiquity. (Such a misunderstanding obviously did not exist between Greek and Rabbinic discourses, which

---

[27] On this concept, see J. H. Waszink, "Some Observations on the Appreciation
of 'the Philosophy of the Barbarians' in Early Christian Literature", In *Mélanges
Christine Mohrmann* (Utrecht, Anvers: Spectrum, 1963), 41-56. See also R. Wilken,
"Wisdom and Philosophy in Early Christianity", in R. Wilken, ed., *Aspects of Wisdom
in Judaism and Early Christianity* (Notre Dame: Notre Dame University Press, 1975). See
further G.G. Stroumsa: "Philosophy of the Barbarians: on Early Christian Ethnological Representations", in H. Cancik, ed., *Festschrift Martin Hengel* (Tübingen: Mohr
[Siebeck], forthcoming).

[28] On Clement's esotericism and the discussion about it, see the important article
of E.L. Fortin, "Clement of Alexandria and the Esoteric Tradition", *Studia Patristica*
IX, vol. 3 (TU 94; Berlin: Akademie Verlag, 1966), 41-56. See also S. Lilla, *Clement
of Alexandria: a Study of Christian Platonism and Gnosticism* (Oxford: Oxford University
Press, 1971), 142-158.

operated at safe distance from one another). This misunderstanding is reflected in the following words of Porphyry:

> Some, in their eagerness to find an explanation of the wickedness of the Jewish writings rather than give them up, had recourse to interpretations that are incompatible and do not harmonize with what has been written, offering not so much a defence of what was outlandish as commendation and praise of their own work. For they boast that the things said plainly by Moses are riddles (*ainigmata gar ta phanèrôs para Môusei legomena einai kompasantes*), treating them as divine oracles full of hidden mysteries, and bewitching the mental judgement by their own pretentious obscurity; and so they put forward their interpretations.[29]

Porphyry is outraged by the Christian claim that the Hebrew Bible should be interpreted as if it were a corpus of myths, to be considered as riddles worthy of a higher, philosophical interpretation. Porphyry sees Origen as the main culprit for this attitude of Christian intellectuals. And indeed, in his *Contra Celsum*, Origen polemicizes against the anti-Christian views of an otherwise unknown second century philosopher, Celsus. In his *Alethès Logos*, Celsus had claimed the existence of a *philosophia perennis*: "Hear Celsus' words, writes Origen, quoting : "There is an ancient doctrine which has existed from the beginning, which has always been maintained by the wisest nations and cities and wise men" . And, Origen adds, he would not speak of the Jews as being *a very wise nation* on a par with "the Egyptians, Assyrians, Indians, Persians, Odrysians, Samothracians, and Eleusinians." [30] In the following chapters, Origen argues against Celsus' opinion, according to which Moses' book is intrinsically different from the books written by the wise men of other nations and hence is unfit for allegorical exegesis: "But later when he criticizes the Mosaic history he finds fault with those who interpret it figuratively and allegorically. Origen claims at some length that various pagan mythologies, which Celsus respects as so many enigmas reflecting the *philosophia perennis*, are intellectually ridiculous and morally reprehensible. He then adds:

> And if the Egyptians relate this mythology, they are believed to be concealing philosophy in obscurity and mysteries; but if Moses wrote for a

---

[29] Porphyry, *Contra Christianos*, 39.14 (quoted by Eusebius, *Hist. Eccl.*, VI.19.4. On this passage, see P.F. Beatrice, "Porphyry's Judgment on Origen", in R.J. Daly, ed., *Origeniana Quinta* (Leuven: Peeters, 1992), 351-367.

[30] Origen, *Contra Celsum*, I.14 (17 Chadwick).

whole nation and left them histories and laws, his words are considered
to be empty myths not even capable of being interpreted allegorically.[31]

It seems that the reason for Celsus' denigration of the Bible comes
precisely from its historical and legal nature: in this, the Bible is intrinsically different from the various mythological traditions of different nations. Implicit in Celsus' attitude is the belief, obvious for a
Greek intellectual, that historical and legal texts should not be interpreted, but understood *au pied de la lettre*. Historical and legal records
are straightforward texts, and are not suitable for allegorical interpretation. A Greek intellectual, even if not prone to anti-Jewish feelings
(as was frequently the case), would naturally be puzzled by the attitude of the Christian towards the Hebrew scriptures, which they
claimed as their own, and even fancied to understand more properly
than the Jews themseves did. The Christians did not follow the Law,
and were not concerned in a direct sense by the history of the Jews.
By offering allegorical interpretations of non-mythical texts, which
dealt with men rather than with the Gods, the Christians were breaking the rules of interpretation in an unacceptable way. Other nations,
such as the Syrians or the Indians, had both myths and interpretive
writings. Similarly, "the Egyptian wise men who have studied their
traditional writings give profound philosophical interpretations of
what they regard as divine, while the common people hear certain
myths of which they were proud, although they do not understand
the meaning" .[32]

It is such conceptions that Christian intellectuals had to confront.
Just like Clement, Origen could neither give up the exegetical drive
nor deny the fact that the Christian writings were written in a 'low
style' . In the eyes of pagan intellectuals, this style related the Christian writings to myth rather than to the philosophical interpretation
of myth. So Origen's solution was to argue that

> our prophets, Jesus and his apostles were careful to use a method of
> teaching which not only contains the truth but is also able to win over
> the multitude...so that the Christian believer can ascend to the hidden
> truths in the words which seem to have a mean style.[33]

---

[31] *Ibid.*, I.20 (21 Chadwick).
[32] *Ibid.*, I.12 (15 Chadwick). On Celsus' fundamental misperception of Christianity, see A. D. Nock, *Conversion: the Old and the New in Religion from Alexander the Great to
Augustine of Hippo* (Oxford: Oxford University Press, 1933), 204-208.
[33] Origen, *Contra Celsum*, VI.2 (316 Chadwick).

For Origen, therefore, as for the other Christian writers cited above, truth could be reached through simple, low language. This attitude implied the death of myth as conceived by Greek intellectuals, i.e., as a riddle to be decoded by the philosopher.

Origen, like Clement and other Christian writers, was put into an awkward position. On the one hand, he could not conceive of the Bible as another corpus of mythical traditions in need of a higher, more sophisticated, esoteric interpretation. On the other hand, in order to be treated with a modicum of intellectual respect by pagan thinkers, he had to read philosophical conceptions into the Biblical text. This situation was further complicated by the fact that, like Clement and other thinkers, he knew of the existence of early Christian esoteric traditions, and was aware of the Jewish origin of some of these traditions as well as of the very methods of Christian esotericism.

Celsus, on his side, had acknowledged that although the Biblical stories could not bear a deeper, esoteric interpretation, "the more reasonable Jews and Christians are ashamed of these things [such as, for instance, God's creation of Eve from Adam's rib] and try somehow to allegorize [*allègoreisthai*] them." To this Origen replies that

> it is not treating the matter fairly to refuse to laugh at the former [Origen refers to the story of Pandora in Hesiod] as being a legend *(muthos)* and to admire the philosophical truths contained in it, and yet to sneer at the biblical stories and think that they are worthless, your judgment being based upon the literal meaning alone.[34]

Towards the end of the same chapter, Origen argues once more against Celsus that it is inconceivable to deny the Jews alone, of all nations, "philosophical truths in a hidden form", while the Greeks, the Egyptians and all barbarians can put their pride in mysteries and in the truth they encapsulate. The same arguments and counter arguments, which are manifestly at the root of the fundamental polemics between Hellenic and Christian intellectuals, reappear elsewhere in the book.[35]

In his response to Celsus' attempt at deprecating and delegitimizing the Hebrew scriptures, Origen insists time and again on the *ethical* character of the Biblical stories, a character totally absent from Greek or barbarian myths:

---

[34] *Ibid.*, IV.38 (213 Chadwick).
[35] See for instance *ibid.*, IV.49-50.

It is the legends of the Greeks which are not only very stupid, but also very impious. For our scriptures have been written to suit exactly the multitude of the simple-minded (*tou plèthous tôn haplousterôn*), a consideration to which no attention was paid by those who made up the fictitious stories of the Greeks.[36]

In other words, the 'low level' of Biblical language renders at the same time a moral reform possible.

But not all believers are simple-minded. For Origen, as for any Platonist, the main criterium of simple-mindedness is the denial of spiritual realities, beyond the corporeal and material realm.[37] There are thus two categories of believers:

And the Gospel so desires wise men among believers that, in order to exercise the understanding of the hearers, it has expressed certain truths in enigmatic forms, and some in the so-called dark sayings, some by oracles, and others by problems.[38]

Origen provides examples of such dark sayings and riddles in the Bible. The *cherubim* in Ezekiel, for instance, "are expressed in an obscure form because of the unworthy and irreligious who are not able to understand the deep meaning and sacredness of the doctrine of God..." [39]

Here again, it seems that Origen, like Clement, contradicts himself. He makes a dual effort to refute the Greek polemist by arguing at once that the Hebrew scriptures are different in nature from pagan mythologies—mainly because of their ethical dimension—and that they should be interpreted according to the same exegetical rules that are applied to the various mythologies. Indeed, both Alexandrian theologians partake of an elitism not unlike that of the Greek philosophers. Yet, the texts adduced here show that this elitism is of a modified or mitigated nature. While they agree that there are two categories of believers, they insist, with all Christian thinkers, that not

---

[36] *Ibid.*, IV.50 (225 Chadwick).

[37] See for instance *Ibid.*, III.47 (161 Chadwick).

[38] Origen, *Contra Celsum*, III.45 (159-160 Chadwick). In *The Earliest Lives of Jesus* (New York: Harper, 1961), 66, Robert Grant points out that for Origen 'riddle' and 'parabol' are equivalent to 'myth' and ' fiction. This seems to reflect a misunderstanding of the fact that *ainigma*, for instance, is used by Origen *in bonam partem*, something he could not do with *muthos*. Cf. M. Eliade, *Aspects du mythe* (Paris: Gallimard, 1963), 199-203.

[39] *Ibid.*, VI.18 (331 Chadwick). Cf. VI.23 (336 Chadwick), where these esoteric doctrines are found in apocryphal writings of Jews and Christians.

only the perfects, or true gnostics, but also the *simpliciores* partake of salvation, offered by Christ to all who believe in him.

The ambivalence of the position of the two Christian theologians reflects the complexity of the milieu in which they operate. Their exegetical attitude is not only a reaction to the Hellenic polemicists. It should also be seen as a direct function of both the ongoing threat of the dualist heretics (the 'so called gnostics') and the esoteric traditions received, both orally and in various writings, from the earliest strata of Christianity.[40]

This is not the place to discuss the nature of the Gnostic threat to Christianity in the making. Nevertheless, it should be noted in the present context that Gnostic staunch esotericism was established on grounds deeply different from those on which the philosophers had founded their own teaching. The nature of the elitist teaching of the Gnostics was soteriological, not anymore primarily epistemological. While the philosophers sought to give a deep intellectual meaning to the exoteric myths told in popular language, the Gnostics seem to have kept secret the myths they invented with much gusto, and to have told them only to initiates. The Valentinian teacher Ptolemaeus, for instance, can thus present an exoteric version of his exegetical and metaphysical teaching to a sympathizing Christian lady, Flora, while insisting that the full-fledged myth (preserved to us by Irenaeus) is to be told only to the members of the sect.[41] Similar protection of the sect's myths is found among Basilides' followers.[42]

Moreover, one of the Coptic texts found at Nag Hammadi, the *Thunder*, a work *sui generis*, seems to be direcly influenced in its literary style by the riddles which had a certain vogue in the Hellenistic world.[43] Yet, if the 'enigmatic genre' permits veiled references to the gnostic myth, this fact entails the esoteric character of the myth itself.

In any case, the Church Fathers were quite conscious that they

---

[40] For Clement's anti-gnostic polemics as the context of his esoteric conceptions, see S. Lilla, *Clement of Alexandria*, 142-159.

[41] Irenaeus, *Adv. Haer.*, I.3.1: The myth was only indicated 'in mystery' (i.e. through parables) in the scriptures, since " not all understand" gnosis.

[42] *Ibid.*, I.24.6 *in finem*.

[43] This argument was convincingly argued by B. Layton, "The Riddle of the Thunder", in C. Hedrick and R. Hodgson, eds., *Gnosticism and Early Christianity* (Peabody, Mass.: Hendrickson, 1986), 35-54. On riddles in the earliest strata of Christian literature, see H. Leroy, *Rätsel und Misverständnis: ein Beitrag zur Formgeschichte des Johannesevangeliums* (Tübingen: [Imprimerie orientale, Louvain], 1967). See further Chapter 3 *supra*.

had to distantiate themselves in a radical way from the gnostic heretics on all grounds, including on their conception of a two-tiered
teaching. More than any other single cause, it is the gnostic challenge
which is responsible for Patristic Christianity eventually 'opting out'
of esoteric conceptions. The constant tension, within early Christianity, between 'pro-esoteric' and 'anti-esoteric' trends, was resolved by
the time of Augustine. True, Augustine's vocabulary retains traces of
the former esoterism, such as 'aenigma' or allegoria' .[44] It is also true
that his intellectual elitism and insightful psychlogy combined do not
permit him to fool either himself or his readers and to claim that
there is only one level of religious teaching. Yet at the same time
Augustine launches violent attacks against the very idea of esoteric
teachings. It is only the level of *teaching* (and not of the doctrines themselves) which should be different according to the level of understanding of the listeners.[45] For him, indeed, it seems that it is through
the soul's inner examination that the scriptures' *aenigmae* find their
solution.[46]

I have alluded above to the Jewish, or Jewish-Christian matrix of
Gnosticism. To paraphrase an *obiter dictum* of A.D. Nock, one could
even say that Gnosticism is Jewish-Christianity run wild. The esoteric
character of early Jewish-Christian teaching has been pointed out on
various occasions. It is also noteworthy that the Elchasaite community
in which Mani grew up partook in this kind of esotericism.[47] This
esotericism was in its turn the direct heir of Jewish esoteric teachings
from the later days of the Second Temple period. These teachings,
carried in both oral traditions and written teachings, the so-called
apocryphal literature, were often known to the Church Fathers. Al-

---

[44] See for instance Augustine, *De catechizandis rudibus*, 9(13): " *unde etiam mysteria vo-
cantur, quid valeant aenigmatum latebrae et amorem veritatis acuendum*" .

[45] Augustine, *In Iohannem*, 98. Cf. J.-P. Schobinger, "Augustins Einkehr als Wirkung
seiner Lektüre *Die Admonitio Verborum*", in H. Holzhey and W. Ch. Zimmerli, eds.,
Esoterik und Exoterik der Philosophie (Basel, Stuttgart: Schwabe Verlag, 1977), 70-100. On
Augustine's attitude to esotericism and allegorical interpretation of the Scriptures, see
also A. Kleinberg, " *De Agone Christiano*: the Preacher and his Audience", *JTS*
38(1987), 16-33, and the seminal study of J. Pépin, "Saint Augustin et la fonction
protreptique de l'allégorie", in *La tradition de l'allégorie*, II, 91-136. One should however point out that Pépin totally ignores the Jewish background of Christian esoteric
traditions. Moreover, while he insists on the similarities between Augustine's attitude
and that of the pagan authors, he does not seem to recognize the fundamental differences betweenthem. See further Chapter 8 *infra*.

[46] See for instance *Confessions*, V.14.24 and XI.22.28.

[47] See Chapter 4 *supra*.

though the origin of these traditions ran counter to the Fathers' conception of Christian esoteric Biblical interpretation as opposed to Jewish 'litteralism', they recognized their importance, and made much use of them, often quite openly. Origen himself is a well-known case in point, as we shall presently see.

Right from the beginning of the first book of the *Stromateis*, Clement states that he is the carrier of an esoteric, oral tradition stemming from the apostles. He is well aware of the great dangers connected with putting truth ino writing, and refers to Plato's *Second Letter* in that context. Therefore, he says, he will use various methods in order to protect the truth from those unfit to hear it. Together with various devices such as allusive or eliptic speech, the judicious use of symbolic language, even apparent contradictions and deliberate omissions, he adds that even the seeming disorder of the text is intended to render the truth at once more difficult of access but more lovable for its seekers. Moreover, the purposeful dispersion of truth within the text is presented by Clement as interspersed seeds of true knowledge:

> Having completed this introduction, and given a summary outline of ethical philosophy, wherin we have scattered (*egkataspeirantes*) the sparks of the true knowledge widely here and there, as we promised, so that it should not be easy for the uninitiated to come across them to discover the holy traditions...[48]

In the following paragraph, Clement adds that the method, which seeks to exercise the intelligence and ingenuity of the readers, is known to the Greeks.[49]

Actually, it seems that we can follow Clement's hint and trace this method of at once saying the truth and hiding it back to the Greek commentaries on the Homeric epics. Heliodorus (who is slightly posterior to Clement since his *floruit* is in the first half of the third century) writes that Homer hints at identifying real visions of gods, but few readers penetrate his riddle. Comprehension remains superficial when one understands the language but is ignorant of the "theology dispersed in the verses, (*tèn de egkatesparmenèn autois theologian)*".[50] The

---

[48] *Strom.*, I.9.43; cf. VI.15.132 and VII.18.111. These methods are all documented in Fortin, "Clement of Alexandria and the Esoteric tradition". For what follows, see further Chapter 7 *infra*.

[49] *Strom.*, VII.18.110-111. Cf .I.12.52.

[50] Heliodorus, *Aethiopica* 3.12.3. This text is quoted in R. Lamberton, *Homer the Theologian*, 151.

fact that both Clement and Heliodorus not only express the same thought, but also use the same verb, entitles us to assume that Clement and Heliodorus probably reflect the same tradition.

A rather similar tradition on the ways in which the scriptures hide truth is preserved by Origen. In the Prologue to his first *Commentary on the Psalms*, preserved in the *Philokalia*, Origen notes that the Scripture, thanks to its darkness, resembles a great many locked rooms in a single house. There is a key next to each door, but it does not open this door. It is indeed a great work to find the keys corresponding to the doors. The keys, in a sense, are dispersed in the building like so many seeds of truth. Yet the direct origin of this last tradition does not come from Greek interpretation of Homer. Origen states that he received this tradition "from the Hebrew", and that it relates to the whole of the Scriptures.[51]

This last tradition shows once more that early Patristic methods of esoteric interpretation are to be found at the confluence of Greek and Jewish influences. I would like to conclude by referring to a much later example of the same care taken in hiding the truth from those unworthy of it. Maimonides, in his Introduction to the *Guide of the Perplexed*, offers an 'Instruction with respect to this treatise'. Maimonides starts this instruction by asking the reader to be extremely careful when reading his book to the placement of every word, even if seemingly out of context. And Maimonides ends the Introduction by comparing the true meaning of terms to a key permitting to unlock the gates to the place of rest of souls.

Although the distance separating Clement from Maimonides is great indeed, it is not to be excluded that there is a link that connects them on this point.[52]

---

[51] See M. Harl, "Origène et les interprétations patristiques grecques de l' 'obscurité' biblique", *VC* 36(1982), 334-371, esp.351.

[52] Although Maimonides openly criticized Christian theology, some Christian influences on his thought have been pointed out, particularly by S. Pines, "Some Traits of Christian Theological Writing in Relation to Moslem Kalam and to Jewish Thought", *Proceedings of the Israel Academy of Sciences and Humanities*, V. 4 (Jerusalem, 1976), 105-125, and most recently by Sarah Stroumsa, "The Impact of Syriac Tradition on Early Judaeo-Arabic Bible Exegesis", *Aram* 3 (1992), 83-96. On the more general question of Eastern Christian influences on the earliest strata of medieval Jewish theology, see S. Stroumsa, *Dawud ibn Marwan al-Muqammis's Twenty Chapters* (Etudes sur le Judaïsme Médiéval 13; Leiden: Brill, 1989), introduction. On a possible link between the philosophical tradition of antiquity and al-Farabi, the originator of medieval Arabic philosophy, see Fortin, art. cit., 54-56.

CHAPTER SEVEN

CLEMENT, ORIGEN, AND JEWISH
ESOTERIC TRADITIONS

As we have seen in the previous chapters, early Christianity had inherited various esoteric traditions from Judaism. Such traditions,
which were developed, sometimes in wild or baroque ways, in gnostic
trends, are reflected in three different ways in ancient Christianity:
esoteric texts, such as the apocalyptic literature, secret oral traditions,
and esoteric Biblical exegesis. The universalist ethos of Christianity,
however, prevented Christians from easily retaining these esoteric
doctrines.

In the Christianity of late antiquity, the boundaries within the
communities were redefined in terms of supererogation rather than as
the special knowledge of an elite group. Rather than the recipients of
a private revelation, theologians and monks defined themselves and
were perceived as virtuosi able to reach ever deeper levels of faith.
Rather than the secrecy of a special revelation, one came to recognize
the secrets hidden in the depth of the heart. Humility became the
new virtue necessary in order to enhance such hidden dimensions.
The change of attitude toward esoteric traditions reflects the process
of interiorization typical of late antiquity.

One can follow in early Christian thought the transition from esoteric doctrines and conceptions (such as those transmitted, for instance, in the *paradosis* of the presbytes and those reflected in various
gnostic texts) to the development of mystical patterns of thought.[1] In
this process, the very meaning of 'inner' beliefs was transformed. In
the emerging Christian mysticism of late antiquity, only the vocabulary reflected traces of the esotericism of old. The secret traditions
were thoroughly interiorized, and the two-tiered teaching, directed to
two levels of understanding among two distinct classes of believers,
became spiritualized in a gradual way, according to the ability and
powers of each individual, but in which the highest levels were, at
least in principle, open to all.

---

[1] See chapter 9 *infra*.

In this deep-seated transformation of religious language and attitudes, Clement of Alexandria and Origen of Caesarea played a major role. Their writings reflect the passage from the former esotericism to the new mysticism. While both are deeply interested in the spiritual understanding of the Holy Writ, both also show a great interest in the preservation of esoteric traditions and patterns of thought.

Clement's and Origen's esotericism, which forms a central aspect of their thought, has often been studied, from various viewpoints. In this chapter, I by no means intend to cover the whole ground anew. Although Clement and Origen reflect a rather different religious and intellectual sensitivity, both stem from the same Alexandrian school of religious thought. The fact that this tradition grew at the confluence of Hellenistic philosophy and Gnostic doctrines is very well known indeed. In relationship to esotericism, in particular, Clement and Origen are usually understood to follow patterns originating in Greek philosophical traditions, especially those stemming from Platonic thought. Both thinkers, and in particular Clement, also retain close links to gnostic milieus and traditions.[2]

Despite the towering figure of Philo, however, and despite the fact, well-known in antiquity, that Clement and Origen had both learned from Jewish masters,[3] the Jewish side of the Alexandrian matrix seems to have remained understudied. Even less studied is the place and function of Jewish *esoteric* traditions in the formation of Alexandrian esotericism. It is easier to deal here with Origen, because of his out-

---

[2] For a general presentation of the intellectual milieu of the two great Alexandrians, H. Chadwick, *Early Christian Thought and the Classical Tradition* (Oxford: Clarendon, 1966), remains a classic. On Clement, see S. Lilla, *Clement of Alexandria: a Study in Christian Platonism and Gnosticism* (Oxford: Oxford University Press, 1971). This book is the best guide to Clement's links to Gnostic patterns of thought. For Origen, one can refer to J. W. Trigg, *Origen: The Bible and Philosophy in the Third-century Church* (Atlanta: J. Knox, 1983), which presents the main results of Origenian scholarship from the last generation. For a rather different interpretation, current in former Catholic scholarship, see J. Lebreton, "Le désaccord de la foi populaire et de la théologie savante dans l'église chrétienne du IIIe siècle", *Revue d'Histoire Ecclésiastique* 19 (1923), 481- 506, and 20 (1924), 5- 37. According to Lebreton, the secret tradition, which belonged at first only to the Gnostics, was only later accepted by Clement and Origen, and then by the latter's disciples, such as Basil of Caesarea, before it disappeared from the church (see esp. 504). See also Lebreton, "La théorie de la connaissance religieuse chez Clément d'Alexandrie", *Revue des Sciences Religieuses* 18 (1928), 457- 488.

[3] Jerome, *Contra Rufinum*, I. 13. (P. Lardet, ed., trans. *Jérome, Contre Rufin* [SC 303; Paris: Cerf, 1983], 36-41). Jerome mentions also Eusebius as having learned from Jewish teachers.

standing interest in, and knowledge of, various Jewish traditions, but Clement's attitude should also be analyzed. Various questions, capital for a full understanding of the nature of Clement's and Origen's esotericism, do not seem to have received enough consideration. I hope to be able to call attention to some intriguing and paradoxical aspects of the discourse of the two great Alexandrian theologians. The discussion will also hopefully shed some light on the similarities and the differences between their conceptions and attitudes.

1. Clement's esotericism and Jewish traditions

In contradistinction to Origen, Clement, who was probably not born a Christian, shows a rather slim interest in the Jewish inheritance of Christianity. Even Philo, to whom he owes so much, remains conspicuously absent from his works.[4] To judge from the quotations in his works and from his vocabulary, he would seem to be moving within the parameters of Hellenistic culture: the authors he refers to are the Greek classics, and much of his religious language is that of the mystery cults. In one of the most typical passages in that respect, Clement compares the difference between baptism and *gnosis* [the last term *in bonam partem*, of course] to that between the smaller and the greater mysteries.[5]

Clement has long been known for his gnostic proclivities. He lived in an intellectual and religious milieu in which the boundaries between heterodoxy and orthodoxy were not yet clearly defined. The importance of esotericism in Clement's thought, as well as in Patristic thought in general, has not always been recognized.[6]

---

[4] See A. van den Hoek, *Clement of Alexandria and his Use of Philo in the Stromateis* (VC Suppl. 3; Leiden: Brill, 1988). While van den Hoek insists on the multiform influence of Philo on Clement, Philo's name appears only very rarely in the whole Clementine corpus.

[5] *Strom.*, V. 11. 71 (A. Le Boulluec, P. Voulet, ed., transl., *Clément d'Alexandrie, Stromates V*; SC 278 [Paris: Cerf, 1981], 142-145). See also, for instance, *Strom.*, I. 1. 14. 1 on the memory of the *thyrsos* (C. Mondésert, M. Caster, ed., transl., *Clément d'Alexandrie, Stromates I*; [SC 30; Paris: Cerf, 1951], 53).

[6] For an instance of such scepticism, reflecting a traditional suspicion of heretical thinking among Catholic scholars, see C. Mondésert, *Clément d'Alexandrie: Introduction à l'étude de sa pensée religieuse* (Théologie 4; Paris: Aubier, 1944), 61: "...il n'y a, chez Clément, qu'une attitude ésotérique, et non pas un ésotérisme proprement dit...". *Ibid.*, 62: this attitude is "réelle, mais superficielle." The same view is partaken by other scholars; see Fortin, 42 (n. 19 *infra*).

As the *secret Gospel of Mark* mentioned by Clement shows in an ir-
refutable manner, he was confronting gnostic teachings, such as those
of the Carpocratians, and sought to protect various esoteric traditions
known in the Church of Alexandria from unworthy ears.[7] His gener-
ous use in the *Stromateis* of the vocabulary typical of the Greek mysteries has brought most scholars to look also in this direction for the
source of his esotericism.[8] There are, however, some major differences
between Clement's esotericism and that of the Gnostics. For instance,
pistis for Clement is a condition *sine qua non* for reaching *gnosis*. And
ethics plays a central role in Clement's worldview, in opposition to
that of the Gnostics.[9]

Clement makes good use of the various ways of protecting secret
doctrines: by keeping them oral, consigning them to esoteric writings,
or alluding to them in writing without revealing them in a clear language, understandable by everybody. He mentions doctrines which
are only transmitted orally, he knows secret texts, such as the *secret
Gospel of Mark*, and he protects truth by "scattering" its elements, a
method he uses in his *Stromateis*.

For Clement, there are two classes of Christians, the simple ones,
or believers, and the perfect ones, or gnostics.[10] Those who know the
secret, reserved teaching, thanks to a specially imparted knowledge,
stand significantly higher than those who accept the popularized message of Christ without recognizing its deeper significance. It may be
worth noting here that for Clement, the Gnostics do not separate
themselves from the simple believers, and help them by showing 'con-
descendence' (*sugkatastasis*) toward them.[11] Clement also insists on the

---

[7] The Gospel is mentioned in a letter of Clement discovered by Morton Smith in
the Mar Saba monastery; see M. Smith, *Clement of Alexandria and a Secret Gospel of Mark*
(Cambridge, Mass: Harvard University Press, 1973). Smith shows beyond reasonable
doubt the authenticity of the letter.

[8] For a recent and thorough study, see Ch. Riedweg, *Mysterienterminologie bei Platon,
Philon und Klemens von Alexandrien* (Untersuchungen zur antiken Literatur und
Geschichte 26; Berlin, New York: de Gruyter, 1987), 116- 161. On Clement's and
Origen's 'mystery' vocabulary, see also A. D. Nock, "Hellenistic Mysteries and Chris-
tian Sacraments", in his *Essays on Religion and the Ancient World*, Z. Stewart, ed., (Ox-
ford: Clarendon, 1972), II, 814- 815.

[9] See *Savoir et Salut*, 145- 162.

[10] See esp. *Strom.*, VI and VII. *Strom.* VII. 14. 84 (60, Stählin) summarizes Clement's teaching about the perfect Gnostic's superiority over the simple believer. Cf.
Lebreton, "Théorie de la connaissance" . See further A. Guillaumont, "Le gnostique
chez Clément d'Alexandrie et chez Evagre le Pontique", *Alexandrina: Mélanges Claude
Mondésert* (Paris: Cerf, 1987), 196- 201.

[11] *Strom.*, VII. 9. 53 (39 Stählin). Cf. *Strom.*, I. 4. 3 (46 Mondésert-Caster). See also

oral character of Gnosis: Gnosis was transmitted orally from the apostles of Christ to a small number of men.[12] Elsewhere, Clement points
out that the secret doctrines of Jesus were told to James, passed in
tradition to John and Peter, then to the other apostles, and later to
the seventy *presbuteroi*, among them Barnabas.[13] In other words, the
secret Gnosis preserves the oldest and the deepest teaching of Christianity, which had been reserved by Jesus to his closest disciples. It
should be pointed out that this conception is by no means unique to
Clement. Rather, it reflects attitudes current in early Christianity. A
similar preference of oral traditions over written texts is shown, for
instance, by Papias of Hierapolis.[14]

To these two categories of Christians correspond two levels of understanding the Scriptures. Those who are unable to understand are
unworthy of hearing the deeper meaning of the Word of God. Hence
esotericism permits one to avoid two different but related dangers: it
protects truth, which would be put in jeopardy by those unworthy of
it, and it protects the weak ones, who would be threatened by a direct
and "unscreened" exposition to divine truth. Scripture is thus endowed with a secret meaning.[15]

Clement's attitude to esoteric traditions has been carefully studied,
in particular by Salvatore Lilla, who was able to draw a concrete and
detailed picture of the intellectual and cultural milieu in which Clement's thought grew.[16] Lilla insists on the gnostic context and on the
Platonic frame of Clement's esotericism. This frame reflects Clement's own consciousness and is concretely underlined by his quotations, references and allusions. Clement, indeed, refers mainly to
Plato,[17] and does not mention, for instance, any Jewish sources that

---

Strom., V. 4. 26. 1, on I Cor 2: 6-7: the Apostle opposes common faith to the perfec-
tion of knowledge. On Rom 1: 11: it is impossible to write certain things, which
should remain oral. Cf. n. 25 *infra*. Eusebius, too, reports that Paul "committed to
writing no more than short epistles" (*H. E.*, III. 24. 4 [250-251 LCL]).

[12] See *Strom.*, VI. 7. 61. 1 (462 Stählin).

[13] See *Hypotyposes*, in Eusebius, *H.E.*, II. 1. 3-5 (104-105 LCL). See also Clement's
comments on Rom 1: 11, in *Strom.*, V. 26. 5: "It was not possible to send you by letter,
openly, these instructions about charisms." Cf. Le Boulluec's commentary on *Strom.*
V, vol. II, 111- 112.

[14] Papias's *floruit* is approximately 140- 150.

[15] *Strom.*, VI. 15. 116. 1- 2. Cf. *Strom.*, I. 1. 13-14 (52-55 Mondésert-Caster): Clement asks for caution in writing, in order to protect both the hearer and truth.

[16] S. Lilla, *Clement of Alexandria*. On Gnosis and esotericism, see esp. 142-159.

[17] He refers also to Pythagoras, who was the first to discover the hidden meaning
of words; see *Eclogae Propheticae* 32 (146-147 Stählin). In *Strom.*, I.1.18. (56 Mondésert-

might have influenced his thought, such as Philo or other Jewish literature.

It is well known that the *Stromateis* follow the structure of philosophical exercises (*askèsis*), a genre well known under the early empire.[18] In an important article on the esoteric traditions in Clement, however, E.L. Fortin has pointed out that Clement's own reasons for concealing his innovations were different from those of the pagan philosophers.[19] For Clement, the language of secrecy is meant not only to hide the experience, but also to prepare it. The *Stromateis*, as Clement himself insists, are purposefully constructed in a complex way, which is meant to protect truth from a complete exposure to those unworthy or unable to grasp it, who could misuse it. But while it is possible, perhaps, to describe mystical experience, it is impossible to lead to it through clear language.

As a consequence of this attitude, Clement proposes in his *Stromateis* an original way of hiding and revealing truth at the same time, by scattering its elements in the text. In this way, truth appears like a riddle, an *ainigma*, to be deciphered by the careful reader.[20] In two important passages, Clement speaks of the truth *scattered* in the *Stromateis*.

Caster), Clement states that in his book, he will reveal truth "veiled and hidden by the dogmas of philosophy". Cf. *Strom.*, I. 19 on the propaedeutic value of Greek philosophy.

[18] See P. Hadot, "Exercices spirituels", *Annuaire de l' EPHE, section des Sciences Religieuses*, 84 (1977), 25-70.

[19] E.L. Fortin, "Clement of Alexandria and the Esoteric Tradition", in F.L. Cross, ed., *Studia Patristica, IX* , 3 (TU 94; Berlin: Akademie Verlag, 1966), 41- 56; cf. esp. 54.

[20] On riddles and enigmatic ways of expression, see chapter 1 *supra*. On seeing God "through a glass and in a riddle" (I Cor 13: 12), see R. Mortley, "Mirror and I Cor 13: 12 in the Epistemology of Clement of Alexandria", *VC* 30 (1976), 109-120; cf. Origen, *C. Cels.* VII. 38 and 50, (H. Chadwick, transl., *Origen, Contra Celsum* [Cambridge: Cambridge U. P., 1953], 425 and 438), and *Com. Joh.*, X. 43. For the use of *ainigma* in Origen's school in Caesarea, see Gregory Thaumaturgus, *Discourse of Thanks*, XV (H. Crouzel, ed., transl., *Origen, Contra Celsum* [Cambridge: Cambridge U. P., 1953], 425 and 438), and *Com. Joh.*, X. 43. For the use of *ainigma* in Origen's school in Caesarea, see Gregory Thaumaturgus, *Discourse of Thanks*, XV (H. Crouzel, ed., transl., *Grégoire le Thaumaturge, Remerciement à Origène* [SC 148; Paris: Cerf, 1969], 180). H. Crouzel has studied the concept of riddle in Origen in his *Origène et la connaissance mystique* (Museum Lessianum 56; Bruges, 1961), 238.

Having completed this introduction, and given a summary outline of ethical philosophy, wherein we have scattered (*egkataspeirantes*) the sparks of the true knowledge widely here and there, as we promised, so that it should not be easy for the uninitiated to come across them to discover the holy traditions...[21]

The method used by Clement in order to preserve truth from unworthy readers is interesting. To use a 'post-modern' metaphor, one might call it a "deconstruction" of the text of truth.

In a less anachronistic vocabulary, however, one could apply to what Clement does, purposefully, in the *Stromateis* a metaphor used by Irenaeus in order to describe—and condemn—the gnostics' misuse of Scripture. Irenaeus describes gnostic biblical interpretation as "dismembering the body of truth," [22] implying that Scripture is like a "body" encompassing the totality of truth (*sôma tès alêtheias*).[23] By their heretical, perverse mode of reading, the gnostics "dismember", as it were, truth. Instead of keeping the naked body intact, Clement, in similar fashion, argues that it should be 'torn apart' in order to be protected.

The purposeful scattering of dismantled elements of truth within the theological text is a rather peculiar method, but it is known elsewhere. Slightly after Clement's days, Heliodorus describes in his *Aethiopica*, how Homer "dispersed" theology in his verses (*tèn de egkatesparmenèn autois theologian*).[24]

Moreover, and perhaps more direcly significant in our present context, exactly the the same method of truth is described by Mai-

---

[21] *Strom.*, VII. 18. 110. 4 (78 Stählin); cf. *Strom.*, I. 12. 56. 3 (89-90 Mondésert-Caster). See chapter 6 *supra*. In the following passage (*Strom.*, I. 13; 91-92 Mondésert-Caster), Clement speaks of the dismemberment of truth into fragments, comparing it to that of Pentheus by the Bacchae and the *sparagmos* of Dionysos in Greek myth. On Paul's secret docrine, which cannot be committed to writing, see for instance *Strom.*, V. 26. 4. 25.

[22] *Adv. Haer.*, I. 8. 1 (A. Rousseau, L. Doutreleau, ed., transl., *Irénée, Contre les Hérésies, I* [SC 264; Paris: Cerf, 1979], 112-117); cf. J.-D. Dubois, "L'exégèse des gnostiques et l'histoire du canon des Ecritures", in M. Tardieu, ed., *Les règles de l'interprétation* (Paris: Cerf, 1987), 89-97.

[23] *Corpus* has already the meaning of a group of texts in classical Latin. Cf. Marc the Gnostic's conception of the *sôma tès alêtheias*. See further chapter 5 *supra*. This mythical conception has been compared to that of the *Shi' ur Komah*. by scholars of early Jewish theological literature, from Gaster to Scholem. See G. Scholem, *Major Trends in Jewish Mysticism* (New York: Schocken, 1946), 63 and notes.

[24] Heliodorus, *Aethiopica*, III. 12. 3. This text is quoted by R. Lamberton, *Homer the Theologian* (Transformation of the Classical Heritage; Berkeley: U. of California Press, 1987), 151.

monides in the Introduction to his *Guide of the Perplexed*. Maimonides requires the reader to exert the greatest care, particularly when words seem to appear out of context.[25] The use of the same method in order to preserve esoteric doctrine by Clement and Maimonides is striking. *Prima facie*, it is hard to see how influences from Clement's side could have reached Maimonides.[26] Barring a coincidence, one should envisage the possibility of the influence on Clement of a Jewish hermeneutical tradition.[27]

There exists, actually, in the *Stromateis* at least one allusion to the possible influence of a Jewish teacher on Clement. In *Strom.*, 1. 11. 1-2, Clement mentions his most important teachers, those who had a decisive influence on his formation and taught him important doctrines. Among his oriental teachers, one came from Assyria, while the other one was originally a Palestinian Jew.[28] The last one of these teachers was the most prominent one according to his [intellectual and spiritual] powers (*hustatôi de perituxôn, dunamei de houtos prôtos èn*). Clement met him in Egypt, where this wise man was hiding (Clement does not tell us why). Once he had met him, he remained by the side of this master. Using a literary topos refering probably to the fact that he was "gathering the spoil of the flowers of the prophetic and apostolic meadows", he calls him a "Sicilian bee", indicating by this the great impression this teacher had made upon him.[29] Although Clement's

---

[25] Maimonides, *Guide of the Perplexed*, Sh. Pines, trad. (Chicago: Chicago University Press, 1963), Epistle dedicatory, pp. 3-4, and "Instruction with regard to this treatise," pp. 15-17.

[26] See chapter 6 *supra*, n. 52.

[27] For J. Daniélou, such a possibility is a certainty: "Cette gnose philonienne est christianisée par Clément. C'est donc chez Clément que les courants issus de l'ésotérisme juif viennent confluer dans le christianisme hellénistique.", in "Aux sources de l'ésotérisme judéo-chrétien", *Archivio de filosofia*, 2-3 (1960), 39-46 (= *Umanesimo e esoterismo* [Padova: CEDAM, 1960]).

[28] *ho de en Palaistinèi hebraios anekathen* (51-52 Mondésert-Caster). The *hebraios* might of course have been a Jewish Christian or a Christian of some other sort. On the semantics of *hebraios* and *ioudaios* in Patristic Greek, one may note that the former is usually used *in bonam partem* and the latter *in malam partem*, refering respectively to Jews before and after Jesus. In the present exemple, Clement's teacher is of course a "good" Jew.

[29] Opinions vary as to the identity of the Jewish teacher. Theophilus of Caesarea and Theodotos the Gnostic have been suggested. Some have proposed to identify "the Sicilian bee" with Pantaenus. See for instance Mondésert-Caster, *Strom.*, I. 51, n. 4; This is based upon a different reading of the text, according to which "the last one" is not "the Hebrew from Palestine". Cf. G. Bardy, "Aux origines de l'école d'Alexandrie", *RSR* 27 (1937), 65-90, esp. 71 ff., and *Vivre et Penser* (1942), 83 ff. For

rather obscure allusion to the identity and nature of the teachings of his Jewish teacher precludes any conclusions, it leaves open the plausibility that among the various teachings which had a formative influence on Clement there were some Jewish (or Jewish-Christian) esoteric traditions.[30]

2. Origen on Jewish esoteric traditions

Origen's interest in Jewish traditions is well known, and has been studied from various angles.[31] His attitude towards these traditions is complex. On the one hand, it reflects the common opinion among early Christian intellectuals about the Jewish reading of the Bible: "The Jew does not understand hidden meaning".[32] According to this opinion, the Jews are only capable of a literal understanding of the Biblical text, and fail to perceive the deeper layers of divine revelation. Their blindness, obviously, stems from their refusal to recognize Jesus Christ as the Messiah of God announced by the prophets. In contradistinction to the Jewish, exterior, superficial, 'carnal' reading

Bardy, "rien n'est moins assuré" than the identification of "the last one" with Pantaenus. See also D. Dawson, *Allegorical Readers and Cultural Revision in Ancient Alexandria* (Berkeley: University of California Press, 1992), 220 and 294, n. 64, who points out rightly that Clement does not identify the "Sicilian bee" he discovered in Egypt as Pantaenus. According to Bardy, Pantaenus himself was probably "one of the presbytes whose doctrine Clement claimed to retain." ("Origines", 74).

[30] On the secrecy inherent to tradition (*paradosis*), see *Strom.*, I.12.55.1 (59 Mondésert-Caster), and *Strom.*, V.10.61. R.P.C. Hanson, *Origen's Doctrine of Tradition* (London: SPCK, 1954), 73 ff.,"Origen's Doctrine of Secret Tradition", points out the Jewish reference of *paradosis* in Origen's works. For one instance of such a secret Jewish *paradosis*, see Origen, *Com. Joh.*, VI. 14. 83 (188-189 Blanc). See also E. Norden, *Agnostos Theos: Untersuchungen zur Formengeschichte religiöser Reden* (Leipzig-Berlin: Teubner, 1913), 288, on the links between *gnosis* and *paradosis* among the Jews. In *Strom.*, VI. 15. 116. 1-2 (Stählin, 490, 15-16), Clement points out that one of the differences between the believer and the gnostic is that the former is able to keep the commandments only from fear of God, not from love. One should compare this to the similar Rabbinic teaching about fear and love of God, and about the superiority of the latter.

[31] The list of relevant studies is large. I refer here only to the important monograph of N. de Lange, *Origen and the Jews: Studies in Jewish-Christian Relations in Third-Century Palestine* (Cambridge: Cambridge U. P., 1976), which includes a detailed bibliography, and to J.A. McGuckin, "Origen and the Jews", in D. Wood, ed., *Christianity and Judaism* (London: Blackwell, 1992), 1- 13; see esp. n. 1 for further bibliographical references.

[32] *Hom. Jeremiah*, XII. 13 (P. Husson, P. Nautin, ed., transl. [SC 238; Paris: Cerf, 1977], 44-45).

of the Biblical text, the Christian understanding of the Bible is interior, deep, hidden, spiritual. The one is lacking, while the other is perfect.[33] It is, indeed, necessary to understand Scripture in a metaphorical, spiritual way. This exegesis is established upon hidden interpretations: one must understand secretly.[34]

The ambivalent relationship shown by Origen toward Judaism and the Jews is usually perceived as consisting in an occasional use of the Jewish sages' knowledge, combined with a criticism of their literal reading of Scripture.[35] This relationship, however, should be understood as a deeper and more complex phenomenon. Although Origen rejects the doctrines professed by contemporaneous Jews as "myths" and "trash", he acknowledges that the Jews also know of a mystical contemplation of the Law and the Prophets: "The Jews said many things according to secret traditions (*paradoseis aporrhètous*)" . [36] Origen recognizes, at least implicitly, that the traditional Christian accusation of literalism thrown at the Jews is not established on facts, when he says that the Jews teach the "double meaning" of texts, both according to the letter and to sense.[37]

One can identify here a major paradox in Origen's approach to Jewish Biblical hermeneutics: on the one hand, the Jewish literal understanding of Scripture prevents any deep interpretation. On the other hand, Origen shows a deep interest in, and a great respect for various Jewish hermeneutical traditions—something that is much more than appreciation for the Rabbis' 'technical' Scriptural knowledge. This paradox reflects two trends inherited by Origen: the (then already) traditional *adversus judaeos* attitude in Patristic literature,[38]

---

[33] *Com. Joh.*, XIII. 16. 98- 18. 109-111 (182-191 Blanc). I quote this text according to C. Blanc, ed., trans., *Origène, Commentaire sur Jean*, in three volumes: I (Livres I-V; SC 120;); II (Livres VI et X; SC 157); III (Livre XIII; SC 222); respectively Paris: Cerf, 1966; 1970; 1975.

[34] *Hom. Jer.*, XII. 13, commenting upon Jer 13: 17 (44- 51 Husson- Nautin).

[35] See for instance M. Harl, ed., transl., *Origène, Philocalie 1-20, Sur les Ecritures* (SC 302; Paris: Cerf, 1983), 49. On Origen's lack of sympathy for myth, se for instance M.J. Edwards, "Gnostics, Greeks, and Origen: the Interpretation of Interpretation", *JTS* 44 (1993), 70-89, esp. 87: "Origen has no ear for myths and mysteries."

[36] *Com. Joh.*, XIX. 15. 92 (315 in E. Preuschen, ed., *Origenes Werke, IV* [GCS; Leipzig: Hinrichs, 1903]).

[37] *C. Cels.*, 7. 20 (411 Chadwick).

[38] On the evolution of this tradition, see G.G. Stroumsa, "From Anti-Judaism to Antisemitism in Early Christianity?", In O. Limor and G.G. Stroumsa, eds., *Contra Judaeos: Ancient and Medieval Polemics between Christians and Jews* (Tübingen: Mohr [Siebeck], 1996), 1-26.

with a subtle undercurrent of respect for the wisdom of the ancients, preserved in various ways by the sages of Israel. Such a positive attitude to the wisdom of the Rabbis, although it represents by no means the common attitude among the Church Fathers, is reflected elsewhere. One can quote here, for instance, a passage from the Origenist Eusebius of Caesarea, who compares the two-tiered education of Christians to that of the Rabbis:

> But those who are in a more advanced condition, and as it were grown grey in mind, are permitted to dive into the deeps, and test the meaning of the words: and these the Hebrews were wont to name 'Deuterotists,' as being interpreters and expounders of the meaning of the Scriptures.[39]

Dealing with the sources of Origen's esoteric exegesis, Jean Daniélou identifies two main sources of "Origen's esoteric interpretations". He refers on the one hand to what he calls "the apocalyptic elements of the Old Testament and their Jewish exegesis", and on the other hand to New Testament apocalypticism. He also mentions the Jewish and Jewish-Christian apocalyptic literature (*ta apokrupha*), as well as the oral tradition, but without giving any detail on the relationships between these *corpora*, and points out that the esoteric doctrine deals with the heavenly world and its inhabitants.[40] Yet for Origen, apocalypticism is not the only, or even the most important source of Jewish esoteric traditions. These are mainly of a hermeneutical nature, i. e. are hidden under the literal sense of Scripture.

The first way in which the Jews maintain their secret traditions is by various esoteric writings, to which Origen refers. In his *Homilies on Jeremiah*, for instance, he states that among the Scriptures there are some esoteric and mystical writings.[41] Some works which are usually called 'apocryphal' (*apokrupha*) contain secret doctrines. Such works are to be taken seriously. Referring to the contemporary discussion among Christians about the possibility of the imminent end of the

---

[39] Eusebius, *Praeparatio Evangelica*, XII. 1. 574 a (621 Gifford, transl.).

[40] J. Daniélou, *Message évangélique et culture hellénistique aux 2e et 3e siècles* (Paris: Desclée, 1961), 447- 448.

[41] *Kai epei tôn legomenôn en tais graphais ha men estin aporrhètotèra kai mustikôtera... Hom. Jer.*, XII. 7 (30-31 Husson-Nautin). Origen also divides here the Scriptures into "those which are secret and 'mystical', and those which are "direcly useful to those who understand them."

world, Origen proposes to check the esoteric writings (*ta aporrhèta*) of the Hebrews. Other secret doctrines of the Jews which are kept in such books deal for instance with Beelzebub, the soul, or with metempsychosis.[42] These books also include secret doctrines about the Messiah.[43] Elsewhere, Origen writes that when the Jews ask John, son of Zacharias, "Are you Elias?", "it is clear that they asked this question because they believed that the doctrine of reincarnation was true, since it was consistent with the tradition of their fathers and in no way different from their esoteric teachings (*tès en aporrhètois didaskalias autôn*)." [44] Here Origen seems to believe that metempsychosis was commonly taught among Jews at the time of Jesus.[45] Origen also speaks about the "deepest truths about the way in which the soul enters into the divine realm... from the books, some of which are Jewish and are read in their synagogues." [46]

Together with these apocryphal writings, some Biblical texts should be mentioned, which are of a distinct esoteric nature. The most important of these texts for Origen is the *Song of Songs*, which offers a broad basis for his mysticism, of his description of the love between God and the soul. His *Commentary* on the text reflects clearly the passage from esotericism to mysticism. The bridal chamber represents the secret interpretation reserved for those advanced in holiness and knowledge.[47]

On this point, the prologue to Origen's *Commentary in the Song of*

---

[42] *Com. Joh.*, XIX. 15. 92-96 (315 Preuschen); metempsychosis is rejected by Clement, see Lebreton, "désaccord", 504. On metempsychosis in Patristic literature, see K. Hoheisel, "Das frühe Christentum und die Seelenwanderung", *JAC* 27-28 (1984-85), 24-46.

[43] *Ibid.*, XIX. 17. 104 (317 Preuschen).

[44] *Com. Joh.*, VI. 12. 73 (182- 183 Blanc).

[45] For a different interpretation of this passage, see R. Roukema, "Reïncarnatie in de oude kerk", *Gereformeerd Theologisch Tijdschrift* 93 (1993), 33-56, esp. 34. [The first part of the article is to be found in *GTT* 92 (1992), 199-218]. I should like to thank Dr. Roukema for calling my attention to this article.

[46] *C. Cels.*, VI. 23 (336 Chadwick). On this tradition about the mysteries discovered in Numbers, Lebreton comments: "Ici encore le grand chrétien s'est laissé prendre aux fantaisies rabbiniques" ("Degrés", 295, n. 2). On another secret tradition of the Hebrews about Elias being identical with Pinehas, see *Com. Joh.*, VI. 14. 83 (188-189 Blanc).

[47] *Com. Cant.*, I. 5 (62 in W.A. Baehrens, ed., *Origenes Werke*, VIII [GCS 33; Leipzig: Hinrichs, 1925]); trad. R.P. Lawson, *Origen, the Song of Songs*, 23. On Origen's mysticism, see B. McGinn, *The Foundations of Mysticism* (New York: Crossroads, 1991), 108-130.

Songs preserves a testimony of capital importance for the early history of Jewish mysticism. Indeed, the great importance of this text of Origen has been recognised for a long time by scholars of Rabbinic Judaism.[48] Origen is here our earliest source on those chapters of the Bible on which the Rabbinic tradition offers an esoteric interpretation. These chapters must be read only by mature persons (*nisi quis ad aetatem perfectam maturamque pervenit*). The four parts of the Bible listed as receiving a particular esoteric interpretation are the first chapters of *Genesis*, which relate the creation of the world, the first and the last chapters of *Ezekiel*, which deal, respectively, with the divine Chariot and with the Temple, and finally the *Song of Songs*.

Beside Jewish apocryphal writings and some Biblical texts endowed with a particularly esoteric meaning, Origen also knows about Jewish esoteric Biblical hermeneutics, which he values. Indeed, Jewish esoteric teachings are mainly expressed in the spiritual hermeneutics of the Old Testament. According to Origen, the veil hiding truth under riddles or parables in Scripture serves two goals. It protects truth from too direct an access on the part of beginners, but it also serves as a pedagogical method in order to encourage spiritual and intellectual progress.[49] Elsewhere, Origen says that Scripture includes various secrets, and that its obscure expression is purposeful. "There is a *nous* (*i. e.*, a meaning) hidden under the letter".[50] Scripture contains deep thoughts hidden under a visible surface; it is compared to a planted field under which a treasure is hidden. The treasure is the thoughts hidden under what is apparent.[51] To give only a few instances of the 'enigmatic' Scriptural hermeneutics: "But all the more mysterious and esoteric truths, which contained ideas beyond the understanding of everyone, [the prophets] expressed by riddles and allegories and what are called dark sayings, and by what are called parables or prov-

---

[48] See for instance G. Scholem, *Gnosticism, Mysticism, and Talmudic Tradition* (New York: Jewish Theological Seminary, 1961), 36-42, and R. Kimmelman, "Rabbi Yohanan and Origen on the Song of Songs", *HTR* 73 (1980), 567-95, with bibliography.

[49] R. Girod, ed., trans., Origène, *Commentaire sur l' Evangile de Matthieu, I* (SC 162; Paris: Cerf, 1970), 53.

[50] *Com. Joh.*, V. 1 (372 Blanc).

[51] *Com. Mat.*, X. 5 (156-59 Girod); cf. *C. Cels.*, V. 60 (310-311 Chadwick), where Origen states that "the meaning of the Mosaic law has been hidden from those who have not eagerly followed the way through Jesus Christ" .

erbs." [52] Or elsewhere: "...And who, on reading the revelations made to John, could fail to be amazed at the deep obscurity of the unspeakable mysteries contained therein, which are evident even to him who does not understand what is written?" [53]

Like the traditional doctrine of all other nations, that of the Jews is established on two levels, the one open to all, expressed in stories understandable by everybody (the Bible, equivalent to other nations' myths), and the other reserved to the sages, offering deep philosophical interpretations of these myths. Thus Origen can state quite squarely that the Jews have secret philosophical doctrines. [54] In the same vein, the Jews teach the "double sense" of the Law, according to the meaning (*pros dianoian*) as well as to the letter (*pros rhèton*). [55] Indeed, there is a hidden treasure in the Bible. [56] Origen speaks elsewhere of the splendors of the doctrines hidden under the letter of the Biblical text, and gives this as a reason for its obscurity. [57] He also specifies that the *simpliciores* deal with ethics, while the *perfecti* understand the divine secrets. [58]

Moses was the first of these teachers to receive from God knowledge of the divine secrets. But he did not reveal to the multitudes every teaching that he received in private. When teaching, he mentioned only what was enough for men, and what simple people could understand. [59] Moses transmitted this doctrine to the priests, whose duty it was to explain the secret meaning of the Law. "According to

---

[52] Cf. *C. Cels.*, VII. 10 (403 Chadwick), cf. *C. Cels.*, III. 45 (159-160 Chadwick). Cf. Stroumsa, "Moses' Riddles", n. 38.

[53] *Peri Archôn*, IV. 2. 3. I quote according to H. Görgemanns-H. Karpp, eds., transl., *Origenes, Vier Bücher von den Prinzipien* (Darmstadt: Wissenschaftliche Buchgesellschaft, 1976), 704-706.

[54] *C. Cels.*, IV. 38-39 (214-216 Chadwick); according to Origen, Plato would have learnt Jewish philosophical (esoteric) hermeneutics during his trip to Egypt. This approach is particularly clear in Origen's apologetics.

[55] *C. Cels.*, VII. 20, where Philo, in all probability, is refered to as the source of the christian belief in a double meaning (literal and spiritual) of the Biblical text (cf. Philo, *de Spec. Leg.*, I. 287, passim). Cf. *C. Cels.*, II. 6 (71 Chadwick), on the double sense of the prophetic writings.

[56] See Girod, Introduction to his edition of *Com. Mat.*, 51 ff.

[57] *Peri Archôn*, IV. 1. 7 (688-691 Görgemanns-Karpp).

[58] In *Hom. Lev.*, XIII. 3 (I quote according to M. Borret, ed., transl., *Origène, Homélies sur le Lévitique* [SC 286-287; Paris: Cerf, 1981], 208-211). This taxonomy is similar to that of Maimonides, for whom the question of good and evil is lower than that of truth and error. For the sources of this idea, see Sh. Pines, "Truth and Falsehood versus Good and Evil", in I. Twersky, ed., *Studies in Maimonides* (Harvard Center for Jewish Studies; Cambridge: Harvard University Press, 1990), 95-157.

[59] *Hom. Num.*, VI. 1, on Num 11: 24; (122- 123 Méhat).

this the priests of the Jews served 'a pattern and shadow of the heavenly things' (Heb 8: 5), discussing in secret the meaning of the Law about sacrifices and the truths of which they were the symbols." [60]

Thus, a secret Judaism existed already in the Biblical times. Those who are Jews secretly (*en tôi kruptôi Ioudaioi*) receive their name not from Judah, son of Jacob, but from a High Priest also named Judah, whose brothers in freedom they are, like him being saved by God from the hand of their enemies.[61] This secret Judaism is very highly prized indeed: the knowledge of the highest secrets of true religion makes the saints of the Old Testament superior to ignorant Christians.[62]

The teachers of the Jews thus had the keys of knowledge, although the Rabbis, who were in charge of keeeping the Law, have given up the deepest knowledge of the word of God, and have become satisfied with the outer sense.[63] Jewish secret doctrines, therefore, are the core of true Judaism, in contradistinction to rabbinic Judaism—although the rabbis are the heirs of these traditions of old and know them. For Origen, true or secret Judaism stands in stark opposition to contemporaneous Judaism:

> If one considers the present condition of the Jews, comparing it with their past condition, one will see how the Lord's herd was crushed.[64]

Interestingly enough, this argument is part of a polemics against *judaizantes* within Origen's audience, i. e., Christians (in this case, Christian women) following Jewish rites, such as eating unleaven bread during Passover or fasting on the Day of Atonement.

The secret meaning of the Bible begins, for Origen, with the 'correspondences', established upon the letters of the Hebrew alphabet, such as the twenty two letters and the twenty two books of the Bible.[65] In the same vein, Origen also discusses the spiritual meaning of the *tau*, the last letter of the Hebrew alphabet; he reports the view of

---

[60] *C. Cels.*, V. 44 (299 Chadwick); cf. *ibid.* II. 6 (71 Chadwick). See also *Hom. Num.*, IV. 3, where the mysteries are said to be reserved to the priests.
[61] *Com. Joh.*, I. 35. 259 (188-189 Blanc).
[62] *Com. Joh.*, I. 7. 37 (80-81 Blanc).
[63] *Philoc.*, II. 2 (242-245 Harl; cf. Harl, introduction, 48).
[64] *Hom. Jer.*, XII. 13 (48-51 Husson-Nautin).
[65] See *Philocalie*, ch. 3, (260-268 Harl).

a Jewish convert to Christianity, according to whom the *tau* is a symbol of the Cross.[66]

According to Origen, the Bible provides various allusions to esoteric teachings about the divinity. One such instance is Isaac's banquet (Gen. 26: 30), which alludes to the banquet attended by the perfect ones, where they discuss about "the wisdom of God hidden in the mystery".[67] Origen also refers to the secret name of God known to the Hebrews.[68] He mentions elsewhere the heavenly counterparts of the cities of the Holy Land as another secret in the Bible.[69]

Perhaps the most striking, and certainly the most beautiful instance of a Jewish tradition of esoteric Biblical interpretation is the tradition reported by Origen in his lost *Commentary on Psalms*, an early work written in Alexandria. The tradition is preserved in the *Philokalia*.[70]

Origen repeats "a very beautiful tradition" (*khariestatèn paradosin*) which he learned "from the Jew (*ho hebraios*)", and which concerns Scripture in general. According to this tradition, Scripture, because of its obscurity, is compared to a house in which there are many locked rooms. There is a key near each room, but it does not fit the lock. It is a difficult work, in Origen's words, to find the key which can open the door of each room. If the Scriptures are so obscure, it is because their interpretive principle is "dispersed" among them (*ekhousôn en autais diesparmenon to exegètikon*). Origen adds that Paul suggests a similar method of Biblical interpretation when he says: "Which things also we speak, not in the words which man's wisdom teacheth, but which the Holy Ghost teacheth; comparing spiritual things with spiritual" (I Cor 2: 13).

This text, according to which the proper method of Biblical hermeneutics involves the reconstruction of a purposefully broken dis-

---

[66] *Com. Ezech.*, IX. 4. For speculations on letters in antiquity, one can still refer with profit to H. Dornseiff, *Das Alphabet in Mystik und Magie* (Stoicheia 7; Berlin: Teubner, 1925).

[67] *Hom. Gen.*, XIV. 4 (344-347 Doutreleau).

[68] *Com. Ezech.*, VIII. 2. These last two passages are reprinted in the pioneering study of Gustave Bardy, "Les traditions juives dans l'oeuvre d'Origène", *RB* 34 (1925), 217-52. The passages in question appear under the numbers 39 and 41, pp. 241- 242 (=318- 454 Baehrens). Daniélou (*op. cit.*, 447) speaks of "numerous allusions to esoteric Jewish interpretation" in Origen's *Commentary on Ezechiel*, but does not give any references.

[69] *Hom. Jos.*, XXIII. 4 (464-469 Jaubert).

[70] *Philocalie*, II. 3 (244-245 Harl).

course, is indeed remarkable. It should be compared to the passage of the *Stromateis* refered to above, where Clement reveals his method of scattering truth in his book in order to protect it from those unfit.[71] I called attention above to a similar conception in Heliodorus, for whom the deeper theological truth was also scattered in the Homeric verses. I also refered, however, to Maimonides' description of his own method of mixing on purpose his philosophical interpretations within the *Guide of the Perpexed*, in order to keep them hidden from those unable to stand truth. Since it is hard to imagine an influence of Clement's view upon Maimonides, I tentatively suggested a possible Jewish source for Clement's view. Origen's testimony about the Jewish origin of a very similar attitude strengthens this hypothesis.

The importance of Origen's testimony about the tradition received from "the Jew" has been recognized. Pierre Nautin, in particular, has insisted upon the "profound influence" of this Jewish master on Origen.[72] Yet, it seems that the similarity between Clement's method and that of Origen's Jewish master has remained hitherto unnoticed.

I have searched in vain for a precise parallel to this tradition of "the Jew" in early Rabbinic literature. The earliest trace of a similar metaphor is in an early medieval Hebrew commentary on *Song of Songs*, attributed to Sa'adya el Fayyumi, where the text is compared to locks whose keys have disappeared.[73] Of course, the lack of an earlier testimony is no argument against our hypothesis of an early

---

[71] *Strom.*, I. 9. 43; see above.

[72] P. Nautin, *Origène: sa vie et son oeuvre* (Christianisme antique 1; Paris: Beauchesne, 1977), 262-75, see esp. 268. See also Trigg, *Origen*, 88. Unfortunately, there is nothing on the Jewish origin of this tradition in Harl's commentary on *Philokalia*, II. 3 (pp. 250-59). On this passage, se also M. Harl, "Origène et les interprétations patristiques grecques de l'obscurité biblique", *VC* 36 (1982), 334-71.

[73] See E. E. Urbach, "The Homiletical Interpretations of the Sages and the Expositions of Origen on Canticles, and the Jewish-Christian Disputation", *Tarbiz* 16 (1945), 283, n. 50 (Hebrew). Urbach's article also appeared in an English translation in J. Heinemann and D. Noy, eds., *Studies in Aggadah and Folk-Literature* (Studia Hierosolymitana 22; Jerusalem: Magnes, 1971), 247-275. Cf. F. Y. Baer, "Israel, the Christian Church and the Roman Empire", in *Studia Hierosolymitana* 7 (1961), 99. The article was originally published in Hebrew in *Zion* 21 (1956), 1-49. The other part of the metaphor, the rooms, is found in a Spanish Kabbalistic text, and represents the multiplicity of the divine names. See Joseph Gikatilla, *Sha'arei Ora* (Jerusalem: Mossad Bialik, 1970), I, 55. I should like to thank Boaz Huss for calling my attention to this text. Cf. G. Scholem, *On the Kabbalah and its Symbolism* (New York: Schocken, 1965), 12-13: "This story ... may give an idea of Kafka's deep roots in the tradition of Jewish mysticism", adding that: "Another formulation of the same idea is frequent in the books of Lurianic Kabbalah."

Alexandrian Jewish esoteric tradition, applying to Biblical exegesis methods developed by the Homeric commentators.

3. True Judaism and Secret Christianity

The secret Judaism described above is the *philosophia perennis*, the tradition of wisdom carried by generations of sages. Origen thus speaks of a spiritual, or interior Judaism. The exterior Jew observes the Law; the interior Jew observes the spiritual Law in secret.

Origen's understanding of true or secret Judaism as identical to the essence of Christianity permits him to present a fresh picture of the origins of Christianity. John the Baptist, already, took care to keep his teaching oral, because of the secrecy involved:

> Moreover, what did "John teach his disciples" concerning prayer, as they came "unto him" to be "baptized" from "Jerusalem, and all Judea, and the region round about", unless it was that, being "much more than a prophet", he saw certain things concerning prayer which, I dare say, he delivered secretly (*aporrhêtôs*), not to all those who were being baptized, but to those who were under instruction as disciples for baptism?[74]

Referring to a passage of Plato's *Letter VII* quoted by Celsus, Origen argues that better than Plato, the Scriptures propound an esoteric doctrine. "... our prophets also had certain truths in their minds that were too exalted to be written down and which they did not record." Ezekiel and John swallowed a book lest they should divulge by writing secret doctrines, Paul heard "unspeakable words which it is not lawful for man to utter" (II Cor 12: 4). Origen adds: "Jesus, who was superior to all these men, is said to have spoken the Word of God to his disciples privately, and especially in places of retreat. But what he said has not been recorded." [75]

Jesus had preached in a synagogue because he wanted neither to dissociate himself from it nor to reject it.[76] It is not only his exoteric teaching to the crowd, but also his esoteric teaching to the disciples,

---

[74] *On Prayer*, II. 4 (243- 243 in Oulton' translation, in J. E. L Oulton and H. Chadwick, *Alexandrian Christianity* [Library of Christian Classics; Philadelphia: Westminster, 1954]).

[75] *Contra Celsum*, VI. 6 (320 Chadwick). On the 7 thunders in Rev 10: 4, cf. chapter 3 *supra*.

[76] *Com. Mat.* X. 16; (212 Girod).

which remained oral and was not committed to writing, that Jesus preached in the synagogue. The Evangelists did not write these teachings down, yet they say that these teachings were so great and so beautiful "that all were astonished; it is also probable that what he said was above what they wrote."

The parables, in particular, which can be easily understood by all, are for the crowd: " *multitudini foris in parabolis loquitur*".[77] Side by side with this exoteric teaching, however, Jesus has an esoteric doctrine which he reveals only to his disciples:

> Jesus spoke these to the people outside (*hôn tois exô*; cf. Mat 13: 36), and kept their explanation for those who had advanced beyond exoteric understanding (*tas exoterikas akoas*) and who came to him privately "in the house."[78]

So Origen states explicitly that Jesus offered a double teaching: He told stories with a common-sense moral for the simple ones, and offered hints of a deeper, more mystical understanding for the spiritual ones (*pneumatikoi*).[79]

The mysteries which Jesus had revealed to His disciples in secret and far from the ears of a crowd which had hardly heard them and had misunderstood them, he orders the disciples to announce to whomever will become light.[80] "Those who have become light" are, in usual Origenian parlance, "the perfect ones" (*hoi teleoi*). These perfect ones can discuss in detail the doctrines about Jesus.[81] By writing the Holy Scriptures in their hearts, they build for themselves a "spiritual Law."[82] The Son and the Holy Spirit are identical to the two cherubs standing above the arch of covenant, and they are said to know the divine secrets.[83]

---

[77] *Hom. Cant.*, II. 7 (O. Rousseau, ed., transl., *Origène, Homélies sur le Cantique des Cantiques* [SC 37; Paris: Cerf, 1953], 92).

[78] *C. Cels.*, III. 21 (140 Chadwick). On the exterior ones (cf. Mark 4: 11), see *Peri Archôn*, III. 1. 17 (200 Görgemanns- Karpp). See also *C. Cels.*, III. 46 (160 Chadwick); *Entretien avec Heraclide*, XV (86- 87 in J. Scherer, ed., transl., *Entretien d' Origène avec Héraclide* [SC 67; Paris: Cerf, 1960]); cf. *Com. Mat.*, X. 1 (140-145 Girod).
On the esoteric/exoteric teachings of Jesus, see further *C. Cels.*, III. 21 and III. 46 (140 and 160 Chadwick).

[79] See *Com. Mat.*, XI. 4. (280-287 Girod).

[80] *Com. Joh.*, II. 28. 173-174 (324-325 Blanc).

[81] Cf. I Cor 2: 6- 8; *C. Cels.*, III. 19 (139 Chadwick).

[82] *Peri Archôn*, IV. 2. 4 (708-709 Görgemanns-Karpp).

Paul, too, knew secrets which he could not reveal to everybody, but only to his closest disciples, Timothy, Luke, and those whom he knew able to receive the ineffable mysteries (*quos sciebat capaces esse ineffabilium sacramentorum*).[84] The importance of esoteric doctrines for Paul stems of course from the 'mysteric' vocabulary of the Pauline corpus, and in particular from the description of his ecstatic ascension to the third heaven (II Cor 12: 1-6).[85]

On Paul, one can refer also to the testimony of Eusebius:

> Thus Paul, the most powerful of all in the preparation of argument and the strongest thinker, committed to writing no more than short epistles, though he had ten thousand ineffable things to say, seeing that he had touched the vision of the third heaven, had been caught up to the divine paradise itself, and was there granted the hearing of ineffable words. Nor were the other pupils of our Saviour without experience of the same things.[86]

Origen speaks of an "intelligible and spiritual (*noètou kai pneumatikou*) Gospel", which implies that the literal level of the Gospels does not reveal the deepest levels of the text, and should be overcome. Above the exterior, public level, there is a Christianity "in the secret" . There are thus two levels of Christianity, just as there were two kinds of Judaism. The recognition of the existence of a secret or "hidden" Judaism, next to visible Judaism, is of a capital importance for Christianity, and the inability to recognize it is identified by Origen as the source of dualist heresy.[87] Christian Gnosis, therefore, in deep contrast to heretical Gnosis, recognizes its true Jewish nature.

Indeed, secret Christianity is also, in a sense, secret Judaism: above the public circumcision, there is a hidden one, and similarly a public and a hidden baptism. Paul and Peter were circumcised Jews in the flesh. They were also made secret Jews by Jesus, through both words

---

[83] *Peri Archôn*, IV. 3. 14 (776-779 Görgemanns-Karpp); this tradition Origen learnt from his Jewish teacher: "Nam et Hebraeus doctor ita tradebat" .

[84] *Hom. Jos.*, XXIII. 4 (466 Jaubert). Cf. *Com. Joh.*, XIII. 18, referring to I Cor 2: 7, on the esoteric teaching of Paul. Cf. the interpretation of the philosopher Jacob Taubes, for whom Paul saw himself as a new Moses, in his posthumous *Die politische Theologie des Paulus* (Munich: Fink, 1993).

[85] See C.R.A. Morray-Jones, "Transformational Mysticism in the Apocalyptic-Merkabah Tradition", *JJS* 43 (1992), 1-31, and his "Paradise Revisited (2 Cor 12:1-12): The Jewish Background of Paul's Apostolate", *HTR* 86 (1993), 177-217 (Part I), 265-292 (Part II).

[86] *H. E.*, III. 24. 4; (I, 250- 251 LCL).

[87] *Philokalia*, I. 30 (230-31 Harl).

and deeds. Paul, for instance, is said to have behaved as a Jew among Jews, in order to win Jews to the faith.[88] The same thing must be said of their Christianity.[89]

Two kinds of Christianity, open and secret, must therefore be practiced in order to win the greatest possible number of converts to the faith.[90] The two kinds of Christianity correspond to the two kinds of Christians. For Origen, the *simpliciores* believe only in the carnal Christ,[91] and are unable to understand His divine nature. In other words, they are similar to the (contemporaneous) Jews, who refuse to recognize the deeper meaning of their own writings.

It should be pointed out that a rather similar, though not identical conception of two levels of Christian teaching is found also elsewhere in early Christianity, for instance in the Syriac *Liber Graduum* (4th century), which makes a distinction between *justi* and *perfecti*, or in John Cassian, who insists on supererogation (which is different from Gnosis).[92] One must, however, insist on the originality of Origen's conception. By his daring parallel between two kinds of Judaism and two kinds of Christianity, he offers a vision of an esoteric and spiritual Christianity quite different from "religion for the masses", and almost unique in the history of Christian theology. But for Origen, esoteric Christianity, in contrast to the various Gnostic groups, should be careful not to cut links with the Christianity of the simple ones.

Conclusions

In Christian mysticism, eventually, the secret is interiorized, and the interior becomes spiritual.[93] Origen states explicitly that "one must understand in a secret sense (*kekrummenôs*)", otherwise one remains unable to understand the meaning of divine revelation.[94] Here Origen's

---

[88] *Com. Rom.*, II. 13 (VI. 122 Lommatzsch).

[89] *Com. Joh.*, I. 7. 41 (82-83 Blanc).

[90] *Com. Joh.*, I. 7. 43 (*id.*).

[91] *Com. Joh.*, II. 3. 29 (224-225 Blanc).

[92] A similar distinction between superficial and true Christians is found in Pseudo-Macarius, for instance *Hom.*, VII.6; see V. Desprez, ed., transl., Ps. Macaire, *Oeuvres Spirituelles* I (SC 275; Paris: Cerf, 1980), 132-137. On the origins of this idea, from Ignatius of Antioch through Origen and Gregory of Nyssa, see *ibid.*, 134, n. 1.

[93] See for instance M. Harl, *Philocalie 1- 20, Sur les Ecritures*, 133-135, on the transposition of metaphorical language.

[94] *Hom. Jer.* XII., 13 (on Jer 13: 17; 44-51 Husson-Nautin).

polemics against Jewish literalism reflects the remnant of earlier polemics. More precisely, this polemics takes with Origen a new meaning: he argues against the Rabbis about the inheritance of the deeper, esoteric Jewish tradition. Like Clement, Origen objects to Gnosis not so much its esotericism as the contradiction it implies or fosters between exoteric teaching, to the neophytes, and secret teaching.

For Daniélou, Origen's "gnosis" belongs to the same intellectual trend as dualist Gnosticism and "rabbinic Kabbalah".[95] This is of course a rather sweeping statement. Nonetheless, such a view seems closer to truth than that of Lebreton, for whom the esotericism of the Alexandrian Fathers stems from the mystery religions. Finally, it might be worth pointing out that the same attitude to "true Judaism", defined as the deepest, esoteric level of the message of Jesus, is also found, in a more developed form, in sixteenth century Christian Kabbalah. For the Christian Kabbalists from the Renaissance onwards, too, true Judaism, i. e. *verus Israel*, is already expressed in the secret traditional teachings of the Jews, which reveal the main tenets of Christian theology, such as Christology and trinitarianism.[96]

What did Origen know of Jewish esoteric doctrines? Probably rather little. After all, he did not know Hebrew.[97] But Origen knew two crucial facts about these doctrines: their existence and their importance. One usually assumes that it is mainly in Caesarea, where the mature Origen had almost daily contacts with Jews, including rabbis, that he learned most of what he knows about Judaism.[98] For instance, it

---

[95] Daniélou, *op. cit.*, 460.

[96] For a topical example, see Pico della Mirandola's famous *Oratio de Dignitate Hominis*, which refers to Origen's conception of Christ's esoteric doctrine and considers the Kabbalistic books to present a religion "non tam Mosaicam quam Christianam." I quote according to the new edition of O. Boulnois and G. Tognon, eds., Jean Pic de la Mirandole, *Oeuvres philosophiques* (Epiméthée; Paris: P.U.F., 1993), 66. This attitude was also partaken by the first modern scholars of Judaism, in the nineteenth century, such as August Friedrich Gfrörer, in his three-volume *Geschichte des Urchristenthums* (Stuttgart: Schweizerbart, 1838). Cf. G.G. Stroumsa, "Gnosis and Judaism in Nineteenth Century Thought", *Journal of Jewish Thought and Philosophy* 2 (1993), 45-62.

[97] See D. Barthélémy, "Est-ce Hoshaya Rabba qui censura le 'Commentaire allégorique'?", in *Philon d'Alexandrie* (Paris: CNRS, 1967), 45-78, reprinted in his *Etudes d'histoire du texte de l'Ancien Testament* (Fribourg, Göttingen: Ed. Univ., Vandenhoeck & Ruprecht, 1978), 140-73.

[98] See for instance P.M. Blowers, "Origen, the Rabbis, and the Bible: Toward a Picture of Judaism and Christianity in Third-Century Palestine", in Ch. Kannengiesser and W.L. Petersen, eds., *Origen of Alexandria: His World and His Legacy* (Christi-

stands to reason that he heard there about the four biblical passages most suited to an esoteric interptetation according to the rabbis. David Halperin argues that Origen learnt Rabbinic esoteric traditions in Caesarea, for instance about the Merkabah.[99] In any case, it is probable that Origen's knowledge and use of Rabbinic exegetical traditions "may largely have come to him sporadically and without system." [100] But another path, less often trodden, should also be mentioned. As we have seen in Clement's case, the Alexandrian milieu was also a multiform source of Jewish esoteric traditions. There too, Origen met Jews (including converts), such as "the Palestinian Jew" to whom he refers, who taught him various traditions. The integration of Platonism and Judaism, indeed, was an Alexandrian phenomenon.

Daniélou states that "à la différence de Clément, Origène s'intéresse à la tradition ésotérique juive plus qu'à la tradition chrétienne." [101] It is true that Origen, much more than Clement, recognizes the true origin of Christian esotericism, and is able, much more than his predecessor, to transform this esotericism into a mysticism, to interiorize the secrets, as it were, into the soul. The main differences between the two thinkers' conceptions of esotericism, therefore, far from being limited to style and tone, also reflect deep intellectual changes in their cultural contexts and frames of reference.

---

anity and Judaism in Antiquity 1; Notre Dame, Indiana: U. of Notre Dame, 1988), 96-116.

[99] D. Halperin, *The Faces of the Chariot: Early Jewish Responses to Ezekiel's Vision* (Tübingen: Mohr (Siebeck), 1988), 322-87.

[100] McGuckin, *art. cit.*, 13.

[101] Daniélou, *op. cit.*, 453.

CHAPTER EIGHT

MILK AND MEAT: AUGUSTINE AND THE END OF ANCIENT ESOTERICISM

1. Mysterium

Jesus Christ, truly God and truly man, who had died on the cross for the salvation of humankind and had been resurrected form the dead, offered salvation to all who believed in him. This simple and paradoxical proposition constituted the very kernel of Christianity. It was so radically novel in the ancient world that early Christian intellectuals found no better word to describe it than the Greek term *musterion*.[1] *Musterion* (or the Latin calque *mysterium*) was of course a very loaded word, which refered first and foremost to various cults inherited from ancient Greece and still extant, to some degree, under the empire. These cults, and hence the word, reflected a long tradition of esotericism: the cult was to be rendered to the deity in secret, or, more precisely, there remained an irradicable distinction between the inner circle and those who took no direct part in the cult.[2] Similar distinctions between esoteric and exoteric cultic behaviour are to be found in various cultures and religions of the ancient Mediterranean and the Near East, for instance those of Iran and Israel.[3]

Esoteric traditions in the ancient world, however, were not restricted to cultic practices (the *dromena*). Parallel to the *behaviour* specific to the group members, there was the *knowledge* of the insiders, not to be divulged to outsiders (the *legoumena*). This secret knowledge could

---

[1] The bibliography on the subject is immense. One of the most illuminating studies remains A. D. Nock, "Hellenistic Mysteries and Christian Sacraments", reprinted in his *Essays on Religion and the Ancient World*, II, Z. Stewart, ed. (Oxford: Clarendon, 1972), 791-820.

[2] See in particular W. Burkert, *Ancient Mystery Cults* (Cambridge, Ma., London: Harvard University Press, 1987).

[3] On Iranian esotericism, see esp. Sh. Shaked, "Esoteric Trends in Iranian Religion", *Proceedings of the Israel Academy of Sciences and Humanities*, 1967. On early Jewish esotericism, see for instance I. Gruenwald, "Two Types of Jewish Esoteric Literature from the Time of the Mishnah and the Talmud", in his *From Apocalypticism to Gnosticism* (Beiträge zur Forschung des alten Testaments und des antiken Judentums, 14; Frankfurt: Lang, 1988), 53-64.

either take the form of myths, of their deeper interpretation (while the story itself was known to all), or of philosophical or religious traditions. There were thus mainly two sorts of esotericism in the ancient world, of a cultual and of an intellectual nature. One could say that in a sense, society was divided in a two-tiered way, according to the knowledge of truth as well as cultural practices.

Now, both the faith and the cult of Christianity ran counter to such basic attitudes: the new religion was open to all, there was to be no difference between Jew and Greek, man and woman, free man and slave: the same redemption was offered to everyone. One of the earliest Christian writings asked that the prophecies be revealed to all: "Seal not the prophecy of this book: for the time is at hand." (Rev. 22: 10). While the inner logic of Christian soteriology was fundamentally anti-esoteric, it was also heir to the *koine* of religious esotericism briefly refered to above, both in the Greek and the Jewish traditions. The deep tension stemming from this dual inheritance is reflected throughout the first centuries of the new religion, and brought about the first, and perhaps also most serious crisis of its history, the Gnostic movement. Indeed, Gnosticism should to a great extent be understood as an outburst of esotericism in early Christianity, mainly through Jewish-Christian traditions.[4] Bernard McGinn has recently pointed out the fact that a major imprint of Gnosticism in the later history of Christian thought was the de-legitimation of esoteric patterns of thought: "...the most important effect that Gnosticism had on the subsequent history of Christian mysticism was to make esotericism of any sort suspect, especially an esotericism based on secret modes of scriptural interpretation." [5]

The Alexandrian Fathers, Clement and Origen, as well as Dydimus the Blind after them, testify to the important role played by esoteric trends in early Christian thought, which was far from limited to the Gnostic milieus.[6] The Christian cult itself retains traces of esoteric vocabulary and attitudes, as, for instance, the request that catechumens leave the church, and its gates be closed, before the eucharist is celebrated. Last but not least, the development of the

---

[4] See chapter 2 *supra.*

[5] McGinn, *The Foundations of Mysticism* (New York: Crossroads, 1991), 99.

[6] See for instance Christoph Riedweg, *Mysterienterminologie bei Platon, Philon und Klemens von Alexandrien* (Untersuchungen zur Antiken Literatur und Geschichte, 26; (Berlin, New York: De Gruyter, 1987). See further chapter 6 *supra.*

concept of *disciplina arcani* in the fourth century, a phenomenon still insufficiently understood, should be perceived in the light of Christian esotericism.[7]

For Leo Strauss, who devoted great efforts to the study of esoteric attitudes among Greek philosophers, Jewish and Muslim medieval philosophers, and also some European thinkers, such as Machiavelli, esotericism was the mark of ancient thought, and anti-esoteric attitudes reflected 'modernity'. Augustine, it has often been said, embodies within his towering personality the passage from Antiquity to the Middle Ages. He can be said to usher out the former, as it were, and to usher in the latter. It is therefore a fact of particular significance that the longest and the most important discussion of esotericism in Patristic literature is found in his writings. The chapters 96 to 98 of Augustine's *Sermons on the Gospel of John*, written after 418, have been characterized as "the most detailed and incisive investigation in Patristic writing of the dangers of esotericism" [8]. These three chapters, originally sermons, form a clear unity, a paradigmatic text which does not seem to have received the attention that it deserves. I know of only two studies dealing with it, and both, to my mind, misinterpret Augustine.[9] Augustine develops in this text a strong opposition to the cultivation of esoteric attitudes, which he claims, on various grounds, run against the grain of the Christian ethos. A close analysis of these three sermons should shed light on some paradoxical repercussions of the 'demoticization' [10] of culture and of religion in late antiquity.

---

[7] Besides the references in chapter 2, see V. Recchia, "L'arcano nell'iniziazione cristiana", *Annali della facolta di magistero dell' universita di Bari*, 4 (1965), 243-273.

[8] B. McGinn, *The Foundations of Mysticism*, 256. The text is found in *PL* 35, 1873-1885, and in the edition of Mayer, *CCL* 36 (1954). There exist translations in various languages. See A. di Bernardino, ed., *Patrologia*, III (Institutum Patristicum Augustinianum; Rome: Marietti, 1978), 374-375. I am quoting according to the translation of J. Gibbs and J. Innes in the *Library of the Nicene and Post Nicene Fathers*, VII. ser. I (New York, 1888, reprinted 1956), 371-380. For the dating of the various tractates, see A. M. La Bonnardière, *Recherches de chronologie augustinienne* (Paris: Etudes augustiniennes, 1965). According to her, the sermons 55-124 were composed between 419 and 420.

[9] See D. B. Capelle, "Le progrès de la connaissance religieuse d'après Saint Augustin", *Recherches de théologie ancienne et médiévale* 2 (1930), 410-419, and A. Kleinberg, " *De Agone Christiano*: the Preacher and his Audience", *JTS* 38 (1987), 16-33. Kleinberg deals with various texts showing the evolution of Augustine's views on the issue of what the preacher can refrain from revealing.

[10] I am using here the term coined by Aleida and Jan Assmann.

2. The text

Augustine begins his discussion with the juxtaposition of two seemingly contradictory Scriptural verses. In John 16: 12, we read: " I
have yet many things to say unto you, but ye cannot bear them now.
(*Adhuc multa habeo vobis dicere, sed non potestis portare modo*)" . This
Augustine reads against John 15: 15b: "for all things that I have heard
of my Father I have made known unto you. (*Omnia quae audivi a Patre
meo, nota feci vobis*)" Does Jesus reveal the whole truth about himself
and about God to his disciples, asks Augustine, or does he keep some
knowledge hidden? On the face of it, the two verses would seem to
reflect two opposite tendencies in the New Testament. This is of
course inacceptable for Augustine, who builds a remarkable hermeneutics in order to harmonize them.

Augustine's solution points to the fact that the two verses do not
describe two classes of men, but rather two moments in time. Indeed,
John 16: 13 reveals this chronological element: "Howbeit when he,
the Spirit of Truth, is come, he will guide you into all truth: for he
shall not speak of himself; but whatsoever he shall hear, *that* shall he
speak: and he will shew you things to come" . The Holy Spirit will
reveal the whole truth, but only when the time will be ripe. There is
only one truth revealed by God, and it is the same for all men and
women. But since not everyone can understand divine truth in all its
infinite richness, it is understood at different levels according to the
growth, or development, of each person. This growth Augustine describes in the first sermon as a growth in love (*charitas*), but this spiritual growth has direct epistemological connotations, since one cannot
know without being possessed by a desire for what is to be known.
Hence, a strong chronological parameter is introduced into the conception of *pistis*, simple faith, as a prerequisite for *gnosis*, the deeper
understanding of Christian doctrine, developed by Clement and
Origen, thus transforming it in a radical way: with time, the individual develops, and his understanding of truth is transformed with him.
One cannot speak anymore, as the Alexandrians did, of two classes
of Christians, the *gnostikoi* versus the *psychikoi*, or *simpliciores*. The lower
level of understanding of the divine realities should rather be conceived as a stage in the development of each individual, which, in
theory at least, should and can be overcome. Augustine recognizes
that there is a certain esotericism in Christianity since catechumens
are not told everything. But, he adds, this hiding of part of the truth

is pure pedagogy; it is temporary, as the status of catechumen itself, and its purpose is to kindle the desire to know more: "in order that they (i. e. the things written after the Lord's ascension) may all the more ardently be desired by them (i. e. the catechumens), they are honorably concealed from their view" (96.3, *in finem*).

In opposition to the absence of secret doctrine in Christianity, Augustine describes in the second sermon the "doctrine of the magical arts with its nefarious rites", which is established on their esoteric teaching by "profane teachers" (97.3). The spiritual growth of the individual, and hence his ability to understand the deepest mysteries of Christian truth, is based upon *charitas*. In contradistinction, the seduction power of the perverse teachers of false secrets is grounded in the *curiositas* of undeveloped minds, still unable to differentiate between good and evil, and a fortiori between truth and falsehood. These people want in their *hubris* to hear what they cannot yet understand and hence are willing to believe seducers with false pretences of science.[11]

In the third sermon, Augustine comes back to the fundamental question: do spiritual people hide their doctrine, or at least some of its aspects, from those who are only "carnals" ? Returning to the seemingly opposed verses refered to at the beginning of his discussion, he offers a clear-cut answer. No, there is no need in Christianity for a secret doctrine, and no possibility of one. The public character of the Christian kerygma insures that only one truth is revealed. If everybody hears the same kerygma, however, not everyone understands the divine mysteries in the same way. Those who are unable to understand what they do not see, i. e. those who are "carnals" rather than " spirituals", understand at a lower, simpler, more concrete and less spiritual level. Following Paul, (I Cor 3: 1-2) Augustine identifies them with babes only able to digest milk. Those who have reached the level of "spirituals", on the other hand, are similar to adults able to digest solid foods, in particular meat. Hence, "Christ crucified is both milk to the sucklings and meat to the more advanced" (98.6).

---

[11] To be sure, Augustine does not use the word.

3. Portare

"I have yet many things to say unto you, but ye cannot bear (portare) them now." How does Augustine understand *portare*? "It may be, indeed, that some among you are fit enough already (*jam*) to comprehend things which are still (*nondum*) beyond the grasp of others" (96.1). Augustine clearly insists on the changes happening with time to the knowledge of the individual. Let us also note that he thinks in terms of a community, and of the responsibility of the teacher to teach at different levels at the same time. Similarly, "...many can now (*jam*) bear those things when the Holy Spirit has been sent." It is only thanks to the Holy Spirit that some points of doctrine may be "borne". As Augustine writes a little further: "For why could [Jesus' disciples] not bear then what is now read in their books, and borne by every one, even though not understood?" (96.3).

To bear, in this sense, is to accept, and the believers accept the veracity of the Scriptures even when they do not understand every single verse. Those who do not accept the Scriptures in their literal sense, on the other side, are the unbelievers and heretics of all kinds. They object to what they do not understand, and reject it as being untrue; they are unable to accept the *mysterium*, that which remains beyond the limits of their understanding. Pagans, Jews, Sabellians, Arians, Photinians, Manichaeans "and all other heretics" object to some aspect of Christology, and hence "cannot bear" the Scriptures (*utique ferrre non possunt, quidquid in Scripturis Sanctis et in fide catholica repetitur*). The Christians on their side "cannot bear their sacrilegious vaporings and mendacious insanities (*sicut nos ferre non possumus sacrilegas eorum vanitates et insanias mendaces*)" (96.3). Toleration of stubborn error, indeed, is not a virtue encouraged by Augustine. In other words, Augustine refers here to two opposite kinds of things which cannot be borne: "the evil things which no human modesty can endure" and "the good things which man's little understanding is unable to bear" (96.5).

To those who are still unable to 'bear' the most sublime aspects of Christian doctrine, Augustine recommends that they should transform themselves by growing in the love of what is only partially known and not fully understood. Through the growth of love "one is led on to a better and fuller knowledge" (96.4). This fuller knowledge of God is not brought by 'outward teachers', but by 'that inward teacher' (*interior magister*), i.e. the Holy Spirit, through whom "we shall attain also to the actual fullness of knowledge" . The inner teacher, in other words, guides us in the recognition of spiritual realities, "scarcely perceivable by the pure mind" (96.5).

4. Spiritual Growth

This growth of love, effected by the 'inward teacher', is not a growth in space; it is of a spiritual, not of a physical nature, a growth of the mind, or of the inner man, "that of an illuminated understanding":

> *In ipsa ergo mente, hoc est in interiore homine, quodammodo crescitur, non solum ut ad cibum a lacte transeatur, verum etiam ut amplius atque amplius cibus ipse sumatur* (97.1, *in finem*).

It is through this spiritual growth, therefore, that the believer can reach, beyond faith, a better understanding of Christian mystery, of the nature of Jesus Christ. Through it he moves, as it were, from the status of a baby, who can be fed only milk, to that of an adult, who can eat solid foods, and in particular meat. This spiritual growth is also a progress in love, through which men can climb on the ladder of understanding. Augustine insists on the dialectical relationship between love and knowledge. In a sense, it may be noted, love is close to faith, *fides*, and stands in the same relationship with knowledge.[12] Although one cannot love what is totally unknown, only love offers the drive to a better and fuller knowledge (96.4). Through spiritual growth, one can love more what was already known, and long after what is still unknown, i. e. spiritual matters, "that life which eye hath not see" (97.1). *Charitas* may here be described as a truly *erotic* force.

Here Augustine clearly paraphrases Paul:

> And I, brethren, could not speak unto you as unto spiritual, but as unto carnal, even as unto babes in Christ. I have fed you with milk, and not with meat: for hitherto ye were not able to bear it, neither yet now are ye able (I Cor 3: 1-2).

Other references to these verses and to the metaphor of the milk and the meat are found elsewhere in Augustine's writings.[13] Similarly,

---

[12] On the relationship between faith and knowledge for Augustine, see esp. *Epistle* 147.

[13] For references, see Capelle, "Le progrès de la connaissance religieuse", 416, n. 10.

various references to I Cor 3: 1-2 occur in Patristic literature before the fourth century.[14] Yet in most of these allusions or references, there seems to be no emphasis on esotericism, the only exception I was able to find being in Origen's *Homilies on Genesis*.[15] The Pauline conception of the difference between *pneumatikoi* and *sarkinoi* as reflecting degrees of spiritual growth is at the core of Augustine's thought in our text. The difference can be described as of a spiritual nature, but only if we understand this as inclusive of intellectual perception: "you still have minds that are incompetent to discriminate between the true and the false", he says to those who "are still children" (97.2). This trait should be underlined: the ability to differentiate between truth and falsehood is an intellectual capacity, which comes at the end of a process. Beginners are only able to distinguish good from evil (98.7). Ethics seems to be here of a lower value than intellectual ability. Or rather, faith, even without understanding, offers everyone the possibility of being able to distinguish good from evil; "Grow in the ability to distinguish good from evil, and cleave more and more to the Mediator, who delivers you from evil" (98.7).

5. *Against secrecy*

Is this conception similar to that of the Alexandrian school, for which there is a deep difference between the *pistis* of the simple and the *gnosis* of the advanced? Not quite, it would seem, since for Augustine the passage from the one to the other is, at least in theory, a matter of education, and is acquired with time. It is through the exercise of the "inner senses of the mind" that one passes from belief to understanding, " *Quod profecto quisquis non solum credit, verum etiam exercitatis interioribus animi sensibus intelligit, percepit, novit*" (98.4). The description of faith, however, as belonging to the moral sphere, and this sphere as possessed of a lower status than that of pure understanding, seems to reflect Augustine's esoteric (or Gnostic) as well as Neoplatonic heritage. What is of particular interest in our present context is precisely that fact: Augustine's criticism of esotericism is that of an

---

[14] See for instance Clement, *Stromateis*, V. 10. 66 (134-135 Le Boulluec, [SC 278; Paris: Cerf, 1981]).

[15] Origène, *Homélies sur la Genèse*, XIV. 4; L. Doutreleau, ed. transl., (SC 7bis; Paris: Cerf, 1976), 344-346. Origen also refers to I Cor 2: 6-10: wisdom is to be preached only among the *teleioi*.

insider, or at least of someone close to the presuppositions of esoteric patterns of thought.

A puzzling parallel in the use of the same metaphor is found in Maimonides's *Guide of the Perplexed*. Maimonides warns the intellectual beginner not to study divine science, which would do him more harm than good:

> In my opinion, an analogous case would be that of someone feeding a suckling with wheaten bread and meat and giving him wine to drink. He would undoubtedly kill him...[16]

Yet the difference between Augustine and Maimonides is fundamental: for the latter, divine science is the study and deciphering of the riddles which protect the hidden sides of Scriptures. These are called, hence, "secrets and mysteries of the Torah". It is striking that Maimonides uses the same metaphor as Augustine, but he does so in order to convey a position quite opposite to that of Augustine as to the desirability of esoteric traditions.

For Augustine there is no need to keep secret the more subtle and spiritual sides of divine doctrine, which are hence more difficult to understand. He who is still lower on the ladder of understanding will "receive them according to the slender level of his capacity" (98.3). No harm will be done to him, and hence "there seems no necessity for any doctrine being retained in silence as secrets, and concealed from infant believers" (*ibid.*). For although Christ reveals Himself to all, He does not appear in the same way to all. Only in a subjective sense can we speak of a 'polymorphy' of Christ, since His appearence depends on the intellectual level of the believer: Christ's flesh

> does not present itself to the minds of the carnal in the same manner as to that of the spiritual, and so to the former it is milk, and to the latter it is meat. For if they do not hear more than others, they understand better (*quia si non audiunt amplius, intellegunt amplius*). For the mind has not

---

[16] *Guide*, I. 33; cf. I. 34, *in finem*, and III. 32, where Maimonides uses the metaphor of milk and meat in order to describe the steps of revelation in history, an *Erziehung des Menschengeschlechts*, to use Lessing's phrase. Such a historical dimension is absent from Augustine's use of the metaphor. The idea that God reveals himself according to the strength of men in general, and to that of each individual in particular, is already found in Philo. See for instance *De Opificio Mundi*, 6: 23. The same theme is also found in the Midrash (see for instance *Mekhilta de-Rabbi Ismael, Parashat Jethro*, 6, and *Exodus Rabba*, 5: 9) it then becomes commonplace in Kabbalistic thought; I should like to thank Boaz Huss for calling my attention to these texts.

equal powers of perception even for that which is equally received by both in faith (98.2).

Christ is thus perceived mainly in His human aspect by the simple believers, while the more advanced understand better His divine nature (98.6): "Christ crucified is both milk to the sucklings and meat to the more advanced" (*ibid.*). Similarly, those who can only perceive Christ's humanness will know Him as Mediator, while those able to recognize His divine aspect will know Him as Creator (*ibid.*). The polarity between these two aspects of the divinity, with the soteriological aspect being the lower one, is worth noting. One could compare it to the Rabbinic polarity between the two sides or *middot* of God, the *middat ha-raḥamim* (YHWH) vs. the *middat ha-din* (Elohim). Furthermore, it is remarkable that these two sides of the divinity, love and justice, are also found in Marcion's thought, but in an reversed hierarchical order: for Marcion, the Just God is lower than the Loving God.

Augustine concludes his argument against the need for esotericism:

> what both [the 'sucking' and the 'advanced'] heard in the same measure when it was publicly spoken, each apprehended in his own measure, *sed quod eodem modo utrique cum palam diceretur audiebant, pro suo modo quique capiebant* (98.2).

This point is crucial in order to understand the foundations of Augustine's reasonning. The lack of esotericism in Christian doctrine is a direct consequence of the character of revelation. Christian *kerugma* is public by nature. The divine revelation and good tidings were proclaimed to all. This is a totally public message. Hence:

> there seems to be no necessity for any matter of doctrine being retained in silence as secrets, and concealed from infant believers, as things to be spoken apart to those who are older, or possessed of a riper understanding; *nulla videtur esse necessitas, ut aliqua secreta doctrinae taceantur, et abscondantur fidelibus parvulis, seorsum dicenda maioribus, hoc est intelligentioribus* (98.3).

These strong statements are quite explicit: there are no doctrines reserved for the advanced, and which should be hidden from the simple ones. Capelle's interpretation of our text is basically correct, yet his statement that one should offer the simple believer the result of theological reflexion "dans la mesure convenable" [17] would appear a little careless, in the sense that it implies that part of this reflexion is with-

held from him. Similarly, Kleinberg sees the main difference between
the two levels of teaching, that to the simple and that to the advanced, as consisting in the addition of data which do not contradict
the lower level, though they deeply change its meaning.[18] Our text
does not seem to permit such an interpretation.

Another character of the revelation which stems from its public
nature is its linguistic form. Although Augustine does not discuss the
language of revelation in our text, he deals with it elsewhere. It is on
purpose that the Gospels are written in popular, rather than in ele-
gant or sublime language. God spoke a language that anyone could
understand, with no riddles and need for constant interpretation. The
Gospels, in opposition to pagan religious texts (i.e., first and foremost,
to the Homeric epics and to Greek mythology) retain a profound
meaning even when understood literally. This is the conception of the
Sermo Humilis, so well studied by Erich Auerbach.[19]

6. Curiositas

As we have seen, it is through a careful process of education that men
reach understanding of spiritual matters, which are difficult because
they are removed from sense perception. Augustine, like anyone else
in antiquity, knows of the dangers inherent in a knowledge imparted
to those who are not fit to hear it. But he understands this knowledge
in what seems tto be a radically new way. These dangers do not lie in
the misinterpretation of truth itself by those who are not fit to hear it,
but in their willingness to listen to false doctrines, to various false
pretentions to truth, hiding under its noble name. At the early stages
of its intellectual and spiritual development, the mind is unable to
recognize truth from falshood. Sometimes, however, the individual is
not disciplined enough to follow the path leading from faith to understanding, but wishes to take shortcuts to a full knowledge of truth.[20]
The impulse to know in such an undisciplined way Augustine calls
curiositas.

---

[17] Capelle, "Le progrès de la connaissance religieuse", 419.

[18] Kleinberg, " *De Agone Christiano*", 30. Kleinberg refers here to *In Johan.* 6 (CCSL 36. 579).

[19] " *Sermo Humilis*" is reprinted, in English translation, in E. Auerbach, *Literary Language and its Public in Late Latin Antiquity and the Middle Ages* (London: Routledge and Kegan Paul, 1965).

Hans Blumenberg has called attention to the classical roots of *curiositas* in Augustine's thought, particularly in Cicero's and Seneca's writings.[21] Yet, as is well known, Augustine gave a new meaning and importance to the term. The grounds for this new meaning are reflected in our text: a crucial role attributed to psychology, combined with a deeply pessimistic view of human motives. Opposed to the inward teacher of truth, the Holy Spirit, there are evil teachers, who convey profane teachings to those who are still immature. They flatter and seduce them through pretenses of secrecy, letting them believe that they are made privy to deeper levels of truth, ignored by most men:

> For by such secrecy profane teachers give a kind of seasoning to their poisons for the curious, that thereby they may imagine that they learn something great, because counted worthy of holding a secret ... (97.2)

These secrets, thus, are "unlawful and punishable" (97.3). Such an esotericism is "not only alien to the reality, but also to the very name of our religion", states Augustine (97.3), and the vehemence of his language indicates that his argument is not only theoretical, but directed against heretics, who claim to be Christians while propounding ideas which run counter to Christian ethos.[22] And indeed his indignation is made explicit against "all these senseless heretics who wish to be styled Christians". Those brought by the impulse of *curiositas* to listen to such false teachings are guilty of nothing less than "lusting after spiritual fornication" (97.4). This *curiositas*, through which they believe the lies of outward teachers, keeps them prisonners of their senses. It is, precisely, a *libido cognoscendi*. They are still unable to recognize the existence of spiritual realities and to believe in the existence of invisible things which they do not see, and conceive good and evil to be substances. Hence, they become easy prey to false claims of scientific explanations of the universe, according to which even God

---

[20] Here too, there are clear parallels in Maimonides.

[21] H. Blumenberg, " *Curiositas* und *veritas*: zur Ideengeschichte von Augustin, *Confessiones* X, 35", in *Studia Patristica* VI, 4, (TU 81; Berlin: Akademie Verlag, 1962), 294-302.

[22] Also elsewhere in Patristic literature, heretics are described as carrying esoteric doctrines. See for instance Jerome, *Comm. in Ionam*, III. 6-9 (CCSL 76, 407-408, quoted by D. Satran, "The Salvation of the Devil: Origen and Origenism in Jerome's Biblical Commentaries", *Studia Patristica* 23 (Leuven: Peeters, 1990), 172-173; see also n. 17, p. 401-402 on parallel accusations of esotericism among heretics.

is material, and endowed with a body. One is reminded here of Kantian epistemology: the basic mistake is the application to extra-sensorial reality of a reasonning valid only within the realm of the senses. Augustine names here his old enemies, the Manichaeans of his youth (98.4). We recognize the core of his argumentation against them, as it appears in the *Confessions* and elsewhere. According to his own testimony, it is only through his recognition of the existence of spiritual substances, thanks to the influence of his Neoplatonist friends in Cassiciacum, that he was able in his youth to break the spell of the false scientific pretenses of Manichaean mythology. The old bishop retains the main thrust of the analysis he had developed many years previously.

"False science", however, is not limited to the Manichaeans. It is also found among all those heretics who claim to offer an interpretation of the Holy Scriptures which is better and deeper than that of the Church tradition. They do that through "profane novelties of words (*profanas verborum novitates*, II Tim 2: 16)", the coining of new words which do not reflect religious reality, such as the *Patris homoousios* of the wicked Arians (97.4). Heresy, indeed, is characterized by a misunderstanding of Scripture by unbelievers, *who cannot bear not to understand* the text, and offer forced interpretations: such are pagans, Jews, Sabellians, Arians, Photinians, Manichaeans "and all others of divers perverse sects" (96.3).

Although so many different kinds of rejection of early Christian orthodoxy are mentioned together, most of the 'heretics' in this list did not develop an esoteric theology. Augustine seems here to be carried away by his rhetoric. The main thrust of Augustine's attack against the perversion of Christian *kerugma* through esotericism is clearly directed against the Manichaeans, in whose thelogy esotericism played a major role, as it had in the doctrines of the early Gnostics. Hence, Augustine's insistence on faith before understanding reflects the tradition of Christian intellectuals, since Clement of Alexandria, in their fight against the dualist Gnostics.

The Augustinian opposition to the 'false science' of the Manichaeans, however, seems to have soon been perceived as a deep mistrust of epistemic research, tainted as this research was by *curiositas*. That Augustine was no fideist needs no further demonstration. For him, faith is the first, necessary step towards understanding, *fides quaerens intellectum*. The question, however, remains: Could Augustine be partly responsible for what is often perceived as the medieval

Christian rejection of, or at least lack of interest in science? In a remarkable article, Carlo Ginzburg has sought the roots of "the theme of forbidden knowledge in the sixteenth and seventeenth centuries" in a semantic mutation dating from the fourth century, in the meaning of *sapere*, as quoted from Rom 11: 20, "Be not highminded, but fear, *noli altum sapere, sed time*", in Jerome's Vulgate.[23] While *sapere* originally had a moral meaning ('to be wise'), it became endowed from the fourth century on with an intellectual one ('to know'). Ginzburg, who was able to document this semantic shift, could not identify the reasons for its occurence.

Through their grand battle against Gnosticism in its various garbs, the Church Fathers developed a suspicious attitude towards claims of higher knowledge made by marginal groups or individuals. The main protection of Christian truth against attempts of perversion from all sides lies precisely in the public character of the *keryuma*.

7. 'Demoticization' of religion

On various levels, Christianity launched in the ancient world a radical 'demoticization of religion'. This demoticisation is not only reflected in the breaking down of traditional ethnic, social and sexual barriers, but also in its very language. The popular language of the Christian writings, which shocked pagan intellectuals, reflected its very strength: the revelation was open to all, fishermen as well as philosophers. It is in their apologetical writings that Christian intellectuals, from the second century on, first developed the idea of the superiority of simplicity over the sophisticated language of Hellenic literature: the defenders of the new religion proudly defended the *philosophia barbarum*.[24]

Another argument was being developed concurrently by the heresiologists against the Gnostics: Christian revelation was not only couched in simple terms; its popular language also reflected the universality of the single truth it revealed. In early Christian thought,

---

[23] C. Ginzburg, "High and Low: the Theme of Forbidden Knowledge in the Sixteenth and Seventeenth Centuries", *Past and Present* 73 (1976), 28-41.

[24] See G.G. Stroumsa, "Philosophy of the Barbarians: on Early Christian Ethnological Representations", in H. Cancik, ed., *Festschrift Martin Hengel* (Tübingen: Mohr [Siebeck], 1996.

anti-esotericism thus reflects the demotic character of the new religion.

But Christianity did not exhibit only demotic aspects. To some extent, it shows a return to priestly aspects which were disappearing from Judaism soon after the destruction of the Temple. The transformed Palestinian Judaism represented in many ways a 'demoticization' of religion. Christian sacrificial language and the role of the priest in the transmission of the apostolic tradition, reflect the hierarchy and the Church elite being built in early Christianity. Although esoteric doctrines were soon chased away thanks to the Gnostic abuses, cultic practices retained much longer, and cultivated, allusions to esoteric patterns of religious thought. Hence, in particular, the development of *disciplina arcani* in the fourth century refered to above.

In a paradoxical or dialectical way, it is through its fight against the esoteric *arcana dei* that early Christian thought developed the concept of *arcana naturae*, of the secrets of nature better left unsearched, since they are irrelevant to salvation. Christian soteriology was established upon the paradoxical reversal of traditional thought patterns: the humility of Christ was hidden to the wise, while it had been revealed to the small ones.

The blossoming Christian culture could not be established upon any secret knowledge only imparted to the elite. It soon became grounded in the exegesis of Scripture, at its two levels, the deeper sense of Old Testament having been already deciphered in the New Testament. More than any other text, it is Augustine's *de Doctrina Christiana* that established the hermeneutical parameters of this new culture. The book can be described as the cornerstone of the western medieval intellectual world. The unending interpretation of the *mysterium* had definitively taken the place of the preservation of the *secretum*. Only the language of the mysteries of old had not completely disappeared. Its traces can be detected in the vocabulary of Christian mysticism.

CHAPTER NINE

FROM ESOTERICISM TO MYSTICISM IN EARLY CHRISTIANITY

The complex question of Early Christian esotericism, its nature and its fate, has been dealt with repeatedly since the seventeenth century.[1] It remains, however, a notoriously vexing problem of religious history, at least in part because the emphasis has been put on cult, to the neglect of esoteric *traditions*. In this chapter, I shall try to focus on the *disappearance* of the early esoteric traditions from ancient Christianity and some of its implications.

I shall first briefly review some of the evidence pointing to the existence of esoteric trends in the earliest strata of Christianity (an existence still ignored or played down by some scholars), then discuss the reasons for their disappearance from mainstream Christian thought.[2] Finally, I shall call attention to the fact that the language of esotericism, and in particular *termini technici* such as *musterion* (Lat. *mysterium*), once emptied of any esoteric reference, became key-words of Christian mysticism in the making. This semantic transformation reflects, to my mind, some deep changes in religious sensitivity and the new subjectivity that was crystallising at the outset of the ancient world. Since I have argued some of these points in the preceding chapters, the evidence will not be brought here in a systematic or exhaustive way, but mainly for illustrative purposes.

1. Early Christian esotericism

a. Cult

Renaissance thinkers such as Pico della Mirandola conceived the truth of revealed religions as reflecting a *theologia pristina*, which had been known since the dawn of humankind to the sages of all nations,

---

[1] For a recent and thorough bibliography, see Christoph Jacob, *"Arkandisziplin'*, *Allegorese, Mystagogie: Ein neuer Zugang sur Theologie des Ambrosius von Mailand* (Theophaneia, 32; Frankfurt a. M.: A. Hain, 1990), 13 -32.

[2] On these trends, see Chapter 2 *supra*.

but veiled in the garbs of their various myths, so that it would remain
hidden from those unable or unfit, intellectually or morally, to grasp
them properly.[3] This original and universal truth could in the course
of history have taken the form of either the secret doctrines of the
Egyptian priests (expressed in the hieroglyphs), Kabbalah, the doctrines of Zoroaster, or those of Hermes Trismegistus. In any case, this
attitude paved the way for a belief among early modern thinkers that
the deepest message of Jesus was also secret by nature, and had been
expressed at two levels, the first, exoteric, for the crowd, and the second, esoteric, revealed only to the inner circle of the disciples. This
idea of an esoteric kernel of Christian doctrine was picked up during
the seventeenth century polemics between Catholics and Protestants
about the true nature of Christianity and the causes of its perversion.
Since that time, scholars have been aware of various esoteric trends
in early Christianity. Born of religious polemics, however, the debate
has often been phrased more in theological than in historical terms:
was it true that the very ethos of Christianity, which offered salvation
for all, prevented or forbade the development of any kind of secret
doctrine or practice? If this were the case, then any kind of esotericism would reflect heresy, rather than the true doctrine of Christ and
his apostles.

   Isaac Casaubon, who was the first to work on the question of the
relationship between 'mystery-terminology' and early Christian use of
the term *musterion*, strongly influenced Jean Daillé's conception of a
disciplina arcani in the first Christian centuries.[4] For these Protestant
scholars, the development of esoteric doctrines or of secret cultic
practices in early Christianity reflected the corruption of the earliest
Christian *kerugma* by the Catholic Church.

   Since then, the idea that one can detect esoteric trends and traditions in early Christianity has appealed to many scholars, but the
problem is still too often formulated within the parameters set by its
first students.[5] In particular, the existence of esoteric traditions, or of

---

   [3] See Ch.B. Schmitt, " *Prisca theologia e philosophia perennis*: due termi del Rinascimento italiano e la loro fortuna", in G. Tarugi, ed., *Il pensiero italiano del Rinascimento
e il tempo nostro* (Florence: Olschki, 1970), 211-236.

   [4] Casaubon's *De rebus sacris et ecclesiastis exercitationes XVI* was published in 1614.
Daillé's *De scriptus quae sub Dionysii Areopagitae circumferentur* appeared in Geneva in
1666. On both, see J.Z. Smith, *Drudgery Divine: on the Comparison of Early Christianities
and the Religions of Late Antiquity* (Chicago: Univ. of Chicago Press, 1991), 54 ff.

   [5] A milestone in scholarship is N. Bonwetsch, "Wesen, Entstehung und Fortgang
der Arkandisziplin", *Zeitschrift für historische Theologie* 43 (1873), 203-299.

layers of the cult, in early Christianity were seen almost exclusively within the context of the Hellenistic mystery cults. I say 'cults', since, as Walter Burkert has recently reminded us, the mysteries were options within the general and vague framework of Greco-Roman paganism, rather than full-fledged religions.[6]

Christianity was born and first grew in a world in which esotericism, religious as well as philosophical, was rife. In the ancient world, it was common for religious groups to define and protect themselves by keeping various sets of beliefs or/and cultic practices secret, to remain unseen or unheard by outsiders. This seems to have been the case around the Mediterranean, as well as throughout the cultures and religions of the Near East.

In the Greek world, at least, it is hard to distinguish clearly between the religious and the intellectual dimensions of ancient esotericism.[7] After all, 'truth' (*alètheia*) retained soteriological dimensions in the thought of the Greek philosophers. This phenomenon is particularly clear, of course, in the case of the Pythagoreans, but not only in their case. The 'masters of truth', as Marcel Detienne has called them, were conscious of the marginal character of their trade, and of its explosive potential. Hence, they took great precautions when expressing their perception of truth: one should weigh carefully to whom, and how, to reveal it. For a proper understanding of secret traditions, it is imperative to recognize the major role played by the ambiguous status of literacy in the ancient world for a proper understanding of secret traditions. Such traditions should be transmitted orally, and not committed to writing, a fact emphasized, in particular, by Plato's second *Letter*.[8]

---

[6] This is the main argument of his *Ancient Mystery Cults* (Cambridge, Ma.: Harvard University Press, 1987); for a recent appraisal of this work, see for instance G. Casadio, "I misteri di Walter Burkert", *Quaderni Urbinati di Cultura Classica*, N. S. 40 (1992), 155-160.

[7] See for instance A.H. Armstrong, "The Hidden and the Open in Helllenic Thought", *Eranos Jahrbuch* 54 (Frankfurt a. M.: Insel Verlag, 1987), 81-117, reprinted in his *Hellenic and Christian Studies* (London: Variorum, 1987). See also J. Pépin, "L'arcane religieux et sa transposition philosophique dans la tradition platonicienne", in *La storia della filosofia come sapere critico* (Milan: Franco Angeli, 1984), 18-35 (*non vidi*).

[8] See Th.A. Szlezák, *Platon und die Schriftlichkeit der Philosophie: Interpretationen zu den frühen und mittleren Dialogen* (Berlin, New York: de Gruyter, 1985), and F. Jürss, "Platon und die Schriftlichkeit", *Phil.* 135 (1991), 167-176; this reference is provided by H. D. Betz, "Secrecy in the Greek Magical Papyri", in *Secrecy and Concealment*, 169, n. 59.

Philosophical esotericism, however, played a less prominent role in the development of religious secret practices than the so-called mystery cults, which grew particularly during the Hellenistic times. These cults have traditionally been seen as the proximate channels through which the vocabulary and the practice of secrecy in religious cult reached Christianity.

Indeed, it is mainly to the Hellenistic 'mysteries' that the Christian *musterion* has been compared.[9] The postulated massive influence of the mystery cults on the origins of the Christian *arcana* has brought scholars seeking to understand the nature of early Christian esotericism to insist on cultic activities, (the *dromena* of the Greek mysteries), rather than on esoteric teachings (the *legoumena*)[10]. The obvious linguistic dependence here encouraged such an orientation in research, which has led to many interesting and important studies, particularly on the 'Mystery-terminology' in Patristic literature and on the so-called *disciplina arcani*, reflecting the secret element in Christian cult and its theoretization.[11] In this regard, however, one should heed to the *caveat*

For a basic bibliography, see Armstrong, art. cit., who points out (p. 99) that the term *esoterikos* appears relatively late, while Pierre Hadot remarks that *mustikos* is used sparingly by philosophers (see B. McGinn, *The Foundations of Mysticism* [New York: Continuum, 1991], 42). On oral and written traditions in early Christianity, see B. Gerhardsson, *Memory and Manuscript: Oral Tradition and Written Transmission in Rabbinic Judaism and Early Christianity* (Acta Seminarii Neotest. Uppsaliensis, 22; Uppsala, Lund: Gleerup, 1961).

[9] Among classical studies, one should mention at least those of A. Loisy, *Les mystères païens et le mystère chrétien* (Paris, 1913), and K. Rahner "Christliche Mysterium und die heidnischen Mysterien", *Eranos Jahrbuch* 11 (1944), 347-449, reprinted in his *Griechische Mythen in christlicher Deutung* (Zurich: Rhein Verlag, 1945), 21-72, and A. D. Nock, "Hellenistic Mysteries and Christian Sacraments", *Mnemosyne* 25 (1953), 177-213, reprinted in his *Essays on Religion and the Ancient World*, ed. Z. Stewart (Oxford: Clarendon, 1972), II, 791-820. See now C. Colpe, "Mysterienkult und Liturgie: zum Vergleich heidnischer Rituale und christlicher Sakramente", in C. Colpe, L. Honnefelder, M. Lutz-Bachmann, eds., *Spätantike und Christentum* (Berlin: Akademie Verlag, 1992), 203-228.

[10] There was no dogma at Eleusis, as Burkert reminds us in his *Homo Necans: the Anthropology of Ancient Greek Sacrificial Ritual and Myth* (Berkeley...: Univ. of California Press, 1983), 294

[11] Among the newer works, see especially Christoph Riedweg, *Mysterienterminologie bei Platon, Philon und Klemens von Alexandrien* (Untersuchungen zur antiken Literatur und Geschichte, 26; Berlin, New York, W. de Gruyter, 1987). For the growing influence of mystery cults terminology, see H.D. Betz, "Magic and Mystery in the Greek Magical Papyri", in Ch.A. Faraone and D. Obbink, eds., *Magika Hiera: Ancient Greek Magic and Religion* (New York, Oxford: Oxford University Press, 1991), 244- 259.

of J.Z. Smith, who argues that much of the past and current work done on terminology, particularly that work which insists on the 'mysteric' terminology of Judaism, is flawed, since it ignores the vast differences between the contexts within which this vocabulary appears.[12] In any case, there has been for some time a prevalent feeling that no satisfactory answer has yet been offered to the question of the existence of an early Christian esoteric teaching.

b. Doctrine

In his seminal article, "Pagan Mysteries and Christian Sacraments", A.D. Nock insisted on the long transformation of the language of secrecy in the Greek cultural orbit. According to him, *musterion* was first of all defined in in Hellenic literature in cultic terms, and reflected secret *rites*, more than ideas. Moreover, he noted that in many cases the use of the term *musterion* was only a "façon de parler".[13] He argued convincingly that the evidence drawn from the semantic connections between Greek pagan and Christian vocabularies was not quite compelling, and drew attention, rather, to the vocabulary of Hellenistic Judaism. It was chiefly from Biblical Greek, for instance, that *musterion* "took the additional sense of 'something secret', without any ceremonial associations".[14] Nock pointed out that the Jewish context of early Christianity, in this respect, seemed to have been deeply understudied.[15] Unfortunately, Nock's lack of familiarity with the Hebrew sources prevented him from fully developing his case.

Although the nature of esoteric cultic attitudes and theological traditions in Judaism remains rather ill-defined, their existence cannot be denied. Esoteric traditions, which appear first in the Apocryphal and Pseudepigraphic writings, can also, in part, be unearthed from various eliptical statements in Talmudic and midrashic texts. Their *locus classicus*, however, remains the *Hekhalot* literature from late antiquity. These texts describe the heavenly journey of the mystic (or of the magician, as Peter Schäfer has claimed), and his vision of the divine palaces, or of the divine chariot described in Ezekiel 1. It is only in the last generation that the philological study of the earliest strata of

---

[12] See J.Z. Smith's study quoted n. 4 above.
[13] Nock, "Religious Symbols and Symbolism. III", in his *Essays*, II, 914.
[14] Nock, art. cit., 798.
[15] In this, Nock has been echoed by J.Z. Smith.

Jewish mysticism has begun in earnest. Scholars, who still disagree about much else, (for instance, the question of dating both the texts and the older oral traditions which they may carry is hotly debated) recognize that these texts clearly reflect esoteric doctrines.[16]

Moreover, the Dead Sea Scrolls have added considerable evidence to our sources. Such vocables as *sod* or *raz*, for instance, which appear time and again in the Qumran texts, seem to refer to a *mysterium* of sorts, difficult to define precisely, but in any case esoteric by nature.[17]

Oddly enough, the major textual discoveries of the last generations have not really eroded the neglect of the Jewish sources by students of early Christian esotericism. Neither the publication of the Dead Sea Scrolls nor the renewed study of Gnosis since the Nag Hammadi discoveries have brought a real change in this regard. This is all the more surprising, since in Protestant theology and scholarship, since the Enlightenment and until the end of the nineteenth century, it was almost a *lieu commun* to trace back to the earliest stages of Kabbalah the roots of the Gnostic teachings of the first Christian centuries.[18]

The reasons for this strange blindness are too complex to be dealt with here.[19] Let us only point out that the discussions have been oc-curring on different levels. The Catholic-Protestant polemic led to a radical distinction between the study of Gnostic origins and that of the *disciplina arcani* in the fourth century. For Protestant theologians such as Gottfried Arnold, the Gnostic and dualist thinkers of the sec-ond century had been heralding or prefiguring the Protestant revolt against the Church hierarchy; and so was Mani, for the Hugenot Isaac de Beausobre.[20] (As is well known, this is also the intellectual and spiritual background for Harnack's attraction to Marcion.) These thinkers, however, did not usually perceive the development of the *disciplina arcani* as having been connected to the esoteric trends in early Christianity. For them, it reflected the spiritual weakness of

---

[16] The latest synthetic study is that of Peter Schäfer, *The Hidden and the Manifest God: some Major Themes in Early Jewish Mysticism* (SUNY Series in Judaism; Albany, N.Y.: SUNY, 1992), with a bibliography.

[17] See for instance E. Vogt, " 'Mysteria' in textibus Qumrân", *Biblica* 37 (1956), 247-257. Cf.*Savoir et salut*, 231-234.

[18] See G.G. Stroumsa, "Gnosis and Judaism in Nineteenth Century Thought", *Journal of Jewish Thought and Philosophy*, 2 (1992), 45- 62.

[19] At least in part, the guilt falls on the marginalization of Jewish learning in late nineteenth century German universities.

[20] See Isaac de Beausobre, *Histoire critique de Manichée et du Manichéisme* (two vols: Amsterdam, 1735-1738).

fourth century Catholicism in the time of Constantine and the origins of Caesaropapism, that is to say a Christianity stained by the invasion of pagan influences. This situation was fundamentally different from the Gnostic movement of the second century, which was perceived as an internal revolt aimed at retaining the deepest and purest elements of the *kerugma*. Catholic scholars brought counter-arguments, showing that the development of mysteric language in Christianity had happened on a grand scale only after the great danger of a powerful and organized paganism had disappeared.[21]

The conjunction of these two trends, i. e., the occultation of the Jewish dimension of early Christian esotericism together with the focus on cultic attitudes rather than on the intellectual content of doctrines, had serious consequences. It explains why research has tended to minimize the question of the possible doctrinal elements of the Christian *arcana*.

These elements, however, could not be totally ignored since some texts, known to all, are quite explicit in this regard. Testimonies about the esoteric dimension of early Christian teachings include some of Jesus's and Paul's dicta or expressions in the New Testament, various Gnostic texts and traditions, as well as the whole ethos of Alexandrian theology (Clement, Origen, Dydimus), and such fourth century figures as Basil the Great, Cyril of Jerusalem, and even John Chrysostom.

One of the most famous texts in this respect is a passage of Cyril of Jerusalem. It shows that the cultic *arcana* cannot be understood without direct reference to theological esotericism. More precisely, we can detect in this text a particular mixture of allusions:

> For to hear the Gospel is not permitted to all: but the glory of the Gospel is reserved for Christ's true children only. Therefore the Lord spoke in parables to those who could not hear: but to the disciples he explained the parables in private; for the brightness of the glory is for those who have been enlightened, the blinding for them that believe not. These mysteries, which the Church now explains to thee who art passing out of the classs of catechumens, it is not the custom to explain to heathen. For to a heathen we do not explain the mysteries concerning Father, Son and Holy Ghost, nor before catechumens do we speak

---

[21] See further P. Battifol, "Arcane", *DTC* I. 2 (1923), 1738-1758. Pagan vocabulary became more visible in the fourth century, "lorsque tout risque d'équivoque aura disparu".

plainly of the mysteries; but many things we often speak in a veiled way, that the believers who know may understand, and they who know not may get no hurt.[22]

In other words, the insistence on the different status of pagans, catechumens and 'insiders', i. e. 'believers', members of the community of the faithful is not only reflected in their participation (or the lack thereof) in the cult, but also in their different exposure to Christian doctrine. More precisely, perhaps, this passage seems to confirm the view that in the fourth century, a vocabulary previously typical of esoteric doctrines came to be used in the context of the various levels of participation in the cult.

Even Celsus, the pagan philosopher and polemicist from the mid-second century, argues against the secret character not only of Christian cult, but also of Christian doctrine, as Origen points out at the beginning of his *Contra Celsum*. For Celsus, the Christians are a secret society, and hence prohibited by law, on account of their secret *doctrines* as well as of the secrecy of their *cult*. To be sure, Celsus does not distinguish between 'main stream' Christians and Gnostics, but it is quite improbable that all such allusions refer only to the Gnostic teachings. A few instances may emphasize this point.[23]

In a short but important testimony, this secret tradition is perceived by Basil the Great as being oral in nature, and coming directly from the apostles:

> Among the doctrines (*dogmata*) and proclamations (*kerugmata*) kept in the Church, some were received from written teaching, and some were transmitted secretly from the apostolic tradition.[24]

The evidence from the writings of the Alexandrian Fathers, in particular Clement and Origen, is so massive that it must be dealt with

---

[22] Cyril of Jerusalem, *Catechesis*, 6. 29 (P. G. 33, 588- 589): the *mustèria* must remain hidden from the *katechumenoi*: *Tauta ta mustèria, ha nun hè Ekklèsia diègeitai soi tôi ek katèxoumenôn metaballomenôi, ouk estin ethos ethnikois diègeisthai* (589 B). This does not seem to refer only to the liturgy. Cf. *Procat.*, 12, *in finem*.

[23] For a more detailed treatment, see Chapter 2 *supra*.

[24] Basil of Caesarea, *On the Holy Spirit*, XXVII. 66 (Pruche, ed., SC 17 bis, Paris: Cerf, 1968; 478-481, cf. 481-483). On the oral traditions transmitted by the *presbuteroi* in the early Church, see also the testimony on Papias, reported by Irenaeus, *Adv. Haer.*, V. 33. 3-4.

in a different context.[25] Let us here only remember that Clement's
Stromateis provide the *locus classicus* of esoteric teaching and its legiti-
mation in Patristic thought. In Book V, for instance, Clement insists
that truth, in order to be protected from those unable to grasp it,
must be hidden by means of a veiled expression. Some mysteries,
which had remained hidden in the Old Testament, have been transmitted by the apostles only to a small group of selected students, and
this only orally, since "the God of the universe, who is beyond any
thought, any notion, cannot become the object of a written teaching" . The Platonic echoes (actually stemming from a Pythagorizing
Platonism)[26] of such a text are obvious. Indeed, Clement quotes here
Plato's *Second Letter*: "The best protection is not to write, but to learn
by heart" .[27] What is even more remarkable, however, is that such
attitudes are not limited to Clement, but can be found also in Gnostic
texts.

Gnostic Apocalypses, i.e., 'revelations', often insist that the secrets
being revealed to the reader have been kept and transmitted only
orally, " neither transcribed in a book nor written down." [28] Such texts
are presented as *apokruphoi*, that is to say 'hidden' . *Apokruphon* actually,
can be translated as "a book of secrets" [29]; To be sure, there was in
early Christian literature, and not only within Gnostic or gnosticising
milieus, a plethora of such apocalypses. The genre itself seems to have
been rather popular: there is no better way to publicise a text than to
prohibit its publication, strongly limit its readership, or insist that it
reveals deep and heavily guarded secrets.

The esoteric traditions transmitted in early Christianity, both those
transmitted orally and those preserved in apocryphal books, clearly
reflect a Jewish origin. In most cases when Origen uses the term *paradosis*, he refers to a Jewish or to a Hebrew tradition.[30]

---

[25] Cf. chapter 6 *supra*.
[26] This is noted by Alain Le Boulluec, in the introduction to his edition of *Stromateis* V (SC 278; Paris, 1981) 19.
[27] Clement, *Strom.*, V. 10. 65 3 (132-133 Le Boulluec). Cf. Eusebius, *Hist. Eccl.*, VI.
13. 9. See above, 37, n. 40.
[28] *Apocalypse of Adam*, NHC V, 85, ll. 3- 7.
[29] So for instance Michel Tardieu translates *Apocryphon of John* as *Livre des secrets de
Jean*. Cf. H.-C. Puech, *En quête de la gnose*, II (Paris: Gallimard, 1978), 97-98, on the
esotericism of the *Gospel of Thomas* and on *apokruphon*, defined as a "recueil de paroles
cachées de Jésus, émises et transmises en secret" .
[30] See R.C.P. Hanson, *Origen's Doctrine of Tradition* (London, 1954), 73. For a recent article on Origen and Jewish traditions, see J.A. McGuckin, "Origen on the

In an interesting study of early Christian esoteric doctrines attributed to the apostles, Jean Daniélou pointed out that in both the apocryphal writings and the (oral) traditions of the Elders (*presbuteroi*), these doctrines referred first of all to the theme of the heavenly journey. Daniélou identified these esoteric apostolic traditions as the continuation of an earlier Jewish esotericism.[31]

From various indications, such as the importance of the traditions attributed to James the Just, the Lord's brother, we can postulate with a reasonable degree of plausibility that it is through Jewish-Christian channels that Gnosticism first developed. It seems also that the Gnostics picked in Jewish-Christian traditions their idea of esotericsm, which they were to develop so well in the second century.

It appears, then, that esoteric trends did exist in early Christianity, and that their direct roots are to be found more in the Jewish heritage of Christianity than in the broader pagan and Hellenic religious milieu.

2. Disappearance of Christian esotericism

a. The fight against gnosticism

In his *Life of Moses*, Gregory of Nyssa states that Moses' knowledge of the hidden mysteries on behalf of the whole people prefigures the 'economy' of the Church: the public appoints someone able to become initiated to the divine secrets (*para tou ta theia muèthentos*), and then trusts him when he reports to them. Gregory adds, however, that "nowadays, this is not observed anymore in many churches" .[32] Such a testimony, then, would seem to reflect the waning of esoteric doctrines in the fourth century—as well as the knowledge that esoteric doctrines had existed in the early Church.

The question, then, becomes that of the end of Christian esotericism. Why and how did esoteric teachings disappear in the ancient Church? Among others, Walter Burkert has noted that except for the

---

Jews", in D. Wood, ed., *Christianity and Judaism* (London: Blackwell, 1992), 1-13, with up-to-date bibliographical references.

[31] J. Daniélou, "Les traditions secrètes des apôtres", *Eranos Jahrbuch* 31 (1962), 199-215.

[32] Gregory of Nyssa, *Vita Mosis*, II. 160-161 (SC 1ter; Daniélou, ed., transl.; Paris: Cerf, 1968), 208-209.

Gnostics, the Christians gave up secrecy in the early centuries.[33] He does not, however, offer an explanation for this fact. Burkert also points out that the Greek mysteries, too, disappeared in late antiquity. If they did not go underground under Christian rule, he suggests, it is because their theology as well as their organization were too complex to offer a plausible competition to Christianity. It may be interesting in our present context to notice this simultaneous disappearance of both Greek mysteries and Christian esotericism. Should this fact be interpreted as a coincidence, or could it point to a similar or identical cause? Some elements of answer to this difficult question will be mentioned in the following paragraphs.

The most developed anti-esoteric argument in Patristic literature can perhaps be found in a sermon of Augustine. The analysis of its argument shows the complexity of the reasons which brought to the disappearance of esoteric traditions from Christian thought in late antiquity.[34] An obvious and simple explanation for this disappearance lies in the transformation brought by the Peace of the Church: when Christianity was no more *religio illicita*, the need to hide was gone. But this explains the end of *cultic* secrecy, not that of *doctrinal* esotericism.

A more convincing answer lies with the fight of the Church Fathers against Gnosticism. Various Gnostic groups seem to have accepted and developed, sometimes in baroque fashion, early Jewish-Christian esoteric traditions.[35] The appropriation of these traditions by the Gnostics made them suspect for 'orthodox' Christian intellectuals. In their merciless fight against the Gnostics, the Church Fathers felt the need to reject these esoteric traditions, which had accompanied Christianity since its beginning, but which had become an embarrassing burden. Victory over Gnosticism thus meant the eradication of esotericism from Christian doctrine.

But this answer, too, is not really satisfying, or at least, it does not solve the whole riddle. There is also a deeper intellectual cause of the phenomenon: the very *ethos* of Christianity is inherently refractory to esoteric doctrines. There is one single salvation, offered to all and sundry, on the condition that one believe in Christ's salvific sacrifice.

---

[33] W. Burkert, *Ancient Mystery Cults* (Cambridge, Mass.: Harvard University Press, 1987), 53.

[34] See chapter 9 *supra*.

[35] See for instance H. W. Attridge, "The Gospel of Truth as an Exoteric Text", in C.W. Hedrick and R. Hodgson, Jr., eds., *Nag Hammadi, Gnosticism, and Early Christianity* (Peabody, MA: Hendrickson, 1986), 239-255.

In this context, the undeniable esoteric elements in the earliest stages of Christianity were an anomaly, condemned to disappear within a short time. And indeed, one can easily find anti-esoteric statements in early Christian literature. Tertullian, for instance, opposes the openness of true Christianity to the esotericism typical of the heretic :

> This wisdom which he says was kept secret is that which has been in things foolish and little and dishonourable, which has also been hidden under figures, both allegories and enigmas, but was afterwards to be revealed in Christ who was set for a light of the gentiles by that creator who by the voice of Isaiah promises that he will open up invisible and secret treasures.[36]

More than a hidden truth which must be at once protected from those who are unfit and taught to insiders, the *exemplum* of Christ, the eternally living pattern of ethical behaviour, stands at the center of the early Christian experience.[37] The follower of Christ is the saint, or the religious virtuoso, to use Max Weber's term, and not the philosopher. The new philosopher, actually, is the monk. Action has now gained preponderance upon knowledge.[38] This attitude reflects the new religious sensitivity of late antiquity, for which there was no need to preserve or cherish esoteric traditions. These traditions finally disappeared, hidden by the veil of the 'mysteric' vocabulary that had once been used to describe them.

b. Interiorization and the new person

A deep and complex transformation of the structures of the personality is at work under the early Empire. A combination of various intellectual trends, partly inherited from the Hellenistic times and partly encouraged by aspects of Christian theology, brought what

---

[36] Tertullian, *Adv. Marcionem*, 5. 6, (II, 540-541 Evans; Oxford, 1972); cf. Minucius Felix, *Octavius*, 10; LCL 338-341): "guilt loves secrecy". For an opposite example, see a Pseudo-Augustinian text quoted by Nock (art. cit., 818, n. 81), which opposes the simplicity and openness of Christian rites to the secrecy of pagan mysteries.

[37] P. Brown, "The Saint as Exemplar in Late Antiquity", *Representations* 1 (1983), 1-25.

[38] See the semantic analysis of A.M. Malingrey, *Philosophia : étude d' un groupe de mots dans la littérature grecque des présocratiques au IVe. siècle après Jésus Christ* (Paris: Klincksieck, 1961). For the medieval semantic development of the term, see J. Leclercq, *The Love of Learning and the Desire for God* (New York: Fordham University Press, 1961), 100-101 and notes [= *L' amour des lettres et le désir de Dieu: initiation aux auteurs monastiques du Moyen Age* (Paris: Cerf: 1957)].

amounted to nothing short of a remodelling of the human person. Man had been created in God's image, the Son of God had been incarnated, and had resurrected from the dead. These three central tenets of Christian theology entailed the attribution of a new nobility to the human body. In some ways, this transformation encouraged the perception of body and soul as a single unit, more clearly than had been the case in Greek thought.[39]

The new stature of the human person fostered the development of a refined sensitivity to the individual subject, capable at once of damning sin and of saving faith. The 'interior man' mentioned in Paul's letters had achieved a new religious importance in the writings of the Church Fathers. Thus did early Christian thought foster the interiorization of religious attitudes. Feelings became more concrete than ever before.

The deeply ambivalent term 'interiorization' perhaps smacks of apologetics: it has almost always been understood *in bonam partem*, as early Christianity was perceived by Christian scholars and thinkers as having encouraged 'interiorized' beliefs, in opposition to the 'exterior' character of Jewish patterns of religious behaviour (or those of Roman paganism).[40] What is important in our context is its bearing on the transformation of esotericism into mysticism in Patristic times. As a 'master metaphor', its importance is capital. The *metanoia* (Lat. *conversio*) upwards, which describes the turning towards God, soon becomes identified with a turn inward, best expressed by Augustine, who calls Christ 'the inner Master', *interior magister*. This 'turning in' is also understood as 'turning from' the outer world of the senses and common experience. Hence, a new vocabulary is developed, of the 'interior senses', through which one can experience the divinity, in particular through spiritual visions.[41] The significance of such meta-

---

[39] See *Savoir et salut*, ch. 11 , pp. 199-223. To be sure, this human unit was broken anew by the original sin, this time in a different, more intimate way. Cf. the argument developed in the item quoted next note.

[40] See G.G. Stroumsa, "Interiorization and Intolerance in Early Christianity", in J. Assmann and Th. Sundermaier, eds., *Die Erfindung des inneren Menschen* (Studien zum Verstehen fremder Religionen 6; Gütersloh: Mohn, 1993), 168-182.

[41] On the interior senses, see M. Canévet, "Sens spirituel", *DS* 14 (1990), 598-617, esp. 598-604, on the origins of the doctrine and the analogy of the spiritual with the bodily senses developed by Origen. On the ambivalent attitude to mystical visions in late antique Christianity, and in particular among the monks, see A. Guillaumont, "Les visions monastiques dans le christianisme oriental ancien", in Guillaumont, *Aux origines du monachisme chrétien: pour une phénoménologie du monachisme* (Spiritualité orientale, 30; Begrolles en Mauges: Abbaye de Bellefontaine, 1979), 136-147.

phors of 'interiorization' for our present context lies in the fact that they are parallel to those of esotericism: what is inside is also what is hidden from the eyes, what cannot be seen, or expressed in words, be it invisible or unspeakable.[42]

3. From musterion to mysterium

a. Musterion

Although it is mainly since the New Testament that the sense of *secret* has been attached to *musterion*, the scholarly focus has been put mainly, as we have seen, on the relationships between the pagan *musteria* and the Christian *musterion*. Moreover, little emphasis has been put on the *esoteric* aspects of the Christian use of the term and on its Jewish background.

Various esoteric traditions were circulating in ancient Jewish literature, mainly in the Apocryphal and Pseudepigraphical writings, on God and the heavenly court (i.e., angels and Satan) as well as on the creation of the world and on its end. It is a truism to state that this literature stands in the background of the New Testament writings. Nevertheless, passions run high among scholars as to the exact measure in which New Testament texts should be read in the light of Jewish esotericism, since most of our sources are later than the New Testament, and since both genres and *Sitz im Leben* are different. In any case, it is reasonable to read various 'esoteric' passages in the Gospels and in the Pauline Epistles *in the cultural and religious context* of Jewish esoteric traditions.

Only two texts will be quoted here in this respect.

> When He was alone, the Twelve and others who were round him questioned him about the parables. He replied: "To you the mystery (*to musterion*) of the kingdom of God has been given; but to those who are

---

[42] For Georg Simmel, secrecy was in early societies linked to relationships between men, and should be conceived as representing a most important moment of the individuation process; established upon social relations of a certain type, and in their turn encouraging such relationships. One cannot here go into a careful reading of Simmels' remarks for our purposes. Suffice it here to point out that the individuation process described by Simmel bears some similarity with the new structure of the human person launched by Christian theology in the making. See G. Simmel, *Soziologie: Untersuchungen über die Vergesellschaftung*, (Munich, Leipzig: Duncker & Humblot, 1923), ch. 5, pp. 257-304.

outside (*ekeinois de tois exô*) everything comes by way of parables, so that (as Scripture says) they may look and look, but see nothing; they may hear and hear, but understand nothing; otherwise they might turn to God and be forgiven" . (Mark 4: 10-12)

This famous text, together with its parallels, has given way to a long tradition of scholarly interpretations, mainly in the context of the so-called ' *Messiasgeheimnis*' question.[43] Another *locus classicus* in the New Testament, in this respect, is provided by the various "spiritual teachings' of Paul, for instance—the origin and precise nature of which are still in need of clarification:

> We impart a secret and hidden wisdom of God... (*alla laloumen theou sophian en mustèriôi tèn apokekrummenèn*... I Cor 2: 7)

Although the vocable *musterion* does not necessarily have the same meaning in these two contexts, both utterances seem to allude to esoteric doctrines, to be shared only within a small and exclusive group of direct disciples, but to remain hidden from the majority.[44] Yet, a long exegetical tradition, already in Patristic hermeneutics of the first centuries, and up to modern New Testament research, has attempted to explain away such verses or minimize their significance. Two main reasons are responsible for this fact. The first is related to the cultural weight of theological perceptions, while the other reflects the ignorance of Jewish sources on the part of many scholars.

A central concept in early Christian parlance, *musterion* alluded to the main events and beliefs upon which the new religion was established.[45] One of the most interesting documents showing the new

---

[43] This question was raised first by S.W. Wrede, *Das Messiasgeheimnis in den Evangelien* (Göttingen: Vandenhoeck & Ruprecht, 1901). For the contemporary literary approach of the question, see for instance F. Kermode, "Secrets and Narrative Sequence", *Critical Inquiry* 7 (1980), 83- 101, and W.H. Kelber, "Narrative and Disclosure: Mechanisms of Concealing, Revealing, and Reveiling", *Semeia* 43 (1988), 1-20. See now G. Theissen, "Die pragmatische Bedeutung der Geheimnismotive im Markusevangelium", in *Secrecy and Concealment*, 225-246.

[44] For a new approach to the the the social role of secret language in the Pauline writings, see D.B. Martin, "Tongues of Angels and Other Status Indicators", *Journal of the American Academy of Religion* 59 (1992), 547 ff.

[45] On the term and its semantical transformations, see G. Bornkamm, " *Musterion*", in *TDNT* 4, 802-828. For bibliographical elements, see A. Solignac, "Mystère", *DS* 12, 1860-1902, reprinted in A. Solignac *et al.*, *Mystère et mystique* (Paris: Beauchesne, 1983), 3-86.

meaning of the term is perhaps the following passage of Ignatius of Antioch's *Letter to the Ephesians*:[46]

> And the virginity of Mary, and her giving birth were hidden from the Prince of this world, as was also the death of the Lord. Three mysteries of a cry (*tria musteria kraugès*) which were wrought in the stillness of God.

'Mystery' is here used in a highly idiosyncratic way: the term refers to events which are *not* kept secret. On the contrary, they represent the apex of God's new revelation to mankind. These events, hence, are highly visible although, through a cunning of sorts, they remain hidden from Satan. The latter hopes to prolong his reign upon earth by preventing the salvation. Such a presentation of things is not unique. One finds it also in Gnostic texts and traditions. During his salvific descent to the earth, the Gnostic Savior must hide in order to escape the evil intentions of the various archons who keep guard at the gates of the different heavens.[47]

For Ignatius, the mystery is part of the manifestation of the divine power:

> How then was he manifested to the world? A star shone in heaven beyond all the stars, and its light was unspeakable (*aneklalèton*), and its newness caused astonishment... And there was perplexity, whence came this new thing, so unlike them...

The 'mystery' is not any more something that should not be spoken about, it is something that *cannot* be entirely described in words, precisely because of its newness.[48]

But the novelty of the phenomenon is also its power: through the appearance of the *musterion*, the world is transformed:

> by this all magic was dissolved and every bond of wickedness vanished away, ignorance was removed, and the old kingdom was destroyed... Hence all things were disturbed, because the abolition of death was being planned.

---

[46] I quote Krissop Lake's translation, in LCL, *The Apostolic Fathers*, vol I, 192- 193.

[47] See for instance the texts discussed in connection with the *Apocalypse of Adam*, in G.G. Stroumsa, *Another Seed: Studies in Gnostic Mythology* (Nag Hammadi Studies 24; Leiden: Brill, 1984), 82-88.

[48] 'New' is an important term in early Christian literature, used both *in bonam* and *in malam partem*. For the positive meaning, see for instance Nock, art. cit., 808. Tertullian, on the other side, cracks jokes on Marcion's insistence on the 'novelty' of Christ's message; see Tertullian, *Adv. Marc., passim*.

The *musterion* is the correct interpretation of the 'cry' which perturbed God's usual silence about the affairs of humankind. This *musterion* brings at the same time the dissolution of the old evil kingdom and of the ignorance that alone had rendered Satan's reign possible.

Hence, what is hidden is also what is revealed, but can be understood only through faith, not through wisdom.

Such an understanding of the term is not peculiar to second century literature. We find it also, more than two centuries later, in an impressive text of Chrysostom:

> The most characteristic trait of mystery is that it is announced everywhere, and nonetheless remains unknown to those who do not think correctly: since it is not through wisdom that it is revealed, but through the Spirit, inasmuch as we can receive it. One would not err in calling the mystery ineffable (*aporrhèton*), since even to us the believers, it is not possible to understand such things in full light and with an exact knowledge.[49]

The ineffable mystery revealed through the Spirit, therefore, will often be identified with baptism. Expressions such as 'the initiated' (*hoi muethentes, hoi memuemenoi*), losing all esoteric allusion, often refer in Patristic literature to the baptised, those who by joining the Christian community will have gained access to spiritual and saving realities. So, for instance, the liturgical prayers of the *Apostolic Constitutions* describe baptism in terms of initiation.[50] In this sense, *musterion* does refer to the mysteries of cult. This conception was given its classical expression by Augustine, for whom the *musterion*, i. e., the *sacramentum*, is identical to the visible form of the Logos, *visibile verbum*.[51] In its metaphorical use, then, *musterion* came to mean exactly the opposite of its original meaning: it is the outward expression of the divine depth, which remains unattainable.

It is precisely after the fourth century, when Christianity becomes secure and organized paganism "was almost everywhere dead"[52] at last, and when the Christians are, for the first time, in no need of

---

[49] John Chrysostom, *Hom. in I Cor.*, VII (*P.G.* 61; 56b).

[50] *Apostolic Constitutions*, VIII. 6. 7; VIII. 8. 2.

[51] Augustine, *In Ioh. Evang.*, Tract. 80. 3. On *sacramentum, secretum* and *mysterium* in the formative period of the Latin theological vocabulary, cf. J. de Ghellinck *et al.*, *Pour l' histoire du mot sacramentum*, I (Louvain, 1924), *non vidi*.

[52] In the terms of Nock, "Hellenistic Mysteries...", 818.

hiding, that the vocabulary of esotericism—for instance the term *mus-tagogia*—becomes prominent in Patristic literature. This paradox, long noticed, has not really been explained.

In this context, Gregory of Nyssa's *Life of Moses* is a capital witness, and may offer some elements of answer. In this text perhaps better than anywhere else, we can detect the passage from esotericism to mysticism. For Gregory, the life of Moses should be understood as a spiritual itinerary. It is thanks to the 'divine initiation' which guided him that Moses was able to climb step by step up to the *theognosia*, the knowledge of God. Here too, the climbing is also described in terms of 'going inside' (*to endoteron*), since the progress is accomplished by the intellectual and spiritual faculties. God remains invisible, and transcends even all intellectual knowledge. Moses, like David, will eventually be initiated in the secret sanctuary to the hidden mysteries (*ho en tô autô adutôi muètheis ta aporrhèta*).[53] The dynamic character of the initiation is essential in Gregory's thought: due to God's infinite nature, this remains an endless process, and the spiritual quest is never completed. The concept of *epektasis* describes the mystic's constant straining towards the divine.

The popularity of terms like *mustagogein* after the fourth century has usually been explained by the fact that since in the Chritianized empire, paganism was not anymore perceived as a threat, the vocabulary of the pagan mysteries could be used much more freely than ever before.[54] Without totally denying the relevance of this interpretation, I would rather stress another point. As long as becoming (and remaining) a Christian was a courageous and often dangerous act, words as loaded as those of 'initiation' could be used in baptismal context. From the fourth century on, however, baptism, the basic element of Christian identity, was partaken of by almost everybody. Hence, new terms of reference had to be found for a lofty vocabulary which could not anymore be applied to baptism. It is in relation to the spiritual man, isolated by his experience from the rest of the community, that such new terms were found. Words, indeed, have a life

---

[53] Gregory of Nyssa, *Vie de Moise*, II. 162-164 (210-213 Daniélou). See also Origen, *Hom. on Numbers*, 27 (A. Méhat, ed., transl., SC 29; Paris: Cerf, 1951). Cf. W. Völker, *Gregor von Nyssa als Mystiker* (Wiesbaden: Steiner, 1955), esp. 167- 174: "der Gnostiker als Deuter des geheimen Schriftsinnes".

[54] See for instance the words of Battifol quoted n. 21 above.

of their own. When they lose their former reference, they have to acquire a new one.

b. mysterium

> But according to Jesus' teaching the one who leads to God initiates who have been purified in soul will say: anyone whose soul has for a long time known nothing of evil, and especially since he came to be healed by the Logos, let him hear even those doctrines which were privately revealed by Jesus to his genuine disciples. Accordingly, in his contrast between the exhortations of those who initiate men among the Greeks and those who teach the doctrines of Jesus, he does not know the difference between calling bad men to be cured and calling those already pure to more mystical doctrines (epi de ta mustikôtera).[55]

This text of Origen is remarkable on various accounts. Arguing against Celsus who accuses the Christians of secret doctrines, Origen does not deny that Jesus revealed deeper truths to his immediate disciples. But he points out that the major difference between the higher doctrines of the Christians and those of the pagans lie in the essential role played by ethics in Christian teaching: only the pure in heart can be initiated into the spiritual realities. This text also reflects the fact that for him, the term mustikos still means 'secret'. As was aptly noted by Bernard McGinn, "Augustine, too, uses the qualifiers mysticus and mystice frequently, keeping to the primary sense of the Greek root, that is, 'hidden' or 'secret', referring to the inner significance of anything related to the mystery of salvation." [56]

The same is true in the vocabulary used by Pseudo Dionysius, whose mustikè theologia retains a deep element of secrecy. It may be noted here that the substantive term, 'mysticism', does not appear before the seventeenth century, a fact pointed out, in particular, by Michel de Certeau.[57] Can we try to follow some of the semantic shifts which permitted the passage from Christian esotericism to Christian mysticism?

Although mystical patterns of thought are common within various religious and cultural traditions, they are not universal, in the sense

---

[55] Origen, Contra Celsum, 3. 60 (H. Chadwick, transl.; Cambridge: Cambridge Univ. Press, 1951), 169.

[56] B. McGinn, The Foundations of Mysticism (New York: Continuum, 1992), 252.

[57] On the history of the term and of research, see the appendix to McGinn's book.

that they characterize only certain stages of religious development.[58] In particular, the desire to become united with the deity, the search for the *unio mystica*, implies a conception of the divine as well as of the human person, and of the relationship between them, which is not found at all stages of intellectual and religious thought.

In an important article which has not elicited enough attention, the late Hans Jonas sought to follow the passage from myth into mysticism in late antiquity.[59] In this article, Jonas focuses on the mystical reinterpretation of Gnostic myths in the writings of Origen, in particular on Origen's conception of the *apokatastasis*. For him, one essential, though implicit, condition for the emergence of mystical thought is the recognition of the individual as subject. This individual is then able to interiorize what had previously been expressed in an 'objective' way through myth. Jonas states that "the objective representation of reality found in myth precedes in time the subjective realization of different stages of being", the latter being a prerequisite for the development of mystical thought. For him, myth and mysticism are rooted in a common existential experience. In his terms, mystical ascent corresponds in mental immanence to the representational transcendance of myth. He perceives Gnostic mythology as a decisive step on the way from mystery to mysticism in late antiquity. The approach followed here is somewhat parallel to that of Jonas: the genesis of Christian mysticism should be understood within the frame of the fading Christian esotericism.

To the best of my knowledge, a major difference between Christian and Jewish mysticism has remained hitherto unexplained. This difference lies the exoteric nature of Christian mysticism, *versus* the esotericism characteristic of Jewish 'mysticism' — a phenomenon which should perhaps rather be called theosophy, since its classical texts describe, rather than a spiritual experience, the 'objective' knowledge of the divinity. This difference, again, seems to stem from the fact that in Judaism, which evolved in the first Christian centuries outside the intellectual frames of reference of Greco-Roman cul-

---

[58] See for instance the remarks of G. Scholem, *Major Trends in Jewish Mysticism* (New York: Schocken, 1944), chapter 1.

[59] H. Jonas, "Myth and Mysticism: a Study of Objectification and Interiorization in Religious Thought", *Journal of Religion* 49 (1969), 315-329. The argument, however, suffers from Jonas's rather opaque language.

ture, no transformation of the person similar the one referred to above happened.[60]

The development of mystical expression began to take shape precisely with the recognition of the limitations of language itself, and its insufficiencies in dealing with the supreme realities of theology. To be sure, this recognition is found also in the texts of the middle Platonists, not only among those of the Christian thinkers.[61] But the latter succeeded better than the former in taking advantage of the new sensitivity to language. Helped by their theology, Christian thinkers developed a new understanding of the interior world of the individual, complete with feelings and even members, which was strikingly different from the Hellenic belief in the soul as the core of the human person.

A statement of Gregory the Great, toward the end of our period, reflects this transformation. According to him, the *Song of Songs* is an interior solemn secret, which can be reached only through the eyes of the intelligence. [62] In this passage, *secretum* is defined not as something that *should not* be revealed to 'those outside', (*hoi exô*), to use the Gospel's expression[63], but as something that *cannot* be expressed in words. It is not, as in the usual conceptions of esotericism in the ancient world, the uninitiated who are outside. Rather, language itself is 'exterior', and therefore cannot grasp the essence of the *secretum*. (As is well known, *musterion* is translated in Christian Latin by *secretum* as well as by *mysterium* and *sacramentum*). This *secretum*, being essentially interior, can be cracked ('penetrated') only by the 'interior senses'.[64]

The interior man can grasp the interior 'secret', i.e., the saving

---

[60] On this point, see chapter 10 *infra*.

[61] See *Savoir et salut*, 183-197.

[62] "Ita cantica canticorum secretum quoddam et sollemne interius est. Quod secretum in occultis intellegentiis penetratur: nam, si exterioribus verbis adtenditur, secretum non est." Gregory the Great, *Commentary in Song of Songs*, 6 (PL 79, 525-533). See also his *Homilies on Ezekiel* and his *Moralia in Job*, where Gregory develops a language fit to express mystical ways of thought. See the introduction of Dom Robert Gillet, O. S. B., in *Grégoire le Grand*, *Morales sur Job*, première partie (S.C. 32 bis; Paris: Cerf, 1975), 20- 81.

[63] See Mark 4: 10-12.

[64] On a similar point, McGinn notes (*op. cit.*, 213) that Ambrose's mysticism offers no hint of elitism or of esotericism. He calls Ambrose's *On Isaac* "a discourse of an initiatory hermetism, adding that its message is hidden only to outsiders; those within the Christian community had been given the keys, both scriptural and sacramental, that would unlock the inner meaning."

message of Jesus Christ, whom Augustine, as mentioned above, calls 'the interior master'. Christian mysticism thus expresses a spiritual experience. We can detect here, already in Patristic literature, the seed of medieval mysticism, a *cognitio Dei experimentalis*, in Jean Gerson's terms.[65]

Gregory's statement represents in a nutshell the last step in the long semantical transformation of a word. Moreover, it reflects the deep change in religious sensitivities at the end of the ancient world, and the passage to the medieval 'imaginary', i. e. the implicit categories through which a civilization perceives the world.[66] 'Mystery', in its Christian garb, has now become something ineffable, which cannot be fully expressed by words, rather than something which must remain hidden. In other words, we witness here the end of ancient esotericism.[67]

---

[65] See "Mystique" (A. Deblaere), in *DS* 12, 1902-1905, reprinted in *Mystère et mystique*, 87-94.

[66] The term is a calque from the French 'l'imaginaire', so well studied by Jacques Le Goff, among others, for the medieval period. See in particular J. Le Goff, *L' imaginaire médiéval* (Paris: Gallimard, 1986). Le Goff points out that he is particularly interested in the gesesis of conceptions, and speaks about a "long moyen âge" extending from the third to the mid-nineteenth century. The genesis of the medieval imaginary, however, is to be searched for in the earliest stages of Christianity.

[67] Medieval philosophical esotericism, developed around the conception of the 'double truth', is of a quite different nature. See for instance L. Strauss, *Persecution and the Art of Writing* (Glencoe, Ill.: Free Press, 1952). On the double faith theory, see H. A. Wolfson, "The Double Faith Theory in Clement, Sa'adia, Averroes and Saint Thomas and its Origins in Aristotle and the Stoics", *Jewish Quarterly Review*, N.S., 32 (1942), 213- 264.

CHAPTER TEN

MYSTICAL DESCENTS

I. Ascent and descent are obviously complementary notions in the
vocabulary of religious experience. Both are used, in various literatures of the ancient world, in two essentially different senses. One
reads, first, about the descent from the heavens to the earth, of a deity
or savior, who comes in order to reveal himself to mankind and offer
salvation to those willing to recognize him or believe in him. This
descensus is often conceived as being secret (in order to avoid those evil
powers that rule the earth), and may be called *absconditus*. After revealing himself, his mission accomplished, the savior can return to
heavens in an *ascensus gloriosus*.[1] In a different pattern, various mythologies of the ancient Near East describe a descent of the god to the
Underworld.[2] Side by side with the descent and ascent of the savior,
we find numerous descriptions, in different cultural and religious contexts, of a descent of the soul to the earth in order to become incarnated within a body, and of its ascent back to heaven after death.
Another pattern, of the soul's descent to the Underworld, whether it
is called Hades, She'ol or Amente, is also to be found in various contexts.

Although the two metaphors of descent and ascent (of the soul or
of a deity) are clearly related to one another, ascents seem to have
elicited more research than descents.[3] This fact can probably be ex-

---

[1] This mythical pattern of descent and ascent of the savior stands at the basis of
the so-called myth of the *salvator salvandus* cherished by the *Religionsgeschichtliche Schule*.
See C. Colpe, *Die religionsgeschichtliche Schule: Darstelllung und Kritik ihres Bildes vom gnostis-
chen Erlösermythus* (FRLANT; Göttingen: Vandenhoeck & Ruprecht, 1961). See further
I.P. Culianu, *Psychanodia I: a Survey of the Evidence Concerning the Ascension of the Soul and
its Relevance* (EPROER, 99; Leiden: Brill, 1983). This work is based upon Culiano's
French thesis, published as *Expériences de l'extase: extase, ascension et récit visionnaire de
l'hellénisme au moyen-âge* (Paris: Payot: 1984).
[2] For traces of such mythologies in the literature of ancient Israel, see for instance
A. Cooper, "Psalm 24: 7-10: Mythology and Exegesis", *JBL* 102 (1983), 37-60.
[3] See for instance A. F. Segal, "Heavenly Ascent in Hellenistic Judaism, Early
Christianity and their Environment", *ANRW* II, 23. 2, 1333-1394. Although Segal
speaks about the "mythical structure of *katabasis* and *anabasis*", his study concentrates
much more on the latter than on the former. Oddly enough, the article does not refer
to the *yordei merkavah*.
For a very rich catalogue of descent experiences in the ancient world, see the bulky

plained, at least in part, by the much more prominent role of ascent
in mystical language. The idea of a mystical descent, in particular,
seems to be a rather strange phenomenon, still only partly understood. It is perhaps nowhere illustrated as clearly as in those hieratic
Hebrew texts of late antiquity which we have come to call *Hekhalot*
literature, and which represent the first strata of the Jewish mystical
tradition. These texts describe the ecstatical experience and mystical
visions of the *yordei merkavah*, those who "descend to the Chariot", a
reference to the vision of the Chariot in *Ezekiel* 1.[4] Despite some new
studies, the puzzling metaphor of descent and its original meaning
are still defying scholars.[5] I hope to be able to suggest here a way to
understand them better.

II. Salmoxis, the mythical Thracian hero cherished by Romanian his-
torians of religion, seems to have been the first person whose *katabasis*
was recorded in the annals of history. Herodotus recounts how he
descended into an underground chamber, or *andreion*, that he had
made, living there for three years (*katabas de katô, es to katagaion oikèma,
diaitato ep' etea tria...*).[6] Herodotus does not tell us what Salmoxis did,

---

work of J. Kroll, *Gott und Hölle: der Mythos von Descensuskampfe* (Studien der Bibliothek
Warburg 20; Leipzig, Berlin: Teubner, 1932). Kroll's extensive research shows that
the *descencus* is usually linked to an *ascensus*. See also Ganschinietz, " *katabasis*", *PW*
X. 2, 2359-2449 (written in 1919). See further J.E. Ménard, "Le *descensus ad inferos*",
in *Ex Orbe Religionum: Studia...Geo Widengren Oblata* (Suppl. to *Numen* 21: Leiden: Brill,
1972), 296-306. For a folk-lore approach, see A.-L. Siikala, "Descent into the Underworld", *Encyclopedia of Religion* IV, 300-304. On the shamanistic character of the 'ascent of the soul', in ancient literature, see C. Colpe, "Die 'Himmelreise der Seele' als
philosophie- und religionsgeschichtliches Problem", in E. Fries, Hrg., *Festschrift für
Joseph Klein zum 70. Geburtstag* (Göttingen: Vandenhoeck & Ruprecht, 1967), 85-104.
    [4] For an introduction to this literature and its problems, see in particular G.
Scholem, *Jewish Gnosticism, Merkavah Mysticism and Talmudic Tradition* (second edition;
New York: Jewish Theological Seminary, 1965), and for a clear presentation, I.
Gruenwald, *Apocalyptic and Merkavah Mysticism* (AGAJU 14; Leiden, Cologne: Brill,
1980). The work of Peter Schaefer and his students has transformed the field. For a
presentation of the texts, see P. Schaefer, "Tradition und Redaktion in Hekhalot Literatur", in his *Hekhalot-Studien* (TSAJ19; Tübingen: Mohr [Siebeck], 1988), 8-16. In
contradistinction to Scholem and other early students of this literature, Schaefer insists on its magical core, rather than on the heavenly vision. See his "The Aim and
Purpose of Early Jewish Mysticism", in *Hekhalot-Studien*, 277-295.
    [5] See A. Kuyt, "Once Again: *yarad* in Hekhalot Literature", *Frankfurter Judaistische
Beiträge* 18 (1990), 45-69. See now her monograph, *The 'Descent' to the Chariot: To-
wards a description of the Terminology, Place, Function and nature of the Yeridah in Hekhalot
Literature* (TSAJ 45; Tübingen: Mohr [Siebeck], 1995).
    [6] Herodotus, *Histories* IV. 95 (LCL, vol. II, 296-297). Cf. F. Hartog, "Salmoxis: le
Pythagore des Gètes ou l'autre de Pythagore", *Annali della Scuola Normale Superiora di*

or saw, during his underground sojourn. But in this *andreion*,[7] he instructed the best among his countrymen, telling them "that they should go to a place where they would live for ever and have all good things" .[8] It may be noted that the verb used is *anadidaskein*, a rather rare verb which seems to indicate a special kind of teaching, implying perhaps repetition, or memorization of an esoteric content.[9] In any case, the story of Salmoxis clearly retains strong shamanistic elements. As we know, archaic Greek shamanism was deeply influenced by Scythian and other traditions, already in the seventh century B.C.[10] Mircea Eliade, among others, has insisted upon the fact that the Greeks were struck by the similarities between Salmoxis and Pythagoras. Both figures reflect a belief in the immortality of the soul and certain initiatory rites.[11]

Pythagoras too, when he came to Crotona, descended into a subterranean dwelling which he had made (*kata gès oikiskon poièsai*) according to Diogenes Laertius, who reports a story told by Hernippus. When he finally came up, "withered and looking like a skeleton", he declared to the assembly that "he had been down to Hades, and even read out his experiences to them." [12]

Pisa, Cl. di lett. e fil. 8 (1978), 15-42, who gives the basic discussion. I wish to thank Professor Aldo Corcella, who kindly sent me the relevant pages of his commentary on Herodotus IV before publication.
On Salmoxis and early Thracian religion, see especially M. Eliade, *Zalmoxis, the Vanishing God: Comparative Studies in the Religions and Folklore of Dacia and Eastern Europe* (Chicago: Chicago University Press, 1972. The book first appeared in French under the title: *De Zalmoxis a Gengis Khan* [Paris: Payot, 1970]). Eliade points out that Strabo (7. 297 ff.) does not mention an "underground chamber", but a cave on mount Kaganoion (p.24).

[7] On this term, see Hartog, *loc. cit.*, 26: "En Crète, le terme désigne le local public où se réunissaient les membres des hétairies...". Eliade, *op. cit.* 24, notes that the underground chamber is reminiscent of the rooms in which the ritual banquets of the secret religious societies took place.

[8] Herodotus, *ibid.*; I quote the LCL translation.

[9] Hartog, *ibid.*, 28, notes that *redoceo, iterum doceo, edoceo*, are given by the *Thesaurus*. Cf. the Hebrew term *mishna*, i. e. *deuterôsis*, 'second teaching', which seems to imply also the idea of a 'deeper', i. e. esoteric teaching, not imparted to all, and perhaps also of an oral teaching, learned by heart. These terms and the history of their semantics deserve further study.

[10] This recognition is due especially to the seminal work of K. Meuli. See for instance his "Scythica", *Hermes* 70 (1935), 121-176. See further Eliade, *op. cit.*.

[11] Eliade, *Zalmoxis*, 23-24.

[12] Diogenes Laertius, *Lives of Eminent Philosophers*, II, LCL, 356-359. On the nature of Pythagoras' *katabasis* and its relationship to religious beliefs, see W. Burkert, "Das Proömium des Parmenides und die *katabasis* des Pythagoras", *Phronesis* 14 (1969),

But this is not the only experience of Pythagoras that involves a *katabasis* experience. While in Crete, the philosopher had gone down into the cave of Ida, together with Epimenides.[13] The fact that Pythagoras would have undergone initiation to the Idean dactyls is not surprising. The Ida cave, indeed, was famous as the place of the oldest attested mystery warrior band, and had served as a cult cave since the Minoan times.[14] The secret character of the cults conducted in the cave, however, has meant that few texts have reached us, which tell about what took place there. Porphyry, on his side, describes the ascetical preparation which Pythagoras underwent prior to his *katabasis* into the cave, and the ritual cycle of three times nine days which he spent there, then making offerings to Zeus and finally seeing the god's throne (*etos thronon etheasato*), as it is spread annually with leaves.[15]

The 'culmination', if one may mix metaphors, of the *katabasis* in the vision of a divine throne is a significant trait, which should be emphasized here, since a similar vision of the divine throne (the *kisse ha-kavod*) also forms the acme of the vision of the Jewish mystics, the *yordei merkavah*.[16] Visions of the god seated on his throne which are found in different religious traditions, might well offer a background in which to see anew the Jewish texts. Already in apocryphal and pseudepigraphic texts such as *I Enoch* or the *Testament of Levi*, the rapture can end in the vision of God seated on his throne of glory.[17] A central place is reserved to Moses' vision of the divine throne by

---

1-30. For Burkert, Pythagoras behaved as the hierophant in a Demeter cult of Asia Minor, while the rites emphasize the secret of death and the belief in reincarnation.

[13] Diogenes Laertius, VIII. 2-3 (II, 322-323 Hicks, LCL).

[14] W. Burkert, *Greek Religion in the Archaic and Classical Age* (Cambridge, Mass.,: Harvard University Press, 1987), 48, 280. On the cultic role of caves in antiquity, see P. Saintyves, "Essai sur les grottes dans les cultes magico-religieux et dans la symbolique primitive", appendix to J. Trabucco, transl., Porphyre, *L'antre des nymphes* (Paris, 1918), 35-262.

[15] Porphyry, *Life of Pythagoras*, 17 (43 Des Places; Paris: Belles Lettres, 1982). For an English translation, see M. Smith and M. Hadas, *Heroes and Gods: Spiritual Biographies in Antiquity* (New York: Harper and Row, 1965), 112-113. See further I. Lévi, *La légende de Pythagore de Grèce en Palestine* (Bibliothèque de l'EPHE, 250; Paris: Champion, 1927), 28ff.

[16] See for instance D. J. Halperin, *The Four Faces of the Chariot: Early Jewish Responses to Ezekiel's Vision* (TSAJ 16; Tübingen: Mohr [Siebeck], 1988).

[17] See for instance I Enoch 14; 8-18, T. Levi 2: 7. See further O. Schnitz, "Thronos", *TDNT* III, 160-167. On these texts and their influence upon the crystallisation of Gnostic mythology, see F.T. Fallon, *The Enthronement of Sabaoth: Jewish Elements in Gnostic Creation Myths* (NHS 10; Leiden: Brill, 1978), 39 ff.

Ezechiel the Tragedian in his *Exagogè*, a play on the Exodus from Egypt written in Hellenistic Alexandria. Pieter van der Horst has shown that the biblical references in the play can be fully understood only in reference to Hekhalot literature, and particularly the Hebrew Book of Enoch (*III Enoch*).[18] There was no doubt a long Israelite and Jewish tradition of reference to and speculation upon the divine throne. Yet, it would seem illegitimate to study the development of this tradition as if it had remained untouched by the overwhelming presence of similar visions of divine thrones in Greek and other literatures and religions.[19]

III. A whole literature with Orphic tendencies , which developed in the Pythagorean tradition, emphasized Orpheus' *katabasis eis Aidou.* This *katabasis* is atttested since the fifth century in literary works which have been described as "apocalypses avant la lettre".[20] This literature seems to have been one of Virgil's main sources in his classic description of Aeneas' visit to the underworld in Book VI of the Aeneid.[21]

Under the Empire, the literary importance of *katabaseis* grew, and they seem to have become particularly fashionable. As is well-known, Aeneas' visit to the Underworld offers a clear parallel to the *Nekyia*, the evocation of the dead in order to know the future, described in Book XI of the *Odyssey*. Aeneas checks out the vast cavern on the hilltop protected by Apollo, which is the secret dwelling of the Sibyl. The description of Aeneas' visit includes visions of the god and references to the Sibyl's 'secret utterances' .

The *Isis Book* in Apuleius' *Metamorphoses* provides another *locus clas-*

---

[18] P. W. van der Horst, "Moses' Throne Vision in Ezechiel the Dramatist", *JJS* 34 (1983), 21-29, esp. 24; reprinted in his *Essays on the Jewish World of Early Christianity* (Freiburg, Schweiz, Göttingen: Universität Verlag Freiburg, Vandenhoeck & Ruprecht, 1990), 63-71; Van der Horst points out that Moses' dream vision has no classical antecedents. See also the commentary of H. Jacobson, *The Exagoge of Ezekiel* (Cambridge: Cambridge University Press, 1983), 89-97.

[19] For a rich analysis of *thronosis* in initiation in Greek religion, see A.D. Nock, "A Cabiric Rite", *American Journal of Archaeology* 45 (1941), 577-581, reprinted in his *Essays on Religion and the Ancient World*, vol. I (Oxford: Oxford University Press, 1972). For a general background, see A. Hug, "*Thronos*", *PW*, II Reihe, VI A, 613-618 (1935).

[20] R. Turcan, "La catabase orphique du papyrus de Bologne", *RHR* 150 (1956), 136-172.

[21] See P. Boyancé, *La religion de Virgile* (Paris: Presses Universitaires de France, 1963), 154 ff.

sicus on the esoteric character of the vision of the gods encountered during the infernal voyage:

> Thou shalt understand that I approached near unto hell, even to the gates of Proserpine, and after that I was ravished throughout all the elements... I saw likewise the gods celestial and the gods infernal, before whom I presented myself and worshipped then. Behold now have I told thee, which although thou hast heard, yet it is necessary that thou conceal it (*quamvis audita, ignotes tamen necesse est*)...[22]

During the first centuries of the common era, the descent into Hades, which had remained a literary *topos* throughout antiquity, became commonly used for descriptions of the good life. In Lucian's parody of the *katabasis* genre, for instance, a text written in the tradition of Menippean satire, the hero goes down to Hades in order to see how one should live, lead by his reluctant guide, the wise wondermaker Mithrobarzanes.[23]

The most famous description, however, of a *katabasis* into the Underworld dating from the empire is probably that of the descent into the crypt of Trophonius at Lebadeia, as reported by Pausanias.[24] We deal here with a direct testimony, describing in detailed fashion the trance and the terror with which the inquirer of the oracle is seized in the course of his descent. After he has set his mind on the descent, and after various preparations by the priests, he is brought down by a rope and descends into the earth through an artificial hole. "The inquirer at the oracle is led at night into a vaulted chamber from which a whirlwind miraculously carries him through a small aperture above the ground." Walter Burkert, whose summary of Pausanias I quote here, follows Nilsson in believing that the theatrical elaboration, including, perhaps, mechanical elements, is a product of the Imperial age.[25] In many places, there seem to have existed "subterranean

---

[22] Apuleius, *Metamorphoses*, XI. 23, *in finem*. I quote the translation of J. Gwyn Griffiths, *Apuleius of Madauros, the Isis Book (Metamorphoses, Book XI)* (EPROER 39; Leiden: Brill, 1975), 296-301.

[23] Lucian, *Menippus, or the Descent into Hades*, 5-6 (IV, 84-85, Hammond; LCL). The text describes the purificating rites undergone by Menippus. Note that the hero comes back to earth through the sanctuary of Trophonius, in Lebadeia. Before his trip to the underworld, Menippus had undertaken an aascent to heaven, in order to discover the truth about the nature of the universe.

[24] Pausanias, *Description of Greece*, IX. 39 (IV. 346-355 LCL).

[25] Burkert, *Greek Religion*, 115 and notes 46-47. See already Burkert, *Lore and Science in Ancient Pythagoreism* (Cambridge, Mass.: Harvard University Press, 1972), 154, who

installations which presented the Underworld in physical form." [26] Such caves (*megara*, sing. *megaron*) or chambers (*aduta*, sing. *aduton*), were places of worship, "into which offertory gifts were lowered." [27]

Another indication of the widespread role of caves in the religious psyche under the Empire comes from the Mithraic cult. The Mithraeum is a cave, which mirrors the cosmos, while the killing of the bull represents the "esoteric philosophy" of these mysteries.[28]

"The classical world was full of holy places", we are reminded by Robert Markus.[29] Among these holy places, pagan holy caves held a place of honour. Speaking of the persistence of subterranean pagan piety in late antiquity, Robin Lane Fox mentions Eusebius' report on Constantine having sent emissaries into "every pagan temple's recess and every gloomy cave", adding: "Their mission was apt, but impossible. Not even the entire army could have covered each cave of the Nymphs, the many caves which claimed Zeus' birthplace, the underground shrines of Mithras, the caves of Cybele and Attis or the many cavernous entries to Hades. Long after Constantine, the old Cretan caves still drew pagan visitors..." [30]

---

refers to M. P. Nilsson, *Geschichte der griechischen Religion*, II, (3 ed.; Handbuch der Altertumswissenschaft; Munich: Beck, 1967), 450. See also Plutarch, *De Genio Socratis* (*Moralia* VII), 589F-593A, where Timarchus is said to have descended into the crypt of Trophonius, where he remained underground for two nights and a day in order to know the nature of Socrates' sign. On Plutarch's knowledge of Orphic *katabaseis*, see Y. Vernière, *Symboles et mythes dans la pensée de Plutarque: essai d' interprétation religieuse des Moralia* (Paris: Belles Lettres, 1977), esp. 286. On p. 289, Vernière refers to the testimony of Clearchus' *Peri Hupnon*, according to which Aristotle would have been taught the new doctine of the other world by a Jewish sage. But she reads in Josephus, *Contra Apionem*, I. 22 more than the text allows: Josephus does not quote enought for us to know what the Jewish sage told Aristotle. She also points out that Clearchus is the first author to give a clear ascensional character to the infernal journey.

On Plutarch's initiatic experience, see Y. Vernière, "Initiation et eschatologie chez Plutarque", in J. Ries and H. Limet, éds., *Les rites d'initiation* (Homo religiosus 13; Louvain-la-Neuve: Centre d'Histoire des Religions, 1986), 335-352.

[26] Burkert, *Lore and Science*, 155.

[27] On *megara*, see P. Chantraine, *Dictionnaire étymologique de la langue grecque*, *s.v.* "*megaron*". Chantraine points out that the word may well be a loan word from a semitic origin, refering to Hebrew *me'ara*, cave. See also *Lidell-Scott-Jones, Oxford Greek Dictionary*, *s.v.* "*megaron*".

[28] See Burkert, *Ancient Mystery Cults*, 83-84.

[29] Markus, *The End of Ancient Christianity* (Cambridge: Cambridge University Press, 1991), 139.

[30] R. Lane Fox, *Pagans and Christians* (Harmondsworth; Penguin, 1986), 673. The text of Eusebius is *Vita Constantini* 3. 57. 4. For other examples of cultic caves under

In his *Life of Isidore*, Damascius tells us of a water stream and an abyss attracting pilgrims, both men and women, as late as in the fifth century. The passage has been recently studied in great detail by Michel Tardieu.[31] The stream, identified by Damascius as the Styx, is actually the Yarmuk, and the location of the place described is not far from Bostra. It is not a *katabasion*, but Damascius' choice of words recalls those used to describe *katabaseis* to caves. He speaks about the 'holy fear' felt by the pilgrims during their descent into the abyss, and about their offerings to the deity and the sacred oaths they swear.[32]

As a last example of this phenomenon, very widespread until late antiquity, I want to mention the text of a Greek magical papyrus. This text, a "charm of Hekate Ereschigal against fear of punishment", was analyzed by H. D. Betz. It contains, as Betz has shown, liturgical tells of a *katabasis* ritual, from the mystery cult of the Idean dactyls:

> I have been initiated, and I went down into the [underground] chamber of the Dactyls, and I saw the other things down below...[33]

But the shamanistic traits of the earlier katabaseis have disappeared here, and the descent into Hekate's realm has been transformed into a metaphor. To summarize the traits encountered in the various *katabasis* texts, we might point out, at least, the following: the descent is the prelude to a vision, it has an esoteric character, and it must be preceded by an ascetical preparation.

IV. It would be a mistake, however, to think that the experience of *katabasis* remained limited to pagan cults and literature. Extrapolating from the mention of the open tombs at the death of Jesus (Mat 27: 52), Christian exegesis had developed very early the theme of Jesus'

---

the Empire, see also D.E. Aune, *Prophecy in Early Christianity and the Ancient Mediterranean World* (Grand Rapids, Michigan: Eerdmans, 1983), 25-30.

[31] M. Tardieu, *Paysages reliques: Routes et haltes syriennes d'Isidore à Simplicius* (Bibliothèque de l'EPHE, Sciences religieuses, 94; Louvain-Paris: Peeters, 1990), 45-69.

[32] *Damascius, Vita Isidori Reliquiae*, Cl. Zintzen, ed., (Hildesheim: G. Holms, 1967), #199, pp. 272-274. A reference was made to this text already by Ganschinietz in his thorough entry on *katabasis* in *PW*, X. 2, 2379-2380.

[33] Translation in H.D. Betz, ed., *The Greek Magical Papyri in Translation* (Chicago and London: University of Chicago Press, 1986), 297-298. Cf. Betz's study of this text, "Fragments from a Catabasis Ritual in a Greek Magical Papyrus", *HR* 19 (1980), 287-295. Cf. my review of I. Gruenwald, *Apocalyptic and Merkavah Mysticism* in *Numen* 29 (1981), 107-109, where I refer to this text and suggest in a nutshell the argument developed here.

descent into hell between his death and his resurrection. The purpose of Jesus' infernal voyage would have been to teach the saints of the Old Testament, who had not had an opportunity to hear His message on earth. Despite various doubts as to its reality (for instance by Abelard, Erasmus, or Calvin), the *descensus ad inferos* was decreed an article of faith by the Council of Trent.[34]

The motif of Christ's *descensus ad inferos* obvioulsy offers very close similarities to some Gnostic conceptions, and perhaps also Christ's descent should be seen at the root of some major Gnostic mythologoumena.[35] The motif is found in different domains of early Christian literature, perhaps nowhere as clearly as in the Syriac milieu. We find the theme of the Savior's *descensus* in the Manichaean *Psalms of Thomas*, which are extant only in Coptic but were written in Aramaic, and in the works of the two great Syriac writers of the fourth century, Aphrahat and Ephrem.[36] The clearest, and the best known, literary evidence from early Christianity on Christ's *descensus*, however, is the apocryphal *Apocalypse of Peter*, where Jesus gives an affirmative answer to a question about whether he had preached to the dead (chapter 41). It is to the credit of Albrecht Dieterich that he recognized in his *Nekyia* the connections between this text and the pagan tradition of *katabasis*.[37] Dieterich recognized that the new text, found in the sands of Akhmim, should be read on the background of the esoteric chtonic cults (*chtonische Geheimkulte*) of antiquity, a tradition going back to Eleusis and Delphi, if not earlier, as shown by Aristophanes' testimony in *The Frogs*. For Dieterich, the *Apocalypse of Peter* reflected a

---

[34] See for instance "Descente de Jésus aux Enfers", *DTC* IV, 565ff. The importance of the conception in early Christianity is emphasized by O. Rousseau, "La descente aux Enfers, fondement sotériologique du baptême chrétien", *RSR* 40 (1952), 273-297. See also O. Michel, "Der aufsteigende und herabsteigende Gesandte", in W. Weinrich, ed., *The New Testament Age: Essays in Honor of Bo Reicke* (Macon, GA: Mercer University Press, 1984), 335-336. The importance of the *descensus ad inferos* as one of the mythical elements of Christianity was already emphasized by H. Gunkel. See further W. Bieder, *Die Vorstellung von der Höllenfahrt Jesu Christi* (Zurich, 1949), *non vidi*. For the early Christian tradition and the polemics with Gnostic conceptions, see A. Orbe, S.J., "El 'Descensus ad inferos' y san Ireneo", *Gregorianum* 68 (1987), 485-522. C.H. Talbert, "The Myth of a Descending-Ascending Redeemer in Mediterranean Antiquity", *NTS* 22 (1976), 418-439, argues that "the early Christian myth of a descending-ascending redeemer was taken over from Hellenistic Judaism."

[35] See for instance M. Peel, "The 'descensus ad inferos' in the *Teachings of Silvanus* (CG VII, 4)", *Numen* 26 (1979), 23-49.

[36] References to texts and studies in *Der Kleine Pauly*, *s. v.* "*katabasis*".

[37] A. Dieterich, *Nekyia: Beiträge zur Erklärung der neuentdeckten Petrusapokalypse* (Leipzig: Teubner, 1893).

Christianized version of "Orphic-Pythagorean Hades books", of a *nekyia* going back to archaic Greece.[38] Dieterich was right in what he saw, but, as Martha Himmelfarb has convincingly argued, he ignored much that could have been of direct relevance to his work. In particular, he had "a nearly blind eye to Jewish sources, [which might have reflected] an expression of a certain kind of history-of-religions anti-Christian (and Jewish), pro-Greek feeling." [39] According to Himmelfarb, "what Dieterich fails to see is that the various motifs in the *Apocalypse of Peter*, whatever their origin, have been shaped in consciousness of a Jewish and Christian tradition." [40]

In contradistinction to Dieterich, Isidore Lévi did make the claim of direct literary connections between Jewish texts and Greek traditions. In particular, he pointed out that the *Revelation of Joshua ben Levi* was an apocalypse "derived from Pythagoras' *katabasis*." [41] Lévi's work, however, was marred by various sweeping and dubious statements, and his insights seem to remain ignored by most scholars to this day. Lévi, moreover, did not know the Hekhalot literature which has become familiar since Scholem's groundbreaking studies "put them on the map of scholarship", as it were.

V. For Scholem, who devoted intensive attention to Hekhalot literature, *yrd* was a puzzling, even paradoxical root in connection to the description of mystical or ecstatic experience finding its acme in heavenly vision. Indeed, the rationale for the use of *yrd* in some of the Hekhalot texts remained unknown to him. It must be said that the poor preservation of the texts makes their study extremely difficult, and renders any conclusions aleatory. This state of affairs was recently changed for the better, however, thanks to both the Synoptic edition and and the Concordance of the Hekhalot literature published by Peter Schäfer and his associates.[42]

New research can now be conducted, on philological ground less

---

[38] See M. Himmelfarb, *Tours of Hell: an Apocalyptic Form in Jewish and Christian Literature* (Philadelphia: University of Pennsylvania Press, 1983), 41.

[39] *Ibid.*, 44, n. 13.

[40] *Ibid.*, 67.

[41] I. Lévi, *La légende de Pythagore*, 8. The *Revelation of Joshua ben Levi* was published by Jellineck, *Beit Ha-Midrash*, II, 48-51. In the Hebrew text, the hero looks for "hell and its treasures."

[42] P. Schäfer, ed., *Synopse der Hekhalot-Literatur* (TSAJ 2; Tübingen: Mohr [Siebeck], 1981); P. Schäfer, *et alia*, ed., *Konkordanz sur Hekhalot-Literatur*, 2 vols. (TSAJ 12, 13; Tübingen: Mohr [Siebeck], 1986, 1988).

shaky than before, leading to more secure, or at least less speculative, conclusions. Annelies Kuyt was thus able to publish recently a remarkable article on the term *yarad* and its semantic field in the Hekhalot texts.[43] Speculation on the meaning of *yarad* has been rife. It has been suggested that the semantic reference of the verb, in Mishnaic Hebrew, is 'to go in', as much as 'to go down'.[44] The expression '*yarad la-merkava*' has also been seen as similar to '*yarad lifne ha-teva*', i. e. "he came down to the altar" [where the Torah is read in a synagogue].[45] The expression *yorde merkavah* has also been compared to that used for those who navigate the sea, *yorde ha-yam*.[46] Yet another explanation, involving reference to theurgic praxis, was suggested by Ithamar Gruenwald.[47] None of these explanations, however, seems to have been accepted as strong enough to carry conviction.

I propose to recognize the root *yrd*, as it is used in the context of the descent into the *merkavah*, as a linguistic calque of *katabasis*, the widely used term for the descent to the Underworld, a theme known since the dawn of Greek civilization and which had under the Roman Empire lost most of its shamanistic features to become a choice metaphor for the mystical voyage ending in the vision of the divine world

---

[43] A. Kuyt, "Once Again: *yarad* in Hekhalot Literature". See n. 5 *supra*.

[44] See for instance the expression *yarad le-gano*: "he came into his garden". Cf. *Mishna, Bikkurim* 3. 1. The argument seems here somewhat weak, since it is of course difficult to know for sure that the act of going into one's garden did not imply an act of descent.

[45] In ancient synagogues, the altar might well have been lower than the ground, instead of being elevated above it, as it is usually today. This has been proposed by Scholem.

[46] D. J. Halperin, *The Faces of the Chariot*, 226-227.

[47] This understanding, reading *yarad* as a *hiph'il*, interprets the expression as a magic practice of the bringing down of the [divine] name. See Gruenwald, *Apocalyptic and Merkavah Mysticism*, 142 ff. This suggestion is accepted by Rachel Elior in her edition of *Hekhalot Zutarti*, 60, comment. on line 6. These references are provided by Kuyt, 64 and n. 132. On the occasion of my preliminary presentation of these findings at a seminar on magical texts led by Hans Dieter Betz at the Hebrew University of Jerusalem in December, 1990, my colleague Shaul Shaked suggested to link *yordei merkava* to the Hebrew expression for sailors: *yordei yam*, referring to Arabic *markab*, ship. (Cf. n. 46 above). The journey of the soul to the Underworld was indeed perceived to have taken place in a ship in various ancient cultures. In Egypt, for instance, the soul goes on a journey in such a vessel after death. One should also in this context refer to the 'vessel of the soul' (*okhèma psuchès*), through which it goes down from heaven before at birth, and up again after the death of the body, in Neoplatonism; see E. R. Dodds, *The Greeks and the Irrational* (Sather Classical Lectures 25; Berkeley: University of California Press, 1951), appendix 2, 283-311; see further H. Lewy, *Chaldaean Oracles and Theurgy* (second edition, M. Tardieu; Paris: Etudes Augustiniennes, 1981), *passim*.

and palaces, or even of the divinity itself, usually seated upon its throne of glory. As we have seen in these pages, the idea of a descent into the divine realm was so widespread in antiquity that there is no reason to ignore the possibility that it was used also by Jews in order to describe their own mystical experiences.

It may seem surprising that no one among the students of early Jewish mysticism appears to have thought of studying its vocabulary and praxis in the context of similar or parallel phenomena and spiritual experiences in the ancient world.[48] To be sure, parallels from diverse or even disparate cultural, religious or linguistic backgrounds do not by themselves explain phenomena, and we should be particularly careful when dealing with esoteric traditions, which by their very nature have left us few secure traces. By no means do I want to suggest that the Hekhalot texts reflect a religious experience identical, or even similar to that of the Greek *katabasis* rituals.[49] Yet in seeking to understand the religious praxis of late antique Judaism, there is no reason a priori to ignore patterns of behavior or traditions of belief current in the *Umwelt* in which Judaism flourished.

VI. In late antiquity, both Augustine and Plotinus seem to reflect a major paradigmatic shift, which was transforming the language of mystical expression and its basic metaphors. In antiquity, as we have seen, the search for the secrets of the universe had retained at least some of the basic metaphors stemming from its mythological and shamanistic heritage. This search was now forgotten, and the soul's adventure became her attempt to merge with the divinity. The esoteric trends that can still be detected in the earliest strata of Christian thought disappeared after the fourth century, while the vocabulary of the ancient mysteries was in some cases re-used to describe the mystical experience.[50] The *unio mystica*, or rather the *way* leading to it, would usually be perceived, from now on, essentially through two

---

[48] The latest monograph on Hekhalot literature, M.D. Swartz, *Mystical Prayer in Ancient Judaism: an Analysis of the Ma'aseh Merkavah* (TSAJ 28; Tübingen: Mohr [Siebeck], 1992), has remarkably little to say about the term: "The term *yrd*, 'to descend', is often employed in *Hekhalot Rabbati* and other texts to refer to the mystical journey." (p. 84).

[49] For a *caveat* on the use and misuse of thematic parallels in the study of Merkavah literature, see P. Schäfer, 'Einleitung', *Hekhalot-Studien* (TSAJ 19; Tübingen: Mohr [Siebeck], 1988), 1-7.

[50] On esoteric trends in early Christianity, see chapters 6 and 7 *supra*.

different but combined metaphors. One is the metaphor of going up, or ascent, and one that of going inside, or interiorization. Augustine expressed this identification of the two metaphors better than anyone else in a lapidary formula: " *Intus Deus altus est*, the God within is the God above", he writes, thus widely disseminating in the religious mentality of the West a fundamentally Plotinian metaphor about the mystical ascent.[51] We might point out here that the same metaphor of elevation is shown by the theurgists of the second century C. E. who have left us the Chaldaean Oracles. The central mystery of these theurgists was the elevation, or *anagogè*, whose goal was the immortalization of the soul. According to Hans Lewy, the term anagoge itself was very probably borrowed "from the terminology concerning the apotheosis of heroized mortals" .[52] This elevation of the soul, disconnected from the body, was accomplished on the 'vehicle of the soul (*okhèma psuchès*), on which it had first come down from its original heavenly abode unto earth.

In the new thought patterns emerging from this transformation, the earlier metaphor of descent into the Underworld retained no clear function, and its *Fortleben* was literary more than religious, directly linked as it was to Virgil's role as model in European medieval literature. This influence, up to Dante, cannot be overemphasized.[53] In later religious thought, indeed, the *descensus ad inferos* seems to play a less and less significant role. Was this paradigmatic change initiated by the transformation in attitudes to the cosmos at the time? More precisely, was the demonization of the cosmos, or the more and more strongly perceived negative attitude to this earth, as a place of demons, ruled by the Prince of Evil, responsible for the insistence on the

---

[51] Augustine, *Homiliae in Psalmos* 130. 12 (PL 37, 1712), quoted by Bernard McGinn, *The Foundations of Mysticism* (New York: Crossroads, 1991), 242. McGinn mentions (p. 205) that Ambrose was the first Latin Christian writer to make the mystical paradigm of ascension available in the West, through his adaptation of Origenist and Plotinian mysticism. The equivalence of the two metaphors was well analyzed by P. Henry in his introduction to a new publication of MacKenna's classic translation of Plotinus' *Enneads*.

[52] H. Lewy, Chaldaean *Oracles and Theurgy*, appendix VIII, 489; cf. chapter III, 177-226.

[53] On the whole tradition, deemed by Cumont "littérature hallucinante" (*Lux perpetua* [Paris: Geuthner, 1949], 245), see already Dieterich, *Nekyia* (1894), and especially H. Diels, "Himmel und Höllen Fahrten von Homer bis Dante", *Neues Jahrbuch für klassische Altertum* (1932), 246-253.

soul's duty to ascend to heaven?[54] Or does the new lack of enthusiasm for the discovery of the secrets of the universe, deemed perverse *curiositas* by Augustine[55], explain the refusal to investigate the entrails of the earth? And does this refusal stem from the growing conception of Hell as an underground, wicked place? It is impossible to deal with this complex issue here, but it would appear that all these reasons did play a role in the transformation which seems to have taken place in late antiquity. It is reasonable to postulate that the same shift of perceptions should be called upon to explain what seems to be a similar shift of vocabulary within the Jewish tradition.

Noting some uncertainty about the use of the descent and of the ascent metaphors to describe the mystical experience in the texts, Gershom Scholem thought that the original term was *'alyia la-merkava*, ascent into the charriot, and that for some reason, *'alyia* became changed into *yerida*, descent. According to Scholem, *yarad* would have replaced *'alah*, and the ascent would have been transformed into a descent, later in the development of this literature, around the year 500. According to him, "in the early literature, the writers always speak of an 'ascent to the Merkabah', a pictorial analogy which has come to seem natural to us." [56] Of his own avowal, Scholem was unable to account for the reasons of this change. On the basis of her rigorous analysis of the texts, Kuyt, however (who mentions at the outset of her article Scholem's puzzlement about the term *yarad*) presents a very strong case against his view of things, and shows that *yarad*, not *'alah*, appears to have been the original term describing the outward journey to the *merkava* in the Hekhalot literature.[57] She thus argues for a later transformation of *yarad* into *'alah*. As to the reason for the use of this word, however, she is unable to propose a clear solution. If Kuyt is correct in her analysis, however, this transformation would fit well within the paradigmatic shift sketched here.

---

[54] See Culianu, *Psychanodia I*, 22, who highlights the importance of Kroll's research in his *Gott und Hölle* on the new demonization of the universe in the early centuries of the common era, and its influence on the *katabasis* patterns.

[55] See H. Blumenberg, " *Curiositas* und *veritas*: zur Ideengeschichte von Augustin, Confessiones X 35", *Studia Patristica* VI. 4 (TUGAL 81 [1962], 294-302.

[56] G. Scholem, *Major Trends in Jewish Mysticism* (New York: Schocken, 1961, 3. ed.), 46-47. No discussion of the 'descent to the Chariot' is found in N. Janowitz, *The Poetics of Ascent: Theories of Language in a Rabbinic Text* (Series in Judaica; Albany: SUNY Press, 1989).

[57] See her conclusions, "Once again: *yarad* in Hekhalot Literature", 67-69.

The above reflections on the use of the descent metaphor in the Jewish mystical literature of late antiquity, as a linguistic calque from *katabasis*, and on the reasons for its transformation into the ascent metaphor, are not offered as the conclusions of an exhaustive study, but mainly as a suggestion for further research.

SOURCES

The studies in this book have originally appeared, in slightly different versions, in the following publications:

Ch. 1:   G. Hasan-Rokem and D. Shulman, eds., *Untying the Knot: on Riddles and Enigmatic Modes* (New York: Oxford University Press, 1996).

Ch. 2:   *Apocrypha* 2 (1991), 133-153 [French].

Ch. 3:   Ch. Elsas et al., eds., *Tradition und Translation, Festschrift Carsten Colpe* (Berlin, New York: de Gruyter, 1994), 26-41.

Ch. 4:   L. Cirillo, ed., *Codex Manichaicus Coloniensis* (Cosenza: Marra, 1986), 153-168.

Ch. 5:   H. Preissler and H. Seiwert, eds., *Gnosisforschung und Religionsgeschichte: Festschrift Kurt Rudolph* (Marburg:Diagonal, 1995), 307-316.

Ch. 6:   Sh. Biedermann and B.A. Scharfstein, eds., *Interpretation in Religion* (Philosophy and Religion 2; Leiden: Brill, 1992), 229-248.

Ch. 7:   G. Dorival and A. le Boulluec, eds., *Origeniana Sexta* (Leuven: Peeters, 1995), 53-70.

Ch. 8:   A. Assmann and J. Assmann, eds., *Das Geheimnis* (Archäologie der literarischen Kommunikation 5; Munich: Fink, forthcoming).

Ch. 9:   H.G. Kippenberg and G.G. Stroumsa, eds., *Secrecy and Concealment: Studies in the History of Mediterranean and Near Eastern Religions* (*Numen* Book Series 65; Leiden, New York, Köln, 1995), 289-309.

Ch. 10: J.J. Collins and M. Fishbane, eds., *Death, Ecstasy and Otherworldly Journeys* (Albany, N.Y.: SUNY Press, 1995), 139-154.

INDICES

I. General Index

allegory 18, 19n., 95, 96, 97, 98, 101,
102, 103, 106, 121, 158
apocalypse 67, 69, 155, 173, 178
apocalypticism 3, 4, 56, 68, 109, 119
apokrypha 29, 38, 39, 40, 41, 43, 73,
93, 104n., 106, 119, 120, 121, 151,
155, 156, 160
aporrhèton 3, 40, 41, 65, 67, 77, 120,
126, 163, 164
arcana 30, 31, 32, 150, 153
arcana dei 2, 9, 94, 146
arcana naturae 2, 23, 93, 146

disciplina arcani 3, 29, 30, 70, 93, 134,
146, 148, 150, 152
docetism 96
dromena 4, 29, 132, 150
dualism 1, 3, 7, 54, 61, 64, 85, 86,
89, 105, 128, 130, 144, 152

enigma 11, 12, 16, 17, 18, 19, 20, 21,
22, 23, 24, 25, 28, 47, 48, 49, 50,
52, 59, 61, 92, 93, 94, 95, 96, 97, 98,
99, 100, 101, 103, 104, 105, 106,
107, 114, 121, 140, 142, 158
eschatology 43, 70

gnosis 36, 37, 38, 45n., 53, 56, 57,
58, 68, 71, 105n., 111, 112, 113, 11-
7n., 128, 129, 130, 135, 139, 152
gnosticism 1, 3, 6, 8, 30, 42, 43, 44,
46, 47, 48, 53, 54, 55, 56, 58, 61,
62, 67, 71, 72, 75, 79, 85, 86, 89, 93,
105, 106, 109, 110, 111, 112, 113,
130, 133, 145, 152, 153, 156, 157,
162, 166, 172, 177

Hekhalot literature 5, 70, 151, 170,
173, 178, 179, 180, 182
heresy 1, 3, 6, 30, 39, 41, 45, 82, 84,
89, 93, 105, 106, 111n., 115, 128,
137, 143, 144, 148, 158

initiation 18, 25, 69, 74, 75, 76, 77,
163, 164, 165, 171, 172, 175n., 176
Islam 1, 45, 66, 87n.

Judaism 1, 3, 4, 12, 28, 29n., 30n.,
31, 33, 41, 42, 43, 45, 54, 61, 63,
78, 83, 84, 89-91, 92, 94, 100, 106,
109, 110, 117-123, 126, 128, 130-
131, 146, 151-152, 155, 156, 159,
160, 179, 180, 182
Judeo-Christianity 39, 43, 56, 67, 74,
75, 85, 93, 106, 116n., 117, 119,
123, 133, 156, 157

Kabbala 8, 42, 125, 130, 140n., 148,
152

legomena 4, 29, 132, 150

ma' asse bereshit,
merkavah 42, 69
magic 5, 46, 49, 136, 162, 170n.,
179n.
manichaeism 6, 8, 63, 64n., 67, 78
Merkavah mystics 70, 131
Midrash 42, 151
Mishna 42, 69, 88, 90-91, 179
monotheism 53, 54, 64, 88
montanism 87, 88
mysteries 2, 4, 21, 25, 29, 30n., 31,
32, 35, 44, 59, 61, 64, 65, 66, 67,
68, 69, 70, 72, 73, 78, 77, 98, 101,
103, 111, 130, 146, 147, 149, 150,
151, 157, 158, 160, 164, 172, 175,
180, 181
mysteries, Christian 2, 3, 4, 5, 8, 9,
29, 30, 31, 32, 34, 36-37, 38, 40,
52, 71, 74, 75, 76, 112, 122, 127,
128, 132, 136, 137, 146, 148, 150,
153, 154, 155, 160, 161, 162, 163,
164, 165, 166, 167, 168
mysteries, Jewish 42, 69, 140, 151,
152, 156

Neoplatonism 139, 179n.

oracle 14, 15, 16, 17, 20, 101, 104
orphism 2, 17, 51, 173, 175n.

II. Names

III. Literature

1. Classical Literature

4. Christian and Gnostic Literature

5. Manichean Literature

STUDIES IN THE HISTORY OF RELIGIONS
NUMEN BOOK SERIES

Recent volumes in the series:

65 H.G. Kippenberg & G.G. Stroumsa (eds.). *Secrecy and Concealment.* Studies in the History of Mediterranean and Near Eastern Religions. 1995. ISBN 90 04 10235 3

66 R. Kloppenborg & W.J. Hanegraaff (eds.). *Female Stereotypes in Religious Traditions*. 1995. ISBN 90 04 10290 6

67 J. Platvoet & K. van der Toorn (eds.). *Pluralism and Identity.* Studies on Ritual Behaviour. 1995. ISBN 90 04 10373 2

68 G. Jonker. *The Topography of Remembrance.* The Dead, Tradition and Collective Memory in Mesopotamia. 1995.
ISBN 90 04 10162 4

69 S. Biderman. *Scripture and Knowledge.* An Essay on Religious Epistemology. 1995. ISBN 90 04 10154 3

70 G.G. Stroumsa. *Hidden Wisdom.* Esoteric Traditions and the Roots of Christian Mysticism. 1996. ISBN 90 04 10504 2

ISSN 0169-8834